KIEREN FALLON

KIEREN FALLON

THE BIOGRAPHY

ANDREW LONGMORE

Copyright © Andrew Longmore 2008

The right of Andrew Longmore to be identified as
the author of this work has been asserted by him in accordance with the
Copyright, Designs and Patents Act 1988.

This edition first published in Great Britain in 2008 by
Orion Books
an imprint of the Orion Publishing Group Ltd
Orion House, 5 Upper St Martin's Lane,
London WC2H 9EA

An Hachette Livre UK Company

1 3 5 7 9 10 8 6 4 2

A CIP catalogue record for this book is available
from the British Library.

ISBN: 978 0 7528 7376 3 (hardback)
ISBN: 978 0 7528 8863 7 (export trade paperback)

Printed in Great Britain by Clays Ltd, St Ives plc

The Orion Publishing Group's policy is to use papers that are natural, renewable and recyclable
and made from wood grown in sustainable forests. The logging and manufacturing processes
are expected to conform to the environmental regulations of the country of origin.

Every effort has been made to fulfil requirements with regard to reproducing copyright material.
The author and publisher will be glad to rectify any omissions at the earliest opportunity.

www.orionbooks.co.uk

To my brother Richard,
who loved his racing

CONTENTS

PREFACE

'It is probable that we who are country born and bred are affected in more ways and more profoundly than we know by our surroundings. The nature of the soil we live on, the absence or presence of running water, of hills, rocks, woods, open spaces; every feature of the landscape, the vegetative and animal life – everything, in fact, that we see, hear, smell and feel – enters not into the body only, but the soul, and helps to shape and colour it.'

W.H. Hudson, *A Traveller in Little Things*, quoted in
The Personality of Ireland by E. Estyn Evans

This is a first draft of Kieren Fallon's life, an attempt to pull together the disparate threads of a controversial, turbulent, brilliant and ultimately doomed career, and to explain why a man who came from nothing, yet was bequeathed every gift imaginable to a jockey, should be so hellbent on returning to oblivion. There will be rewrites, revisions, and, in time, Fallon's own version. It is primarily a racing biography, not just because Fallon's tangled private life has largely defied analysis, but because he is at his most expressive on horseback. Take away Fallon's right to speak in the one arena in which his eloquence is unsurpassed and he is left defenceless against his demons. His riding represents the full confession of a personality. But Fallon's extraordinary life story needs to be set into context, against the background of his own capricious nature and of a sport being coaxed, bullied and swept into change by forces way beyond its control. The advent of the exchanges has changed the landscape of betting forever, and racing has been as slow as Fallon himself to react to the new geography.

Better judges than I am can place Kieren Fallon in the pantheon of great jockeys. On his day, he was the equal of Lester Piggott, but Piggott was at the peak of his profession for almost five decades. Fallon's career has flourished and withered over barely fifteen years, although no one would rule out the possibility of a late bloom. He can still claim fifteen English Classics, including three Derbies and two Oaks–Derby doubles, and two Arcs among a handsome collection of Group One winners, the second of them quite possibly his last ride on a racetrack. But the measure of the rider could equally be found on wet days at Pontefract or Bath, Salisbury or Musselburgh. To Fallon, the challenge came from the horse and finding a way to win, however grand or humble the race. As long as his mount gave its all, winning and losing could take care of itself. In that, above all, he was worthy of the blind patronage of the millions of high-street punters who roared home his every winner as if it was a personal strike against penury. Fallon was a man you would entrust to ride for your life.

For three seasons, he rode successive double centuries, a feat achieved previously only by Sir Gordon Richards and Fred Archer. But it is the whiff of danger that has made Fallon an hypnotic figure in a sport that thrives on scandal. From the day he hauled a rival jockey off his horse at Beverley in 1994, Fallon has danced with the devil. Too often, the devil has won. The devil that made him a peerless race-rider is the same devil that lured him to the brink of self-destruction away from the track, into rehabilitation from alcohol and drug abuse and into a wilful disregard for authority.

Initial suspicion of this project in Fallon's mind has been replaced at least by tacit acceptance. I have never sought Fallon's help, although Jim Regan and Stephen Cunningham, who agreed to talk to me about Fallon's early life, were granted permission to do so by Fallon himself. That is the way it works in the closed communities of rural Ireland and British racing. But this is an unofficial biography. At times, it has been difficult to know which of us has been the hunter and which the hunted. Fallon commands a fierce loyalty within racing, particularly among the rank and file, so in tracing his footsteps I often gained the uncomfortable feeling that I too was being tracked. In Jim Regan, a man with a handshake befitting a middleweight boxer and an independent mind, and Stephen Cunningham, I found two people who were willing to record their experiences of the young Fallon. Charlie Swan, who shared an apprenticeship with Fallon at Kevin Prendergast's yard on the Curragh, and a few scrapes as well, was also generous with his memories and his time. The late Gabriel 'Squibs' Curran, Kevin Prendergast's stable jockey when Fallon arrived in the yard, talked to me just a few months before his untimely and sudden death.

My colleagues in the press box have been patient guides through a world of baffling language and ritual, in particular Sue Montgomery, Paul Wheeler, Tony Coleman and Jonathan Powell. Brough Scott, who writes as freshly about racing as when he first began a near lifetime ago, has been a constant source of energy, advice and guidance. Alan Lee, one of the few journalists who has tried to understand Fallon, has been free with his insights as has Tom O'Ryan, who knew Fallon in his days at Norton Grange with Jimmy Fitzgerald and gave me a long lease on his extensive cuttings library. Mark Dwyer provided further background to Fallon's early days in the north. David Walsh, my colleague at the *Sunday Times*, has allowed me to quarry from his many interviews with Fallon over the years. Henry Cecil, Aidan O'Brien, the owners of Coolmore and Jack Ramsden all refused to co-operate with the biography, but Sir Michael Stoute provided some critical insights on Fallon's time at Freemason Lodge.

Further thanks should go to John Lowe, Frank Conlan, Dallas Toddywalla, Jacqui King, Tim Cox for the use of the best racing library in the country, Slade Callaghan, Philip Robinson, Michael Bell, Michael Caulfield, Ben Cecil, Donn McClean, Eric Alston, Jason Weaver, Greg Wood, Andrew Balding, Clare Balding, Dietrich von Boettischer and Daniela Nowara of the beautiful Ammerland Stud, Andre Fabre for his recollections of Hurricane Run's Arc, Frankie Dettori for his thoughts on a career-long rivalry and friendship, Cash Asmussen and Gary Stevens, David O'Reilly and Mark Davies of Betfair, Tom Clarke, my former sports editor at *The Times* and editor of the *Sporting Life*, David

Ashforth of the *Racing Post* for his help with the trial and many others who were willing to talk but did not want to be named. Thanks to Ian Marshall of Orion Books for his patience, to David Luxton for his calm support and to my wife, Jane, for spending one holiday in pursuit of deadends in the depths of County Clare and sacrificing another to the demands of a deadline.

Reigate, Surrey
April 2008

1

THE BOY FROM CRUSHEEN

'He's never forgotten his roots, never forgotten where he came from.'

Jim Regan

Jim Regan can remember the little figure now, sitting on a stool in the front room of his house, waif-like and pale, his feet barely touching the floor. He'd often wonder whether the boy didn't need a good meal once in a while and he still wonders what might have happened if Kieren Fallon had stuck to boxing instead of becoming a jockey. He had all the basic skills – the courage, the coolness, the aggression and, most surprising of all, the power. Mossey Clabby's wife said she felt sorry for young Kieren because the gloves looked so big on him, but Regan had seen the Fallon boy fight and that was enough to know the truth. He remembers a representative boxing match, Connacht Under-13s v Munster Under-13s, when Kieren was due to box an older, bigger and more experienced opponent. Regan had warned the Munster coach that he would pull his fellow out if the going got too rough. He'd said the same to Kieren. 'He's only got two hands, same as me,' Kieren had said.

'But, you know, Kieren pulled the house down that night,' Regan recalls. 'The other fella came out like a tornado, throwing punches from everywhere, and Kieren came back to his stool at the end of the first round and said he'd never felt a thing. Kieren knocked him out in the third round. "He's only got two hands, same as me." I'll never forget that.'

5

When he wanted something badly, Kieren Fallon could be disciplined enough and he liked boxing, liked the physical buzz and the sense of danger. Some boys had talent but no discipline. You had to look out for those, persuade them to come and train. But you never had to worry with Kieren. He'd be there, in the hall at the college in Gort, on the dot of 7.30 and he would always be the last to leave. One time Regan's assistant trainer, Michael, was driving home from training and noticed a familiar figure walking along the road out of town towards Crusheen. It was Fallon. When Regan asked later what he was doing, Fallon replied: 'Well, Michael didn't say anything about giving me a lift, so I thought I'd walk it anyway.' Gort to Crusheen is a good seven miles and it was getting late.

The boy still comes back to visit. After he won the Oaks on Reams of Verse, he brought a photograph, which is now hanging up on the wall of his old school. He would sit on the stage and the boys would gather round, curious to hear his tale. One of their own had gone away and was starting to make a decent life for himself somewhere else. 'It's not all roses,' Fallon would tell them, 'you have to clean the shit out as well.' But, Regan remembers, Fallon was able to attract people to him in that quiet way of his and he would always be courteous and always pay a visit to see Jim's mother. 'That little lad came by again,' she'd say, though he was close to being the champion jockey by then.

Fallon was brought up just outside Crusheen, on the road from Ennis to Gort, the unloved N18, which trips across the border from County Clare into Galway just a few miles beyond Crusheen. In February 1965, when Kieren Francis Fallon was born, Crusheen was still a place straddling a major road to somewhere else. Not many people stayed long in Crusheen, though if you turned off the main road and then left towards Ballinruan and climbed the hill past the smallholding where Frank ('Buddy' to everyone in Crusheen) and Maureen Fallon brought up their six children, the view to the west from the playground of the old National School takes the breath away. The population of Crusheen has grown hugely in the last ten years or so – by 25 per cent in five years from 1997 alone – but back in the sixties and seventies, long before the tiger economy made Ireland an attractive new home for foreigners, it was a typical Irish settlement, not quite a town but rather more than a village, a place where everyone knew everyone else and most of their business as well. It is still a place that withholds its secrets from outsiders.

By his own admission, Kieren Fallon was an 'academic disaster'. In fact, when he left Our Lady's College in Gort, he was barely able to read or write, a result of dyslexia, a problem officially recognised now but not then, more than any lack of intelligence. 'He was bright enough, but studying wasn't his thing,' Regan explains. 'Education is one thing, intuition is another. Kieren was always willing and able to learn. But survival was his thing.' Survival in his career and survival in life. Fallon was certainly bright enough to know that a life in Crusheen was not for him. Like Jim Regan, he'd go away and make a name for himself and then come back. He was brought up in the outdoors, playing in the woods and fields, and playing sport. A photograph of the young Fallon hangs in Fogarty's pub at the far end of Crusheen, just before the garage. It shows the Crusheen Under-18 hurling team, which won the Minor Championship in 1980. Fallon is in the middle of the front row, the slightest figure in the whole team, and the youngest. 'He was a corner forward,' says Tony O'Donnell, the team manager. 'Small and skilful and awful determined. He was only fifteen then, but he fitted right in with the team. He was a very courageous and determined young lad, that's all I can say.' And that's what makes the rise of Kieren Fallon all the more extraordinary.

Crusheen is hurling country, a stronghold of the Gaelic Athletic Association and a centre for pre-season training for many of the county hurling and Gaelic football squads. Racing folk come from across the border, towards Galway where the racetrack hosts the summer festival. Only when Fallon became a champion in England did attention begin to shift, at least in the public bar at Fogarty's, away from the fortunes of the local hurling teams and towards the distant horizons of Newmarket. Unlike many of his contemporaries, men such as Mick Kinane, Charlie Swan, Pat Eddery, Richard Hughes, the Swinburns, who had horseracing in their DNA, Fallon had no grounding, no background and no understanding of the ways or the language of racing. The farmer-trainers who peppered the landscape in other counties were markedly absent from the west of Clare, and there was no pony racing. Horses were used on the land not in the frivolous pursuit of racing.

Fallon came from so far outside the normal parameters of his sport that he never felt truly comfortable with its society, even when he was the champion. 'It's all right for you up there,' he once told a journalist. 'It's much harder for us down here.' He was talking about social status, not height. Only later in his life, when he had checked himself in to a rehabilitation clinic and listened to other people talk about their addictions, did Fallon start to understand the extent of his own insecurity, which can be traced back to his childhood in hurling country. 'It [the drink] gave me confidence, allowed me to be comfortable in situations where I wouldn't otherwise be comfortable,' he told *Sunday Times* journalist David Walsh in the New Year of 2003. By then, he was the five-times champion jockey and one of the most respected riders in the history of the sport, but he was still searching for confidence at the bottom of a bottle. Yet the edginess, the non-conformity, the vulnerability, the need to prove himself every day of the week also put Fallon directly in the line of legendarily uncompromising Irish sportsmen such as A.P. McCoy and Roy Keane. No less than them, Fallon was fiercely proud of who he was and where he came from. He just held on a little too tight to the way of life that defined him.

The family were well known in the district. Kieren's grandfather, Fergus, had served in the First World War and, according to the locals, had won a medal for bravery. The military records do indeed record that a Fergus Fallon, a Gunner in 250 Brigade of the Northumbrian Regiment, won a British medal for his service in the trenches in 1918. The Royal Munster Fusiliers amalgamated with the Northumbrian Artillery Regiment, whose ranks had been decimated on the Somme, late in the war, and so it's quite possible that this is Kieren's grandfather, but no place or date of birth is recorded. One of Fergus's four sons, Patrick, emigrated to America where the Fallon family have become pillars of the local Catholic Church in Des Plaines, a suburb of Chicago. Patrick Fallon died at the age of 80 in 2006, but among his thirteen grandchildren there is a Kieran, which means 'dark-haired one' or the 'little dark one' in Gaelic.

Quite where Fallon unearthed his love of horses is a matter for debate. The family kept cows, sheep and chickens in Ballinruan and one story has it that Fallon would hop on the back of the most docile cow and pretend to ride it for all he was worth with an imaginary whip. The family had a couple of Connemara ponies and Fallon loved to ride those, too, clinging on to the mane, gripping with his legs, for as long as possible across the fields. His father took him to Galway Races once, but, in the rare moments when he recalls his childhood, he does not regard either that visit or the Irish love of a bet as being significant in his choice of dream.

He does record the fact, almost shocking now, that, at times, he had to share a bed with two of his brothers. A plasterer's wages did not always cover the living expenses of a large family and so the Fallons' existence, always loving and warm, was often hand to mouth. Turf for the fire had to be cut and hauled into the outhouse for winter and drinking water carried from the well. There were no tractors to ease the legwork around the farm, so the children all helped with humping the bales of hay for the feed, and Fallon's father was often away, following the work to London or Dublin. The Fallons' house was one of the more modern ones, built in the 1940s with two storeys, but young Kieren, together with his brothers – Fergus, Michael and Dermot – and sisters – Geraldine and Nora – learned to fend for himself. The strength of Fallon's body and legs, which characterised his style of riding, can be traced directly back to the natural fitness developed in childhood.

'I have a picture of this young lad with his schoolbag on his back, walking up the hill to school on a wet and wintry morning,' recalled Stephen Cunningham, a member of Crusheen's championship-winning hurling team. 'That was Kieren.'

Cunningham was a few years older than Kieren, but played on the same team and knew all the Fallon boys. He too had plodded up that hill, haversack on his back, homework half done, fearful of the reception he would receive from his teacher, Taidh McNamara, who ruled the classroom at the old National School with pre-enlightenment authority.

'I don't have the fondest memories of the place, but it possibly got a bit kinder when Kieren was there,' said Cunningham. 'If you hadn't done your schoolwork, you'd get a good slap, and then if you told your mother or father at home that you'd got a slap, they'd give you another for getting slapped at school. You went to school and you went to Church and you did your work around the farm. They were tough times, you know, and Kieren would have known exactly the same sort of discipline.'

Sport and the countryside were the twin sanctuaries of life in Crusheen. 'The countryside was your own,' recalls Cunningham. 'You could go to the lough to swim or fish, or walk up to Ballinruan and into the mountains. A few would have bikes maybe, but mainly it was walking. If your neighbours had a wall, it wouldn't stop you. No one would chase you off the land or say where you could or couldn't go. Of an evening after school we'd gather in one of the fields to play hurling or football. Kieren would be there with his brothers. He was a tricky little corner forward at hurling, though I saw him in the goals a few times, too. He was a lovely little ball player and he'd be in there, right in the middle of the contest, that's for sure.'

Some people in the area had gone away and come back. Jim Regan left Ireland in 1953 and returned to Gort twenty-two years later. He'd worked in Broadmoor as a psychiatric nurse, had a trial with Reading FC and boxed as a middleweight to a decent amateur level. He left with no more than a small suitcase and a ticket to London, where his first job was digging the tunnels for the underground. He never forgot the thrill of receiving his first pay packet – just £15 but he felt like a prince. On the way home he stopped off to buy a new suit, then he sent £2 home to his mother, as he did every week thereafter.

'We needed the money at home, that was the basis of it,' he says. 'But I always had the ambition to improve myself and it was the same with Kieren. Jane, my wife, and I helped Kieren at the start, but he helped himself mostly. He wasn't educated but he had a good solid grounding of life and living.'

In Jim Regan, Fallon found – and still finds, because he keeps in regular touch – a man who would give his dreams of becoming a jockey proper consideration and encouragement. He wanted to know how Regan had done it and what England was really like. It was not just that he sensed a big wide world out there, but that his ambitions could not be contained forever within the confines of Crusheen. Fallon found an outlet for his mounting frustration in the boxing gym and on the hurling field.

'Boxing helped me develop as a sportsman. Skipping and sparring made me more agile. I also acquired a certain confidence when confronted by physical aggression. I was still very small for my age and the techniques and disciplines learned in the boxing ring provided me with a psychological edge. I could look after myself even though I was small and shy.'

Who wrote that? Roy Keane. But it could just as easily have been Fallon. Translate Keane's conviction, his will, tenacity and anger into Fallon's slim frame and you have the genesis of the six-times champion jockey. In place of Keane haranguing the referee in a fit of rage, you have Fallon pulling Stuart Webster off his horse at a nondescript meeting at Beverley in 1994, an act of violence prompted not just by a surge of anger but a sense of how justice really worked in the ring and in life. It was a matter of SOS, according to Regan – Stretch Or Starve. Stretch for the last piece of bread or starve. Fallon turned the racetrack into a form of hand-to-hand combat, asserting his will on his rivals every afternoon of the week, daring them to snatch the last crumb. If someone tried to get in your way, then retaliation was compulsory, a matter of instinct and honour. Keane played like that and Fallon, at his height, when alcohol hadn't dulled his senses, rode like that, with a drive and a wit that mocked racing's unpredictability.

But Fallon and his fellow Irishman were different in one significant way. The Keane family were steeped in football – Keane just took the family's talent on to a much bigger stage. Fallon had no such support, not because his family didn't care but because they didn't know. 'Loyalty to family and friends remains a cornerstone of my life,' Keane writes. Fallon would share the same philosophy. Keane just developed a better understanding of how the outside world worked than Fallon did. Fallon always seemed shy and self-conscious of his own success.

'I'd put him right up there with Keane,' says Regan. 'They're streets apart from anyone else in their field. With them both, there's a strong sense of taking life as it is because things could be a lot worse. That's inherent, perhaps because we were so long in oppression and we weren't able to express ourselves so strongly. You knew with Kieren that he would always give his best, you would never be ashamed of him.'

Regan brings his knowledge of Freudian psychology to bear on the little boy who listened so attentively in his front room all those years ago. It's when the id, the pleasurable impulse, suppresses the super ego, the rational understanding of reality, that Fallon is liable to court trouble, according to Regan. The simple truth is that Fallon has never fully understood himself, id or no id. He certainly could not be accused of having a super ego in the common use of the phrase. Modesty is one of Fallon's prime virtues. Alan Lee, racing correspondent of *The Times* and one of the few journalists to have taken the trouble to understand Fallon the man not just Fallon the rider, believes that beneath the bravado lies a complex and vulnerable character, still bewildered by the success he's enjoyed and equally by the opprobrium and trouble he's attracted along the way.

'He doesn't think he's going to be recognised anywhere and so he has this endearing and infuriating habit of being unable to see what he should and shouldn't be doing,' says Lee. 'Reading is a problem for him – it's a form of dyslexia – but it makes the world a frightening place, particularly with those he sees as educated and in authority. He likes having people around him who, in his view, are supportive, but that can attract the wrong type of person. I believe he thinks he has loads of friends, but I'm not sure he has. He sees his life as a triumph against the odds.'

So what did Fallon have in his rucksack when he left Crusheen to find his fortune? Not much in the way of qualifications, not from the class-room, and no experience of horses. He had no academic certificates, except in woodwork. He would have passed in cooking, had there been such an exam at the time. Fallon, to everyone's surprise, is still a good cook. What he did have was a dream, and a desire to succeed. He had presence and character, strength, courage, a love of nature and a naïve belief in his own destiny. He didn't know quite what that was or how far it would take him, but he certainly hadn't found anything to keep him in Crusheen. That he did know.

The only book he ever brought back from school was entitled *How To Become A Jockey*. It included a list of names and addresses of major trainers and Fallon's mother wrote off to five of them – Andrew McNamara, Edward O'Grady, Dermot Weld, Jim Bolger and Kevin Prendergast – asking if they would take her son as an apprentice. Only Kevin Prendergast replied. Donn McLean, racing correspondent of the *Sunday Times* in Ireland, once asked Fallon what would have happened if Prendergast hadn't replied. 'I could have ended up on the building sites or something,' Fallon said. 'But I believe if you have a gift, it will come through in some way.' The feeling was shared among the elders of the community. Stephen Cunningham can remember his father and neighbours saying that young Kieren Fallon would make something of himself, whatever he did. Anyone who had the ambition to leave the village had the best wishes of the whole community and Fallon was no different. They knew they'd hear more of young Kieren.

One other factor was working in Fallon's favour, although he knew nothing about it. The steady trickle of Irish jockeys riding in England had become a flow. There was Pat Eddery and young Walter Swinburn. Mick Kinane, though always based in Ireland, was much in demand for the big races overseas, and Ray Cochrane was about to become stable jockey to the powerful Sussex stable of Guy Harwood. Irish jockeys were fashionable, so, not for the last time, Fallon's timing was good. It still didn't make the road out of Crusheen any smoother.

'Coming from where he has, it would have been a huge achievement if he'd become a top jockey in Ireland,' says Stephen Cunningham. 'But to hit the dizzy heights he's done, Jeezus, it's an incredible story.'

2

APPRENTICE YEARS

'If you dared Kieren to do something, he'd do something mad all right.'

Charlie Swan

Fallon arrived on the Curragh, five stone wet through and with five pounds in his pocket, in February of 1983. His 18th birthday was still two weeks away, which meant that, not for the first or last time in his life, he started a few years behind the rest. Whether he knew it or not – and the chances are he did not – Fallon had been pitched without ceremony and without any discernible training straight into the heart of Irish racing. No less than Newmarket, the centre of flat racing in England, the Curragh is the spiritual home of the Irish turf, 5,000 acres of well-drained common land between the towns of Newbridge and Kildare dedicated to the well being of the Thoroughbred, a flat, green, business park for a multi-million pound industry. The Curragh means the 'place of the running horse' in Gaelic and connections with the racetrack, one of the finest in the world, can be traced back to the early eighteenth century. If Fallon was to make it as a jockey in his native land, this is where, sooner or later, he had to come.

The Curragh was dotted with training yards and Fallon could have landed at the door of any one of them. But, by luck or design, his mother had picked one of the best, a yard run with a benevolent eye and Dickensian discipline by Kevin Prendergast, a member of one of Ireland's great racing dynasties. Paddy Prendergast, Kevin's father, had been Britain's champion trainer for three consecutive years between 1963 and 1965, a remarkable feat for an Irish trainer, given the depth of the competition back then and the greater difficulty in travelling with the horses. There was never much doubt that Kevin would inherit the training gene and, having learnt his trade in Australia in the early fifties and been assistant to his father for ten years, he set up on his own in the midsixties. By the time his father died in 1980, on the same day that Ardross, a horse Paddy had bred and Kevin had once trained, was narrowly beaten in the Gold Cup at Ascot, Kevin had already established himself as a leading trainer in his own right.

For a young apprentice who had barely sat on a pony let alone soothed the brow of a tetchy two-year-old, this was a demanding school. Enlightenment of a sort might have penetrated the schoolrooms of Ireland by the early eighties, but their racing yards were still regarded as houses of correction as much as of education. There was a rigid hierarchy, strict and unwritten rules of observance and a rhythm of working that has characterised racing yards since the very first days of the Curragh. A glimpse of the way of life in an Irish yard can be found in the pages of the autobiography of another champion, Tony McCoy. His master was Jim Bolger, a trainer of the same old school as Kevin Prendergast. In an early chapter, McCoy describes a typical morning at Bolger's yard in Coolcullen.

> About 23 to 30 horses would be walking around the yard and the lads would be talking freely until they heard the metallic clang of the catch on the gate at the bottom of the yard, which signalled the arrival of the boss. Then there was absolute silence … there was no speaking until you were spoken to. I don't think it's exaggerating to say that if we were not exactly frightened of him, we were certainly in awe of him. Everything had to be right.*

The same regimental discipline was applied at Kevin Prendergast's, as Fallon quickly and instinctively understood.

*McCoy: The Autobiography, Michael Joseph 2002

'Kevin was a very nice man and really good trainer,' recalled Charlie Swan, who came to Prendergast's the year after Fallon. 'Some people might describe him as a loveable rogue. Put it this way, he'd call a spade a spade. You always knew where you stood with him, but he'd say it to you straight and not hold a grudge. If he liked you, he liked you.'

Two qualities made the new boy from County Clare stand out from many of the other lads in the yard. One was that he had a prodigious appetite for work and the other, noticed quickly by Swan on his arrival, was a natural facility for handling difficult horses. Swan was particularly taken by Fallon's ability to tame the yearlings, which was always one of the jobs of the apprentices.

'Me and Kieren would have to ride the breakers, the yearlings who'd just been broken,' Swan explained. 'We'd be riding them for the first time and they'd be bucking and plunging and rearing and whatever. We'd take them out on to the Curragh, trying to get their mouths organised and teaching them a bit about the business. Kieren was a real natural at it. He'd ride any rough one and we'd be jumping them over the bushes and everything. He had loads of guts and was a good rough rider. He'd ride anything.'

In a later interview with David Walsh of the *Sunday Times*, Fallon spoke of those early, lonely days in Kildare. He shared a room with three other stable lads. On the first night, one of them asked him for a loan. Fallon obliged, as he tended to do for anyone who asked throughout his life.

On the first day in the yard, Tom Fitzgerald, the head lad, took Fallon under his wing, put him up on one of the more docile horses in the yard and told him the secret of riding. 'Just find your natural rhythm,' he said. 'It will take time.' But not too long. In a week, no more than two, certainly quicker than Tom Fitzgerald had anticipated, Fallon was able to ride work with the rest of the yard and look as though he had spent much of his life on horseback, which was very far from the truth. Fallon, Fitzgerald also noted, was a natural.

If that earned him respect among the thirty or so lads and lasses in Kevin Prendergast's care at the time, it did not earn him any special dispensation when the list of jobs was being handed out. Accommodation was Spartan, and the working day began at 7 a.m., mucking out four or five stalls before tacking up for first lot. Only when the stables were spotless could any of the stable staff disperse for lunch. Then it was back in for evening stables. Monday mornings were the worst because the horses hadn't been mucked out on Sunday, so there was twice the muck to carry out.

'We had to muck out with muck sacks,' Swan recalled. 'The head man would cut off a roll of sack and you'd shovel the straw and shit on to the sack and carry it on your back down the yard. On Mondays, it would be dripping down the back of your neck. Tom [Fitzgerald] was a hard man, old school, if you like. He'd sack you if you weren't up to scratch in any way, but Kieren got on well with him. Kieren was a good worker, now, but always a bit of a character. If you'd dare him to do something, he'd do something mad all right.'

Legend has it that, on his first morning, Fallon was so anxious to impress, he mucked out ten stables on his own. The story is not too far-fetched. Laziness is not one of Fallon's faults, as Gabriel 'Squibs' Curran, Prendergast's stable jockey at the time, remembered.

'Kieren always had a spring in his step round the yard, and anyone with a bit of get up and go about him, you notice,' Curran said. 'But if you didn't graft at Kevin's, you didn't last long, and if you didn't learn anything, you wouldn't learn anywhere. Kieren grafted and he learnt. He always had a mind of his own, but he was a great worker.'

The lure for every apprentice, though, is a ride on the racetrack. The majority of stable lads are failed jockeys – very few who come into the sport with big dreams manage to fulfil them – and for much of his time with Kevin Prendergast, it seemed that Kieren Fallon would be just another rider who didn't quite make the grade. Despite the support of Tom Fitzgerald, Prendergast appeared unimpressed by the new boy's skills or his slightly cocky attitude. Either way, Fallon had to wait nearly a year for his first ride in public, and until 19 June 1984 for his first winner, Piccadilly Lord at Navan.

'He was a little chestnut colt, very nervous, and Kieren rode him in a mile and a quarter race,' Gabriel Curran said. 'Navan's a lovely galloping track but Piccadilly Lord was quite nervous and needed a bit of settling. Kieren rode him beautifully, very naturally. He dawdled along at the back and just let him go when the moment was right. He always had soft hands. You're either heavy-handed or you're soft-handed. It's a gift and Kieren had it, like Mick Kinane and Walter Swinburn.'

By this time, Charlie Swan had joined the yard's two main apprentices, Fallon and Eddie Leonard. Charlie, a teenager blessed with a choirboy's face and a velvet touch, could not have come from a background more different from Fallon's. Where Fallon had no racing blood and very little obvious advantage in life, Swan came from the landed gentry and was brought up to the sounds and rhythms of the racing yard run by his father, Donald, a former captain in the Queen's Dragoon Guards. Swan was sent away to Dublin for his schooling; Fallon can remember very little schooling to speak of. Swan began riding a pony when he was four and, not long after that, was walking a two-year-old out on the roads and giving him a bit of a canter across the gallops. Fallon was pretending to race-ride cows and Connemara ponies in a field out the back. Like so many of his contemporaries, Swan graduated through pony racing and by the time he reached the gates of Prendergast's Friarstown yard he had already ridden a handful of winners for his father. Although nearly three years Fallon's junior, he was far advanced in terms of experience.

Perhaps it was that balancing of abilities that shaped one of the most unlikely friendships in racing. You wonder what on earth Fallon would have made of the weekend he was invited back to the Swans' ancestral home, a sturdy, stone-built mansion just outside Cloughjordan in County Tipperary, for the 21st birthday party of Charlie's sister. It was fancy dress, but Charlie forgot to tell Kieren, perhaps for fear that such a shy country boy might refuse to come. From the outside, it seemed that they had a talent in common but little else. Yet their friendship has endured to this day. Even now, Fallon still remembers his apprentice days fondly. Life did not seem so complicated back then.

After a while, Fallon moved out of the stable accommodation and into a flat above the butcher's shop in Kildare. Charlie Swan was his flat-mate, which would make for possibly the most prolific flat-sharing arrangement in the history of racing – Swan, the most successful

National Hunt rider in Ireland, and Fallon, the six-times flat champion in England.

'Charlie Swan was probably the most talented jockey I ever had here,' said Kevin Prendergast in the spring of 2007. 'Gabriel Curran was a fine rider who won the Guineas for me, and Kieren Fallon was an apprentice here for five years, too.' He did add, 'He [Kieren] is a great jockey...' but the order of priority betrayed Prendergast's way of thinking, now and then. For some reason that Swan cannot quite understand, Fallon never quite commanded the same confidence or gained the same opportunities as Swan did.

'A woman who used to work with my father was married to Gabriel Curran,' said Swan. 'He said there was only one apprentice in the yard and he wasn't getting many rides. That was Kieren Fallon. I remember thinking, "Jeezus, I wonder what Kieren will think about me coming in," but he was very good about it and we always got on well. You'd always be a little afraid that I was coming to take his rides, which I probably was.'

One ride of Swan's must have hurt Fallon more than most. It came in the Naas November Handicap, a race with decent prize money, which Swan won on Piccadilly Lord, Fallon's first winner. Swan does not know to this day why Fallon didn't keep the ride, but he wasn't about to question the decision, and he recalls two things that stand out about that victory. One is that Fallon was the first person to congratulate him back in the yard. The second is that he won on Piccadilly Lord again soon after.

Gabriel Curran was aware of Fallon's difficulties. 'I helped to get Charlie the job at Kevin's and he would have had it a lot easier than Kieren, for sure,' said Curran. 'Kevin might say differently now but he didn't see eye to eye with Kieren at all. He didn't. Kieren, how best to say this, could be an arrogant little fella at the time, very strong-willed, and it was hard to come into a yard like that and ride alongside boys who had been riding since they were small.'

In a hint of difficult relationships to come, Fallon did not always see eye to eye with the stable jockey either, as Curran recalls. 'I think he thought I was trying to take his rides or something, so one day I said to him, "Kieren, are we going to go on like this, going left and right all the time, or are we going to shake hands on it and become friends." We shook hands and we've been friends ever since. We wouldn't be the best of mates, but we meet when we can. The thing about Kieren is that he's got nothing easily, he's had to work for everything he's got.'

Progress was certainly slow for Fallon as an apprentice. He and Swan played a lot of pool together, which Fallon tended to win, and there were plenty of evenings out in Kildare, which could be lively on a Saturday night. Swan was smart enough to stay on the right side of a man who had a short temper and quick fists.

'Kieren never had a chip on his shoulder,' Swan said. 'You know he's actually quite quiet, quite a shy person, way shier than people would think, but he'd either like you or he wouldn't, and he'd tell you if he didn't like you. He's a tough man, well able to take care of himself, which was important in that environment. I used to stand behind him because Kildare would be rough enough when we were stable lads, the odd scuffle or whatever, and Kieren would look after himself and his friends around him. He'd be a loyal fellow, now, he would be. But people knew he had that sort of temperament, a bit volatile, and they'd be egging him on.

'I've heard some bad things about him, but I've never seen that side of him. I'd say he had trouble trusting people. If he trusted you, you'd be fine. If not... But he was very good in the yard. He'd get on well enough with everyone, brushing one here, mucking out one there. He was always busy. Kieren was very smart that way. He was just unfortunate. He was just slow to get going for some reason.'

It took Fallon two years to reach double figures in a season, his ten for the 1986 flat year bringing him seventh place in the apprentices' table. The following year, he began at last to make a breakthrough, finishing runner-up to Kevin Manning, the champion apprentice. But despite posting one of his biggest wins on Pylon Sparks in the November Handicap at Leopardstown in the final days of the 1987 season, Fallon knew deep down that his days on the Curragh were numbered and that his future lay in England, where there were two or three meetings every day and far less of a closed shop. Plenty of talented

Irish jockeys had made their fortune across the Irish Sea, most notably Pat Eddery and Walter Swinburn.

'He'd had a good grounding at Kevin's,' said Gabriel Curran. 'He saw how horses should be treated and how to be a horseman as well as a jockey, but if he was going to get anywhere, he had to go to England. Kieren had to make the break to get away. He was clever enough to see that.'

The connection still had to be made and it was here that Fallon's luck held good. Staying two doors down from Fallon and Swan in Kildare was Dessie Scahill, racing journalist and commentator. If anyone could make a connection across the Irish Sea it was Dessie, who had already negotiated a similar move for Mark Dwyer and would later help both Tony McCoy and Adrian Maguire on their way to the top. Through Dwyer, with whom he'd once shared digs, Scahill knew that there was a vacancy for a flat rider at Jimmy Fitzgerald's yard in the North Yorkshire town of Malton, which was at the time, before the rise of Mark Johnston at Middleham, the epicentre of racing in the north of England. Scahill had noticed Fallon's style and thought he had potential, greater potential certainly than was being exploited by Kevin Prendergast. He rang Fitzgerald, suggesting that Fallon was a talented young rider who needed a break and who, he thought, would do well in the north.

'Tell him to be here by Monday,' barked Fitzgerald. Fallon arrived on Wednesday, having gone back home first to tell his parents of the new move in his career.

'Jimmy will be a tough taskmaster,' Scahill said to Fallon, 'but if you work for him, he'll look after you.'

At Malton, Fallon found a yard different in size but not much different in terms of style or discipline from Friarstown. Like the Curragh, Malton was a town twinned with racing. In the *Directory of the Turf*, the bible of international racing, which includes the names and addresses of almost every trainer, jockey, owner, journalist and breeder in racing throughout the world, only four training centres in the UK – Newmarket, Lambourn, Malton and Middleham – are accorded the privilege of a special map detailing the yards. Only the Curragh qualifies for the same treatment in Ireland. By the time the 23-year-old Fallon arrived in town, Malton was in decline, but two things would have made him feel close to home. One was the rolling countryside of North Yorkshire, the other the despotic rule of Jimmy Fitzgerald.

Fitzgerald, like Kevin Prendergast, ran his yard with a traditional crack of the whip. He was that rarity in modern racing, a genuine dual-purpose trainer, and although Fitzgerald's star was on the wane by the time the unknown young Irishman with the piercing blue eyes and the winning smile arrived at Norton Grange Stables, Fitzgerald still knew a decent jockey when he saw one, and certainly retained the knack of setting up a decent betting coup.

In Fitzgerald, Fallon recognised a fellow traveller, older and wiser, for sure, but from the same stock. Fitzgerald loved to tell the story of how a friend bet him £5 that he would not take the Dublin–Liverpool ferry that night and follow the road to fame and fortune in England. He accepted the bet and, having ridden more than 200 winners as a National Hunt rider before his career was cut short by injury, comfort-ably won his wager. After that, he set up, a trifle reluctantly, as a trainer in Malton in the early sixties. That he arrived in Liverpool with £5 in his pocket and no idea of his destiny would have struck an echo with Fallon, whose own finances were not much more handsome on his arrival in Malton.

'When I joined him I was quite heavy,' Fallon recalled in his tribute to Fitzgerald in 2004. 'He was a very funny man and he just looked at me and said, "It's a bloody flat jockey I want, not a bloody jump jockey. I've got plenty of those." He was unbelievable as a trainer, just as good whether it was with a Gold Cup horse, such as Forgive 'N' Forget, or a two-year-old at somewhere like Hamilton or Musselburgh.'

At the time, Fitzgerald was still one of the most powerful trainers in the north, even if the days of Forgive 'N' Forget, who won the Gold Cup so memorably in 1985, were over. Fitzy could assess a horse's natural ability with uncanny accuracy, a skill that allowed him to mount some extravagant gambles in his time. It was the way the bills were paid. Besides, caning the bookmakers was one of the delights of the profes-sion and Fitzgerald was never happier than when plotting their downfall with a horse such as Trainglot, which won the 1990 Cesarewitch, or Sapience, who was backed down from 40–1 to 15–2 to win the Ebor. But Fitzy was no sentimentalist, either. By rights, Sapience should have been ridden by Fallon in the 1989 Ebor. Instead, Fitzgerald gave the ride to Pat Eddery, a slight that Fallon might have forgiven but certainly never forgot. It was a constant source of reference in subsequent interviews, a constant reminder of a saying that old Tom Fitzgerald (no relation) would recite in the tack room at Friarstown – 'Remember, Kieren, life's a rat race and the biggest rat wins.' The disappointment of being 'jocked off' Sapience haunted Fallon ever after, not least when he was able to do the same to lesser-known jockeys during his championship years.

At Norton Grange, Fallon found a yard long on mediocrity and short on stars, but at least he was guaranteed a few more rides than he had been getting in Ireland. Yet Malton was still one of the powerhouses of northern racing, as competitive as Newmarket in its way, with trainers of the stature of Bill Elsey, Jimmy Etherington, the Easterbys and Malcolm Jefferson all based in or around the historic old Roman town. Fallon moved into a whitewashed cottage at the top of the town and began to assess his new life. In many ways it was not much different from his old one, except that the emphasis had shifted subtly. He was no longer a mere stablehand, he was stable jockey, and although with Fitzgerald that still meant driving back from the races to do his turn at evening stables, he had his foot on the bottom rung of a very long ladder. He was able to advertise his talent most afternoons on the racetracks of the north. Fallon certainly made an instant impression on the stable as much for his appearance as his natural ability on a difficult Thoroughbred.

'He was always tidy and immaculate,' recalls Tom O'Ryan, award-winning racing writer, who was a work rider at the time. 'To make an impression, you've got to stand out from the crowd, and Kieren understood that. He always wore matching waterproofs and jacket, shiny boots and nice gloves. But he also had huge patience with the horses. He was very quiet on them, trying to nurture them rather than bully them.

'At Fitzy's, it was an hour and a quarter ride to the gallops across the town and if you had a two-year-old jig-jigging all the way, it would drive you crackers. But Kieren always seemed very calm on a horse. He'd use that time to educate the horses and get to know them. He was riding jumpers as well, so he was getting a good education. But he came as a pretty polished jockey, not as a greenhorn.

'Fitzy had this way of looking at you when it was best to keep your head down. He'd go red and purple in the face and the colours would deepen as the morning wore on. Half of it was bluff, but Fitzy was pretty quick to identify a horseman and so Kieren might well have taken more than his share of stick, because Jimmy had identified him as a real talent. Kieren would travel with Jimmy to the races and there he'd probably see a different side of the man, with Fitzy calmly smoking his cigar. If you've got half a brain, you'd learn, but Kieren had to develop a thick skin just like the rest of us.'

At the time, O'Ryan was living in a three-bedroomed semi-detached house on an estate close to the yard, but a 'for sale' sign outside notified others of his intention to move on. One evening, a knock came on the door. O'Ryan, who was on the phone, answered it only to find a familiar figure on the doorstep. Neither man knows which of them was more surprised by the meeting, but Fallon, never one to mess about with the detail, had a quick look round the house and told O'Ryan he would buy it.

'Kieren went off to India for the winter after that, but the deal was concluded as soon as he came back,' O'Ryan recalls.

It was a significant step for Fallon, the first sign of financial security in a precarious profession. The pair have kept in touch ever since. O'Ryan, who became the Horserace Writers' Association journalist of the year, charted Fallon's rise with an acute eye and without ever betraying the trust earned the hard way on cold mornings at Norton Grange.

Another witness to Fallon's early days in English racing was Mark Dwyer, who had made the same journey across the Irish Sea six years earlier and had established himself in the very top rank of National Hunt riders by the late eighties. One of eight children from a town ten miles outside Dublin, Dwyer shares a tough rural background with

Fallon, and has the same piercing blue eyes, but from somewhere along the line Dwyer inherited sound common sense, and developed a real understanding of the ways of the world, which has largely eluded Fallon. If there was dangerous company to be kept, Fallon would risk it; Dwyer would walk the other way. Dwyer graduated through the ranks via the academy run by Liam Browne on the Curragh, and was good enough on the flat to ride sixty-six winners in Ireland before his five-feet ten-inch frame filled out and turned him into a jump jockey, still able to do 10 stone 1lb throughout most of his career. Dwyer knew exactly where Fallon had come from and exactly what racing education he would have undergone on the Curragh because he had been there himself.

'Kieren came from a good school in Kevin Prendergast's,' he said. 'Liam Browne and Prendergast would be the two toughest guys on the Curragh back then. They were fair but tough. You learnt the whole package, not just tightening up your riding, but how to address people off the horse as well. I just kept working away, coming in early on Mondays when you could earn a few bob more for doing some extra jobs, just doing a bit more than the others. If it didn't work out, what else were you going to do? I left school at fourteen and though there was mention of night classes, the thought didn't appeal to me much.'

When the chance came to move to the north of England with Jimmy Fitzgerald, Dwyer, like Fallon, took it. At the age of 19, he rode Forgive 'N' Forget to land a memorable gamble for the yard in the 1983 Coral Hurdle Final at Cheltenham. Given the importance of the race, it was a tribute to Dwyer's nerve, and to Fitzgerald's confidence in the young Irishman, that he claimed the ride at such a tender age. The biggest prize of all followed two years later when Dwyer and Forgive 'N' Forget won the Cheltenham Gold Cup, a victory he repeated eight years later on Jodami for Peter Beaumont. At his peak, before an elbow injury curtailed his career, Dwyer was a powerful and astute race-rider, right up there with the best of his generation, especially on the big days when a quick brain and strong nerve could make all the difference.

'The only way you can find out precisely how well Mark is going in a race would be to stop and ask him,' one rival said, a quality echoed in Frankie Dettori's judgement of Fallon, his most persistent foe over twenty years on the flat. No less than Fallon, Dwyer was brought up to look after himself around the yard and in his dealings with other people. Although his success at the Festival helped to balance the relationship between master and pupil in those early years, a long-standing friendship with Fitzy was not won without a struggle.

'Fitzy was a hard man, a very hard man,' said Dwyer. 'It would be similar to Liam Browne's yard on the Curragh but not as educational. You'd get a bollocking from Jimmy but you wouldn't be any wiser about why by the end of it. I got on very well with him. I didn't have a retainer. I just took my chance. The only bad memory was that Jimmy called me a liar one day and he was wrong. That never left me, but I have loads of good memories. Jimmy was as soft as a brush when you got him away from the yard. In the early days, you were the boy and he was the master, but eventually he mellowed, and in later years we were good friends. It was probably much the same for Kieren.

'Jimmy and Kieren fought like cat and dog. I don't know how they didn't kill each other because they were two strong personalities together. I wasn't there quite so much when Kieren came, I wasn't as tied to the yard, but the exchanges were memorable, that's all I can say. Kieren was very strong-willed. It would be water off a duck's back. He wouldn't give a damn what anyone said. But they got on despite their differences. There was respect on both sides, particularly when Kieren had moved on and become more successful. They always kept in contact.'

If there was a source of tension between Fitzgerald and Dwyer, it came in their different appreciation of the way horses should be ridden. Fitzgerald liked his horses to be close to the pace, whereas Dwyer, more Timmy Murphy than A.P. McCoy, preferred to let them settle and then get into the race. Fallon's instinct was much the same, but it wasn't until he joined the stable of Jack and Lynda Ramsden that he was able to develop the style of race-riding from off the pace that later became his trademark. What he did learn at Norton Grange was the mastery of a horse, not just for a brief turn on the gallops and back to the yard, but over that long morning walk to and from the gallops, which helped both the conditioning and education of Fitzgerald's horses. As relevant to Fallon's development was the camber and incline of the two main gallops across town, known locally as Ponte A and Ponte B because of their similarity to the rising ground on the straight at Pontefract. Fallon learnt to judge pace over the terrain so precisely that, not long after, when the winners began to flow, he became the self-styled 'King of Ponte'.

In the spring of 1988, Fallon, at the age of 23, was the oldest five-pound claimer in the weighing-room. His career was at the first of many crossroads. Unknown and unheralded, he had a wide horizon ahead of him but only a narrow window of opportunity through which to view it. Fitzgerald was a canny trainer, a good judge of a horse and rider, popular and well connected, but he did not have the strongest flat string in Malton, let alone the north. It is perhaps indicative that no other more established northern jockey had snapped at the chance of riding for Jimmy Fitzgerald, but the assessment of one of them, John Lowe, perhaps suggests why.

'I always felt sorry for those who worked for Fitzy,' he explained. 'He was a very good trainer, but a hard taskmaster. You were really only a working jockey there. You'd never get a big head riding for Fitzy. None of this riding at Thirsk and not going back for evening stables. It didn't matter who you were, he was pretty hard on his staff, and Kieren was no exception.'

Fallon had been well educated in the ways of a racing yard at Friarstown and had a strong enough character to take the constant harrying. It was just the discipline, the respect for authority, the subservience that he found hard to master. A deep anti-authoritarian streak lies at the heart of Fallon's nature, a stubbornness that meant in those early days he would not back down from confrontation, either in the yard or on the racetrack. It made him a formidable foe in both arenas, and dangerous company on a night out in Kildare or Malton. Although he may have had some vague idea of how he might reach the top of his profession, in reality his chances of surviving in the world of northern racing were odds against and the chances of becoming a champion virtually negligible. Not being one to look beyond the day in most things – and particularly his chaotic time-keeping – Fallon had a natural buttress against the prevailing winds. So, armed with a prodigious if largely untapped talent, a rough self-belief borne in part of naïvete and in part of a refusal to accept defeat in any form, he set off up the ladder. The early portents were not auspicious.

After eight chances for his new stable, Fallon had yet to ride a winner when Fitzgerald took a temperamental if talented four-year-old called Evichstar to Thirsk for his seasonal debut. Evichstar, as Fallon was to find out memorably later that April, was not an easy ride. In racing parlance, even at the age of four, he had developed his own ideas about the game and they did not always conform to those of the trainer or jockey. However, these were just the sort of horses that Fallon loved to ride, and the pair had already found some sort of understanding on the gallops above Malton.

The Thirsk Hall EBF Stakes over six furlongs was the feature race on the card on Saturday, 16 April, with a prize fund of just under £9,000 proving a lure for a couple of powerful southern trainers, notably Paul Cole, who saddled the favourite, Jannubi, ridden by Richard Quinn. Bill Watts, Mick Easterby, Jimmy Etherington and Fitzgerald led the northern defence, with Evichstar being backed heavily from 14–1 to 11–2. Fallon was clearly at the sharp end of a good old-fashioned betting coup, nurtured by the residents of Norton Grange. The money was rarely in doubt. From the furlong pole, there were only two possible winners – Richard Quinn was already hard at work on Jannubi while Fallon, more upright and less elegant in the saddle, was about to unleash Evichstar for his final challenge. Once he did, the race was swiftly decided, Fallon and Evichstar running out comfortable winners by a length and a half to bring Fitzgerald and the owners a handsome reward and Fallon his first winner on English soil.

The celebrations that night in Malton would have been better than routine. Fitzgerald 'certainly knew how to celebrate a good victory', as Mark Dwyer noted later – Fallon, too – but for any jockey, a first winner is a cause for a proper and time-honoured memorial. And there was no Sunday racing in those days.

Two weeks later, Fallon and Evichstar were reunited for an ambitious tilt at a listed race at Haydock. Prince Rupert, a French-bred colt, travelled north for Barry Hills and the 9–4 favourite was Heroes Sash, who had recently finished third in the European Free Handicap at Newmarket – unremarkable perhaps, except for the jockey, a brash young apprentice with an ebullient manner and talent to spare, who had come north to ride for Luca Cumani. No less than Fallon, L. Dettori was just starting to make his way in a tough world, although his background, if not his nationality, and his connection with a powerful yard in Newmarket, seemed to promise a more conventional route to the top. Few at Haydock that day would have spotted the genesis of a great rivalry, not least because Evichstar suffered one of his more temperamental days and, having boiled over in the parade ring, bolted before the start, depositing Fallon over the railings. The scar on Fallon's face still bears witness to the incident, but the flailing that the jockey took from Fitzgerald would have left the more lasting mark. Evichstar, while not heavily fancied at 6–1, promised to be one of the stalwarts of the Fitzgerald stable through the 1988 season, and after his withdrawal at Haydock, plans had to be put on hold. The only slice of good news was that both horse and jockey returned relatively unscathed.

It may have been mere coincidence, but Fallon was not given another ride for the stable for ten days. After that, he soon began adding to his tally for the season, first on Saladan Knight in the Houghton Stakes at Beverley for Fitzgerald. More significantly, he began to pick up several rides for outside stables, always a decent measure of a jockey's rising status. None were exactly powerhouse stables, but in Colin Tinkler, Eric Alston and Neville Callaghan, Fallon had valuable support at a time when he needed every ounce of it.

To say that the winners flowed through that debut season would not be strictly true – a steady trickle might be a more accurate description.In June and July, Fallon won on Persistent Bell twice, Balkan Leader and White Sapphire, all for Fitzgerald, on Thirteenth Friday for William Pearce and on Steele's for Neville Callaghan, also twice. Fallon, remember, was still learning the northern tracks, with their quirks and subtleties, and he was up against riders of the calibre of John Lowe, who had been plying his trade in the north for much longer. The difference in age and experience did not stop a burgeoning and unlikely friendship between those two.

'By the time Kieren came, I was well entrenched,' Lowe recalled. 'I'd started in 1969–70 after a few years at Newmarket. My first winner came in 1968, but when Jack Watts retired, I moved up north to ride for his son, Bill. The mood was certainly different from in the south. There was a strong sense of camaraderie. It was one big party really, but a tough old slog, mind you.'

The slog wouldn't have bothered Fallon. He was used to it. Mussel-burgh, Hamilton, Redcar, Beverley, Thirsk down to Nottingham and across to Haydock, northern jockeys would travel prodigious distances just for a ride, let alone the odd winner. Only occasionally did Fallon cross the great divide and ride in the south. On 5 August he made his debut at Newmarket in an evening meeting, riding Notion to finish third for Neville Callaghan. A week later came another significant booking with a ride on Optimism Flamed for Mrs J.R. Ramsden at Haydock. The five-year-old finished eighth of 19, but the trainer noted the quiet confidence of the new young Irishman at Jimmy Fitzgerald's and quickly came calling.

On Saturday, 17 August Fallon passed another milestone, his first double in England, for Bill Elsey and Steve Muldoon, winners 17 and 18 for the season. A month later, victory on Greek Flutter at Redcar reduced Fallon's claim from five to three pounds, and although winners were difficult to find through the closing weeks of the season as Norton Grange turned its attention to the jumps, Fallon finished his first year in England with a highly respectable tally of 31 winners. More importantly, he was gaining a priceless education in the art of race-riding, learning to master the different tracks in the north and gaining a reputation for both his strength of mind on the track and his studious demeanour in the weighing-room. He was also about to learn another hard truth, one which bore out the old Tom Fitzgerald adage about life and rats.

Sapience had made his debut quietly at Beverley midway through 1988, ridden by Mark Birch, Fitzgerald's former stable jockey. There was no sign either in that run or in the market for his next race, a maiden at Chester, that Sapience was anything out of the ordinary. He went to post a 20–1 shot in a sixteen-runner field headed by a well-bred newcomer from Newmarket trained by Ben Hanbury. In Fallon's absence through suspension, Dean McKeown took the ride. The formbook puts it succinctly enough: 'headway and sixth straight, quickened to lead inside final furlong, comfortable'. Actually, the standard shorthand is simply 'comf', a word that suggests the Marquesa de Moratella's new two-year-old had plenty up for his sleeve for another time. Fitzgerald was as astonished by the performance as anyone. There was no doubting that, at last, he had unearthed a gem in the midst of the mediocrity at Norton Grange. Sapience was bred to stay for longer distances, a lot longer, yet he had spreadeagled some decent juveniles over seven furlongs on a fast track. The plotting began. Sapience was taken to Epsom for his first trip over a mile, and although hard ridden in the final furlong, he stayed on well enough to beat the favourite, Leading Bird, trained by Henry Cecil. Fallon had driven down to Epsom with Fitzgerald to ride Miracle of Love in the apprentice handicap, which he won, his first winner on the Derby course. Fitzgerald had hired Walter Swinburn to ride Sapience in the prized race of the afternoon.

Fallon was on board for Sapience's last outing of the season, a mile nursery at Ayr, but the pair finished thirteenth and the horse did not appear on a racetrack again until the following June when, again ridden by Fallon, he finished second of six over a mile and four furlongs at Beverley. The trip was significant. Fitzgerald had the Ebor – one of a trio of great long-distance handicaps – at York in his sights. An abortive outing in a handicap at Royal Ascot ensured a decent weight for the big day and the plot was laid. For Fallon, this promised to be a potential breakthrough, the moment that his fortunes finally took an upward turn, on a televised afternoon at a major summer meeting. Careers can hang on such slender threads. So Fallon, who had looked after the horse through much of his short career and ridden him most mornings on the gallops, waited for the call. It never came. A few days before the Ebor, Fitzgerald told him that Pat Eddery had been booked to ride. While Fallon watched on television, the champion and Sapience, his ride, won the Ebor at 15–2. John Lowe knew the feeling only too well.

'I had the same sort of thing with Edward Hide,' he said. 'Eddie got me riding for some other trainers in the north and I got on a horse called

Fearless Lad, I think it was, a giant chestnut sprinter, and I was winning on him. He was going to the King's Stand at Royal Ascot and had his last race before it at Beverley. I got a suspension and couldn't ride him. Who rode him that day? Edward. Who rode him at Ascot? Edward. What happened? He won. You can't have a go at the owners or anyone. You just have to suffer. You've got to work harder and show them you can ride just as well as the other guy. To be fair to Kieren, he did that.'

To be fair to Fitzgerald, Fallon was back in the saddle on Sapience for the St Leger and the Jockey Club Cup at Newmarket. Both times they finished second, but when Sapience graduated to Group One class at Longchamp in the Prix Royal-Oak at the very backend of the season, Willie Carson was given the ride. Fitzgerald's confidence in his stable jockey, who was still an apprentice, it should be remembered, had limits. Sapience went on to run three times in the King George at Ascot, and in the Prix de l'Arc de Triomphe won by Subotica in 1992. After being switched to David Elsworth's stable, he was beaten a short-head by Rock Hopper in the Hardwicke Stakes at Royal Ascot, ending his career with five wins from thirty-five starts, and having earned nearly half a million pounds in prize money. Fallon's association with the colt had ended long before that, but the memory of it never left him. In 1998, Fallon finally won the Ebor on Henry Cecil's Tuning.

'Thank God,' he said afterwards. 'I've wanted to win this race for so many years. I missed out when Pat jocked me off Sapience. He might have forgotten it, but I haven't. I had to watch the race on television and ever since I wanted to win it for myself.'

However, precious few horses of the calibre or consistency of Sapience bolstered Fitzgerald's armoury at the end of the eighties. Trainglot came later, illuminating a career already in its twilight. On reflection, Mark Dwyer wondered whether times moved on too fast for an old-fashioned trainer such as Fitzgerald.

'When I was there, we had plenty of meetings about changing a few things and it would be all agreed,' he said, 'but it never happened, which used to frustrate me a bit. Fitzy was very set in his ways.'

The statistics of Fallon's career tell of a man marking time – 28 winners in 1989, 39 in 1990, 29 in 1991 hardly make the graphic curve of a future champion. Not until Fallon decided to go freelance, as Dwyer had done before him, did his numbers begin to pick up and his name become more widely publicised. Yet there were little signs of progress.

In Eric Alston, Fallon had a confirmed supporter almost from his first day in the north. Alston, like Fitzgerald, is an old-fashioned type of trainer, with a canny eye for a good sprinter and a decent young jockey. When he was called up by Dave Pollington, Fallon's long-standing agent, and offered a five-pound claimer with a decent record in Ireland, Alston was only too happy to offer him a few rides. It was through one of them, a sprinting filly called Stack Rock, that the partnership was truly forged. From May 1991 to her retirement in September 1994, Fallon rode the filly twenty-four times and won seven races. Yet Stack Rock's finest hour came in defeat in the Prix de l'Abbaye in October 1993 when she was beaten by the flying Lochsong in a Group One over five furlongs at Longchamp in Fallon's first ride on the Continent.

The one race Alston remembers most clearly involved Fallon. 'It was at Ripon and he got off our horse to ride something else,' Alston said. 'Frankie Dettori rode ours and Kieren beat us by a head. I've never forgotten it. But we used Kieren from day one. He was great. Even back then, he would win on horses that others wouldn't have won on. People would think he was pushing them, but he wasn't. He'd just be niggling them along, keeping them interested. He was a very quiet lad, a man of few words, but if he told you something about your horse, it was generally worth listening to.'

Fallon learnt a lot from riding Stack Rock, in particular how to judge a race from the front. 'She mainly made all because she was very big and could jump out and gallop,' says Alston. Stack Rock died recently at the age of 16.

The partnership between Fallon and Alston, one of the game's great survivors and one of its most underrated trainers, has endured. Fallon still rode for his old friend on his trips to the north from Newmarket, on one condition at least – that Alston provided him with a winner. 'I've been training for over twenty-five years and to me Kieren's the best, that's all there is to it,' Alston added.

Strangely, because he is not a personal friend, Dwyer has also remained a fan of Fallon's. 'I mean, we wouldn't be on each other's Christmas card lists, put it that way,' he says, 'but if I had a horse that I thought would go all the way, Kieren would be the first on the list to ride him. He's as good and competitive as anyone out there.' Dwyer makes the distinction between Fallon the man and Fallon the jockey. Having retired from race-riding in 1996 after suffering an elbow injury – he still can't straighten the joint – Dwyer set up a highly successful business buying, selling and educating horses from a farm he bought during his riding days close to Malton. He keeps a close eye on the world of racing, although he is rarely tempted to go to the races himself these days. 'Kieren's determination and his ability marked him out from the rest,' he said. 'He has this instinct for knowing what and when to do things in a race. He is very seldom in the wrong place and I wouldn't like to be upsides of him in a finish, either. You'd back him most times, wouldn't you? He can get his horses switched off. It's a knack, and not everyone can do it. Even though he looks busy, when he wants them to change gear, they'll change gear. He's a bit in the Willie Carson mode – it looked as though they were going flat out but when Willie really wanted to go for it, there would be another gear. The same with Kieren. It will be strength as much as anything.

'Forgive 'N' Forget was a very free-running horse. With horses like that you're trying to get a rhythm going, trying to settle them so they've got something left to give at the business end of the race. It's getting them to switch off in their minds that's a challenge, and can't really be taught. You can shout till you're blue in the face but if a young lad hasn't got it, he hasn't got it. It's a natural ability and Kieren had it.

'To be honest, I have been surprised by his success. Once he was there at the top he was entitled to be there – it was the getting there that surprised me more than anything. I didn't think it would happen, more from what he did off the horse than on it. Even when he was at Malton he would hang around with the wrong people, and he seemed happy in their company. That's him and he's still the same. The self-destruct button was never far away.' This is the late eighties and already a prominent fault line in Fallon's character had been exposed.

Dwyer knew every contour of the road Fallon was travelling because he had passed that way himself, which makes him a robust and reliable witness to Fallon's early life in the north. Even then, Fallon had an instinct for dangerous company and an eye for trouble. News of some scrapes and scraps filtered back to Dessie Scahill in Ireland, and would not have caused much surprise on the cherubic features of Charlie Swan, who was making his own way rapidly to the top. Fallon would stand up for himself, as Swan noted, and would be egged on by others to see when he would snap. One of Fallon's party tricks at the end of a good night out was to walk down the middle of the road and flag down passing cars, but if there was a scrap to be had – and Malton no less than Newmarket was a tough racing town – he would not usually turn the other cheek.

It is to Fallon's credit that once he had left the north for Newmarket and far greater riches, he never forgot his old mentor at Norton Grange. Fitzgerald, he knew, would always tell it to him straight. It was up to him whether he listened or not. 'He was like a father to me ever since I came over to England,' Fallon said on news of Fitzgerald's death in October 2004. 'He still watched every race I rode in. Without him, I probably wouldn't still be in the game. He was always there when I went off the rails.'

By the time Fallon had cut his regular ties with Norton Grange, he had lost his claim and gained a solid foothold in a precarious profession. The 23-year-old apprentice had been transformed into the 26-year-old journeyman. He knew it was time to move on.

3

A LONG HOLIDAY

'If you smoothed off the rough edges and turned him into an angel, you'd kill off the jockey.'

Michael Caulfield

As Fallon drove to Beverley racetrack on the morning of Wednesday, 14 September 1994, at the wheel of his turbo injection model Toyota Supra, a car he treasured but could only just afford, he could reflect that life in England had turned out for the best. He was married to Julie Bowker, one of the top northern women riders, and had a young daughter, Natalie. He had marked himself out as a rider of verve, skill and talent, a cut above the rest of the young graduates of the northern weighing-room. He still owed his old boss and mentor, Jimmy Fitzgerald, pretty well everything, but he had new ambitions and, after a season as a freelance, he had joined Breckenbrough Stables, a thriving new set-up that would lift him one more rung up a dauntingly high ladder. He was well on the way not quite to being champion but to making a decent living, which, from a standing start, was a considerable achievement. He could take the added responsibilities of family life and hefty mortgage repayments in his stride.

He was in his second season as Lynda and Jack Ramsden's retained jockey, and victories in the Gimcrack on Chilly Billy and on Rafferty's Rules in the Hopeful Stakes, a listed race at Newmarket, had advertised

36

not only his own capabilities but the growing confidence of his yard in themselves and in him. Lynda Ramsden, tall, elegant and icily cool, was very far from being the traditional northern trainer, and Jack, a formidable gambler, was very far from being the traditional northern trainer's other half, but together they were starting to disprove a number of theories about the right and wrong way to train racehorses. Lynda did the training and the mothering, Jack did the timing and the plotting, and, after the departure to the south of Alan Munro, Fallon did the riding. The yard was, recalls John Lowe, a closed shop.

'I rode a few winners for them,' he says, 'but I never rode work. I asked, but they always said no thanks. They only invited people they trusted one hundred per cent, who weren't going to shout their mouths off about any of the horses that had been working well. I talked too much for them.'

Fallon fitted the bill perfectly for the Ramsden team. He was quiet, shy, underrated and ambitious. Like Jack Ramsden, he didn't have much time for authority or much use for a rulebook. An interview in the *Sporting Life* in mid-August 1994 was the first sign that people south of Pontefract were beginning to take notice of a rising talent. The only problem was that Fallon was advertised as 'first jockey to Lynda Ramsden and a regular visitor to the northern stewards' rooms'. Fallon's gift for getting into trouble was already becoming an integral part of his story.

By late summer, as the hectic schedule of evening meetings came to an end, Fallon's disciplinary record read: two suspensions of seven days each, two four-day bans and a two-day break for further misuse of the whip. The first of his week-long suspensions had been incurred for striking a fellow jockey, Keith Rutter, with his whip during a race at Thirsk. 'All I did was give the lad a smack to wake him up,' explained Fallon. The second might just have crossed Fallon's mind as he made his way to Beverley that day in September. It had come at Southwell in early July for irresponsible riding on a horse called Heart Broken. Heart Broken had won the race but had been disqualified and placed last. The horse promoted to first place was Sailormaite ridden by Stuart Webster. Sailormaite was Webster's ride again in the third race of the afternoon at Beverley. Revenge was in the air over the Yorkshire track and one of the lessons Fallon had not been taught in his childhood was how to back away from a decent feud.

According to Webster and sources within the weighing-room, the pair had been out to get each other for a few seasons now, the result of some off-track dealings that had spilled into the weighing-room and on to the racetrack. Usually, racing deals with such issues unofficially, through an unwritten set of rules dictated by daily exposure to a dangerous profession and ruthlessly enforced by the senior pros in the weighing-room in much the same way front-row forwards enforce a stringent code of conduct in rugby. But by the time Fallon had taken his mount, Gymcrak Flyer, down to the mile start for the John Mangles Memorial Handicap, the red mist had fallen across his brow and no senior pro was going to stop him from imposing his own crude form of justice on a man who had crossed him.

The race itself was relatively uneventful and was won quite comfortably in the end by Webster on board Sailormaite. Fallon finished well down the field. Sailormaite was a notoriously free-running horse, and may have impeded Fallon and his mount at some stage, but no one was anticipating what happened next. As Webster was pulling up after the finishing post, Fallon came alongside him and, in full view of the stands, grabbed his rival and pulled him out of the saddle. Webster landed on his feet, still holding the reins. He was stunned, so were onlookers, but some in the weighing-room were perhaps less so. In his relatively brief apprenticeship in a tough school, Fallon had established a reputation for being a loyal friend and colleague off the track and a hot-headed opponent on it. Most knew of his antagonism for Webster and, knowing the Irishman's short fuse, they feared the worst. The reaction back in the weighing-room, though, as Fallon came back in, was still one of shock.

This was Webster's account in the *News of the World* of what followed: 'When I walked into the weighing-room, Fallon had his back to me. As I went past, he suddenly turned round, grabbed me by the collar and smashed his forehead into my face. I was pouring blood. I knew my nose was broken and I fell on all fours. Then he jumped on my back and started punching me again and again in the face. He must have hit me a dozen times before Paul Eddery [Pat's brother] managed to pull him off. He was the only one of about fifty people in the weighing-room who did anything to help. Everyone else was too terrified to take on Fallon in that mood.'

According to Webster's subsequent account, he went to a wash basin to clean away the blood and found Nicky Connorton, a fellow rider, throwing up in the next basin. 'Nicky said it was the crunching sound of my nose breaking that made him sick.'

The jockeys present that day have kept remarkably silent on the matter over the past fourteen years. Webster, a journeyman jockey and a difficult and combative character, would not have won any popularity contest within the northern weighing-room. Trouble with his weight had contributed to his belief that the world was against him, and his willingness to ride any horse anywhere regardless of its reputation was deemed reckless at best, downright dangerous at worst, for everyone. Although he liked a drink, he would not necessarily be the first to buy one. Fallon, in contrast, was liked and respected by almost everyone, for his generosity as much as anything. He was still a relative newcomer to the northern scene, at 29 years old no longer an apprentice, but only recently coming into his own as a force in the saddle. Webster was not the worst jockey in the world, not by a long way, but Fallon was better by a country mile and everyone knew it. Fallon could be around for a long time. Besides, he had that look in his eye. The door to the outside world slammed shut. Not even John Lowe would open his mouth to reveal the truth. If the law of omerta, common to most sporting communities, is almost unbreakable in racing, the long arm of the law seemed equally reluctant to breach the inner sanctum. Webster, to his eternal regret, did not press charges, partly because he could not summon enough witnesses to support his side of the story.

Racing, as usual, barely blinked an eye. Despite his reckless treatment of another rider, there for everyone to see on 'News at Ten' that night, Fallon was back riding the next day as if nothing had happened. The following week he was given rides by both John Dunlop and Barry Hills, a silent endorsement by two of the most respected trainers in racing. The sport, so proud of its self-regulatory mechanism, simply turned its head away and got on with the daily business of finding winners. Webster did not ride again until a meeting at Nottingham six days later, and only on the following Friday, nine days after the Beverley incident, did Fallon and Webster contest the same race, at Redcar.

Fallon knew a long suspension was heading his way when he travelled down to Jockey Club headquarters in London's Portman Square on 27 September. Not much of a defence could be mounted against the inevitable six-month ban, the most severe punishment handed down to a rider since Billy Newnes was banned for three years for receiving money for information in 1983. John Lowe's reaction to the ban at the time, and his analysis of his friend's future, proved highly prescient. 'I honestly thought he would get three months, but I suppose his record didn't help him. Let's hope that such a talented jockey learns from this. In my opinion, he's one of the best jockeys I've seen riding. But you get these lads who have this self-destruct button. I just hope that Kieren gets rid of that.'

Not all the news was bad for Fallon. First, no further action was taken over the brawl in the weighing-room for lack of evidence, and second, Fallon was found not guilty on another charge of reckless riding at Ayr a few days after Beverley. The stewards clearly could not be bothered with such a minor offence when Fallon would be off the track for six months anyway. In all the concentration on Fallon, his loss of earnings and the potential long-term damage to his career, not much notice was taken of Webster, who was arguably never the same jockey or man again. Webster's solicitor, Peter McCormick, was damning of the culture of silence in the weighing-room. 'I'm unhappy, as a lawyer, with a situation where a number of men, grown men, are in a room and clearly see something and none of them have the fortitude or decency to come forward and tell a tribunal what occurred,' he said.

The Jockey Club did not seem much inclined to pursue such an unsavoury matter to a proper conclusion, either. 'When you get a closed community, when people ride against each other every day, maybe it is difficult to come forward and say what happened,' said David Pipe, the Jockey Club's Director of Publicity, weakly. The Jockey Club gave the distinct impression that they wanted it all just to go away.

McCormick was wrong in one respect. One jockey did come forward. Lindsay Charnock testified on Fallon's behalf. Fallon, he claimed, had been provoked. A few years later, when one of the prizes for winning the championship was a top of the range Saab, Fallon gave the car to Charnock as a reward for his support. With Fallon as patron, the weighing-room began to resemble a feudal barony.

As head of the Jockeys' Association, Michael Caulfield, 'Corky' to everyone in racing, was thrust into the middle of the controversy. It was his first real contact with Fallon, but decidedly not his last. With two of his members in the national headlines and a plain old-fashioned racing feud on his hands, Caulfield had to maintain a scrupulously straight course between the two sides, which was not easy, even for the son of a High Court judge. Caulfield is now a highly respected sports psychologist. He remembers quite clearly his first impressions of the fiery Irishman who seemed to be gaining so much unwanted publicity, and the sense that he was intercepting Fallon at the crossroads of an uncertain career.

'The suspension was one of the big turning points for Kieren,' he said. 'He had to think hard about what he wanted to do. Do I want to be a professional jockey? Yes or no. Yes, I want it. What I saw back then was a very intense, quite quiet and private person, but he had that absolute Roy Keane type fire. That was when the lid could come off the kettle.

'A.P. [McCoy] says that every sportsman should be like Roy Keane, and Kieren was. The trick is not to quash the fire, but to channel it in the right way. I remember saying to A.P., "You can be an angry jockey, but what's the point of being an angry jockey if you're suspended?" I got him to write down all the bad things about being suspended, which he often was in the early days. He wrote, "I miss rides, I miss winners, Pipey [Martin Pipe, his trainer] gets pissed off, other jockeys nick my rides, I lose five, ten grand in earnings, whatever it costs me, I get heavy, I get bored, I get more angry." "OK, right," I told him. "Now let's put down the good things." Blank piece of paper. A.P. is just as aggressive now but he very rarely gets suspended. Kieren learnt that side of it in time and actually became very good with the stewards, but he never learnt the other bit, the bit about surrounding himself with the right people.

'Through my years with the Jockeys' Association, I got to know Kieren pretty well. He was one of the most interesting people to work with, never foul-mouthed, never bad-tempered. He was very good at analysing information, very straightforward and easy to forgive if he was late, which he could be. Anything to do with a horse or racing issues, he was clear thinking and sensible. But there wasn't much middle ground with him. With Kieren, you're either in or you're out. And he was naturally suspicious of officialdom and some of the media.

'At the height of his powers, when he moved down south, Kieren was like McCoy, a powerful force in the weighing-room, mainly for good. He was interested in the other jockeys. But he would always wind me up, moaning on about going to some far-off track for one ride and losing money, and he would always make out he was a pound worse off than he was. He was always slightly on your case. Jockeys – like any sportsmen – play up to their image, don't they? A.P. is Mr Grumpy. Kieren saw himself as a tough street fighter, standing up against authority, the rough, tough diamond of the weighing-room. It was an image he had to portray, but if you smoothed off the rough edges and turned him into an angel, you'd kill the jockey.'

There was no danger of wings sprouting on the 29-year-old who headed back into obscurity for the long winter of 1994–95. He had become established as a top rider in the north, but did not have the body of winners behind him or the unfailing support that would guarantee his position for his return. Two things worked in his favour. One was that he was banned for the most part through the winter months. The other was that the Ramsdens were fellow travellers when it came to snubbing authority. They had very quickly confirmed their support for their stable jockey and saw no problem in him returning to them to resume the upward curve of his career in the spring. The problem for Fallon was that he could no longer take up his retainer with Dallas Toddywalla, champion trainer in Bombay, for whom he had ridden for the past five seasons and with whom he had formed an important and fruitful partnership. Toddywalla, in fact, can lay claim to being the first person in racing to discover the true depths of Fallon's talent, long before the Ramsdens or Henry Cecil came calling.

Fallon had arrived in Calcutta in the winter of 1989, which was the first season of the all-weather track in England. He could not understand why any jockey would want to ride on cold afternoons at Lingfield or Southwell when there were adventures to be had and lessons to be learnt in warmer climes. Although barely two seasons into his career in the north of England, Fallon was initially persuaded to take up an offer to ride in India by his fellow jockey, Simon Whitworth, who had found a more lucrative engagement in Saudi Arabia. At short notice, Fallon packed his riding boots and headed east to ride for a trainer called L.C. Gupte. He knew no one other than the Indian regulars, including John Lowe, and no one knew him, but it was typical of his nature that he was ready for the challenge. Fallon was always alert to chance and, more especially, to the chance that he might improve.

In Calcutta that first year, he met Dallas Toddywalla, a tall and elegant young trainer who had once been Gupte's assistant but who had now set up on his own in Bombay, home of the Royal Western India Turf Club. Dallas Toddywalla had split with his stable jockey the previous season and was searching for a replacement.

'I'd never heard of Kieren when he came to ride in Calcutta,' he recalled, 'but he finished second in the 2000 Guineas on one of mine. I had no rapport with him, I didn't know him, but he obeyed my instructions to a tee and we finished second to a horse that went on to win the Triple Crown. He gave my horse a superb ride. I'd moved across to Bombay in 1985 and I needed a jockey, so I recommended Kieren to one of my biggest owners. When I went over to England in the summer, I found Kieren at Southwell one day and I approached him to ride for me in the winter. It wasn't a very big retainer or anything. Soon after, his career began to take off back in England – sixty winners, ninety, a hundred and then he got the job with Cecil and he wasn't able to come any more.

'Kieren looked after the horses, that's what I liked about him. He was very unselfish. He rode for the horse and the yard, not for himself all the time. He became a special friend more than anything, and he was honest, that's the irony of it, given what's happened to him. He never went against my stable owners. We have a four-bedroomed flat in Bombay and in the winter one room was Kieren's. He always stayed with me. If he was a thief or whatever, I would know. He was very quiet back then, didn't say much. He could get a bit wild when he partied, but he was still on the road to success. That makes a big difference. Yet to me, even when he was a champion, he never changed. I'd call him five times a month or so.

'Kieren first came over with a decent crop of jockeys – John Lowe and Richard Hughes, and Jimmy Fortune came a bit later. Kieren wanted to know why anyone wanted to stay riding on the all-weather in the cold when you could have a lovely summer job in the sunshine. He'd ride out two hours in the morning and then the rest of the day was his. We lived right opposite the Breach Candy Pool and he would spend most of the day there.'

Toddywalla recalls one horse, New Power Generation, not a particularly good horse, but good enough to win a race. On his first outing, Fallon rode him quite tenderly and the trainer wanted to know why.

'I got upset with him and said he should have won that race. He said he could have beaten the horse up and then we wouldn't have a horse for the rest of the season. New Power Generation won three on the trot after that and so I started to listen to Kieren. By the end, I had blind faith in him.'

With Fallon in the saddle and around the yard each morning, Toddywalla's career began to prosper. Although not backed by one of the very big owners in the west, he won the trainers' championship, in large part, he says, because of Fallon's instinctive understanding of a horse's capabilities, a talent that Michael Stoute would treasure a few years later.

'I was as raw and immature as Kieren was,' Toddywalla admitted, 'but he made a big difference to my career, which is why I'll never forget him and why I'll always be blind to his faults. He's unselfish, that's part of the problem. He wants to look after the whole world.'

Life in India suited Fallon admirably, all bar the food, according to Lowe, a veteran of twenty-four Indian summers. 'In my prime,' Lowe recalled, 'I had the pick of rides before Mick Kinane and Kieren. I wouldn't get that in England, but I did in India. When Kieren first came out, he wouldn't eat any Indian food. He used to go down to the shop to buy chocolate and cake. Kieren spent a lot of time with Dallas, not only riding the horses, but helping to prepare and train them. He never missed track work. He would be there every morning at six and he wouldn't leave until ten. He was always the last one at the swimming pool.'

Walking away from the disciplinary hearing in Portman Square that autumn day, his notoriety now stamped with an official seal, Fallon knew deep down that something in his nature would have to change. A winter without regular work loomed and Fallon's first thoughts revolved around the size of his monthly mortgage payments (£600) and how he would meet them in the absence of any regular income. Jack Ramsden, aware that Fallon needed to be kept busy, advised him to head west to California, where he would find a different racing culture and could still enjoy the sunshine. Fallon took the advice and began a love–hate relationship with the United States that endured throughout his career. In times of trouble, which were plentiful, Fallon's immediate reaction was invariably to head for America, where, he claimed, they left him in peace and let him get on with his riding.

'I'm just learning all the time,' he told the *Guardian*'s Greg Wood in the New Year of 2005. 'All the best jockeys are here – Edgar Prado, Jerry Bailey, Jose Santos. Look at Prado, he always seems to be first out of the gate. The only way I can ever match that is to be there alongside him, practising again and again.'

Within a few weeks of that revealing interview, Fallon was back home, to the bemusement of his American agent and the racing public at Gulfstream Park, who were beginning to warm to the idiosyncratic skills of the champ from across the Pond. If Fallon liked the way the Americans ran their racing, with 'pony guys' to guide every horse to the start and 'gate guys' to get you into the stalls, he was less enamoured by the kickback on the dirt tracks, which make up 90 per cent of US racing. It was typically unrealistic of Fallon to believe, as he stated to Wood, that he could make it in the US solely as a turf rider but, as ever with Fallon, it sounded plausible at the time. Somewhere in Fallon's complex mind, America is the land of the free, the land of opportunity. But he never stayed long.

Back in 1994, Fallon was just another rider from somewhere else who wanted to make a name for himself around the training barns on the back stretch. There is no tougher school in racing than the American way, nor many trainers as tough or as old school as Rodney Rash, who agreed to take on the explosive young Irishman and broaden his racing education for the winter. Rash had once been assistant to Charlie Whittingham, the former US Marine who became all-time leading trainer at Santa Anita and Hollywood Park during a forty-nine-year career. Rash branched out on his own in 1991, handling a medium-sized yard of thirty-five or so horses out of Santa Anita for five years before he died from a rare blood disorder at a tragically young age, just when the future was starting to look bright. Like the young Irishman now in his yard, Rash had a wild streak in him, but he knew how to train.

'Rodney started as a groom with Charlie and worked his way up the ladder, and he trained like Charlie,' recalled Ben Cecil, who took over the yard on Rash's death. 'He would certainly let you know if you did something wrong. Kieren wasn't the prettiest on a horse, by any means, and unlike Frankie he never did pick up the US style. Most people said, "What does he look like?" but Kieren didn't seem to mind too much. Kieren would have ridden out mostly for Rodney around Santa Anita where there would have been 2,500 horses on the grounds. Maybe he'd have ridden six to ten each morning. He would have ridden a lot of horses, but the good thing was you didn't have to muck out any of them. You just had to get on, ride and get off.'

Fallon has often said that his time in America turned him into a proper jockey. On the flat, left-handed ovals of American racing, timing is everything. Races are shorter, more dynamic and certainly more formulaic. Starts are critical and being able to clock precise timings for each quarter mile in your head is the prerequisite for any jockey from Hollywood Park to Hicksville. Jockeys learn about timing from riding work in the mornings, where an English trainer's swinging canter would be translated into split seconds by any American handler. Woe betide the rider who slips more than a beat out of time with the stopwatch.

'Some of the better riders out here will be able to tell you to a fifth of a second how fast they went,' explained Cecil. 'So if you're in the lead in a race and you're going too quick, you know it, and you know where to be in a race and how to pace it and which others are going too quick. It was one of the things that made Steve Cauthen such a success in Europe. He had a good clock in his head. It's the best place in the world to learn about timing.'

As Fallon would have noted, it's also the best place in the world to earn good money, staggeringly good money compared to the daily bread of English racing – $264,586,468 worth of good money to quote the figure that Pat Day, a quiet, rhythmic rider in the Fallon mould, earned for the owners to break the prize-money record in 2002. Take the jockey's 10 per cent of the earnings and it's still an amazingly good living by European standards. The downside, as Ben Cecil also acknowledged, is that racing five days a week, three months in a row, on the same track can get very dull, whatever the savings on fuel and frustration of a life without traffic jams.

Fallon's flirtation with American racing lasted throughout his career. He was still poignantly talking about 'sorting out my life and maybe going to America' in the aftermath of an eighteen-month ban for a second positive test for cocaine in the fraught winter of 2007–08, after he had lost his job with Coolmore. The genesis of his brilliant victories in the Breeders' Cup on Islington and Ouija Board can be found on those bright mornings riding work round the dirt oval of Santa Anita for the irascible Rodney Rash. Even so, Fallon was acutely aware that his style was the antithesis of the American way and that he would always have to persuade the grizzled sceptics in the stands that his upright, bouncing seat could work as effectively at Santa Anita as it could at Newmarket. The extra significance of the start and the ability to change the horse's lead leg coming off the turn, a skill that is second nature to all top-class American riders but not essential to riding the more varied tracks in Britain, roused Fallon's curiosity as much as his sense of perfection. Like any craftsman, he wanted to master a new technique.

'Coming off the left-hand turn, the horse will be leading with its near fore – front left – leg,' explained Jason Weaver, the former champion jockey, who spent many of his formative years riding in America. 'So you ask the horse to stretch for three or four strides coming into the turn, and then ask it to switch to leading with the off fore – front right – leg. By the end of the turn, the left lead leg is getting tired, so by switching to the fresh lead leg you can get extra momentum for the home stretch. It's a matter of shifting body weight on the horse and pulling on the reins. The older professional horses will respond effort-lessly, like a dressage horse, but sometimes you have to exaggerate the body movement to get the switch. It's a skill you teach horses on the gallops. The boys who have been to the States would understand it, but why doesn't every jockey here know about it? You wouldn't want a horse changing legs going into the dip at Newmarket, for example, but after the long sweeping turn at York you've got to switch to the right lead.

'By the time he'd come back from America, Kieren knew about it and about the importance of timing. If a trainer in the States asks you to go five furlongs in a minute and you're more than two ticks out, you've pretty well ruined what he was trying to get from the gallop. If you've got that clock in your head, you instinctively know whether you're going too fast or too slow. Kieren doesn't often make the running, but if he goes to the front, it's because he knows that the gallop's not fast enough and he has the confidence to make the move at the right time.'

By 2003 and Islington's famous victory in the Breeders' Cup back in Santa Anita, American journalists were beginning to understand a little about the stylistic subtleties of the English champion. It took a while. 'With the great European rider, Kieren Fallon, rhythmically flailing and bouncing in unison with the filly through the stretch, onlookers saw the beauty and athleticism of the European riding style at its best,' recorded the official newsletter of the Louisville Thoroughbred Club. Perhaps the writer was just being kind or had his tongue firmly in his cheek. Richard Edmondson, writing for the *Independent on Sunday* in London, called it a little differently:

> The Americans hold limited affection for Fallon's crashing style but once he produced Islington there was no man, at this racecourse or any other, more capable of getting her home. It was not pretty, particularly

in comparison with Edgar Prado's tight style on the runner-up, L'Ancresse, but they will not mention that in the formbook. Instead, they will detail the winner.

'Crashing' and 'flailing' would not have been the adjectives chosen by Fallon perhaps, but the time for change had long since passed by then.

Fallon spent November, December and most of January 1995 in America, returning home at the end of January before spending a month with Toddywalla in India, where he had treatment for a troublesome ulcer. By the time he was back in the north, at his home in Thirsk, the spring was back in his step and the past was another country. This was the first of a number of new dawns.

'I learnt so much in the States,' he told Tom O'Ryan on the eve of the new season. 'I'll definitely be a better jockey as a result. In some ways, I feel my suspension has been a blessing in disguise.' He even issued a placatory message to his old friends in the stewards' room: 'I don't think they were picking on me. I just feel I went through a bad patch. It's not something I want to dwell on.'

Whether he wanted to dwell on it or not was largely irrelevant. The events of September 1994 became an integral part of the Fallon story, a blueprint for the future, the first major link in a long chain of controversy. Neither Webster nor Fallon had the option of erasing the past. Their careers took markedly different paths out of Beverley that evening. Fallon became champion jockey three years later, while Webster slid slowly towards obscurity. His weight rose, the number of rides declined until retirement was no longer an option, simply a matter of fact. Like a boxer suffering too many blows to the head, Webster now suffers from short-term memory loss, but his self-confidence and his trust in his fellow riders never recovered from that moment.

The legacy for Fallon is more complex. In a ruthless profession, Fallon had shown a complete disregard for the written and unwritten rules of racing. Like Roy Keane, Fallon had asked his rivals a searching question. How far are you prepared to go to be the best? Like Lester Piggott in his early days, Fallon's readiness to go further than anyone else in pursuit of his ambitions gave him an advantage every afternoon on the racetrack, where no amount of cameras can capture the subtleties of law enforcement. If Fallon wanted room, it was best to let him have it or he would take it anyway, and every jockey in the weighing-room would think twice about impeding Fallon, which gave him a psychological edge. It was not planned. That was what he was taught to do back in Ireland, fight your corner.

Yet the shadow that fell over him in the autumn of 1994 was never truly cast off. The rules in England, the culture of the track, were subtly different. He might have returned to the north for the following season a more rounded jockey, but he was the same man and the stewards were still watching. The new Fallon, the first of many, as it turned out, looked remarkably like the old one.

4

COCK OF THE NORTH

'Kieren might be a little disorganised in his life out of the saddle, but in it he's a bloody star.'

Jack Ramsden

No sooner had Fallon returned from suspension to pick up his riding career with the Ramsdens in North Yorkshire than he was embroiled in further controversy, this time over the riding of Top Cees. By the end of a versatile career on the flat and over hurdles, this quirky and deeply talented horse numbered two victories in the Chester Cup and one at the Cheltenham Festival among his successes, but two races in particular were the cause of the row. The running and riding of Top Cees in the Swaffham Handicap at Newmarket on 18 April 1995, and the subsequent runaway success in the Chester Cup the following month, led to one of the most celebrated cases in racing history coming to court three years later. However, there were a lot of races to be won before then.

Fallon first moved to Breckenbrough Stables, in the tiny village of Sandhutton, just outside Thirsk, in late 1992. He was freelance at the time, and still riding for Jimmy Fitzgerald whenever he was available, but the opportunity to further his career with the Ramsdens was too good to miss and his old mentor knew it. Despite the steady increase in winners through the early part of the decade, there was little chance of Fallon's ambitions or talent being fulfilled in Malton.

A 'lifestyles' feature published in the 7 November 1992 edition of the *Sporting Life* profiles a 27-year-old journeyman jockey called 'Kieran' Fallon, and reveals someone capable of serious comment on his profession. 'Favourite Comedian: Del Boy or Jimmy Fitzgerald on the way to the gallops. He's a born comedian. Alternative career: A carpenter. My grandfather was a skilled joiner and it was a toss up whether I became a DIY expert or took up racing. I don't think I chose wrongly.' He couldn't, he said, afford a holiday, and his car was a Honda Accord. Even then, Fallon was not short of opinion or advice. Asked what he would do if he was appointed senior steward, Fallon answered:

> Instruct the local stewards to do what they know is right and not allow their decisions to be influenced by what the public might think. At Leicester recently, I was disciplined for smacking an unruly two-year-old who was playing up at the start and wouldn't enter the stalls. My action was nothing more than a parent might have given a naughty child. The officials said they understood my point of view but what I'd done was bad for the public image and that as it would be widely seen on SIS, they had to be seen to be taking action. Stewards should not be influenced in this way.

That typically thoughtful and intelligent response was fashioned by personal experience, and there is little doubt he was right. Yet Fallon's inability to see the wider picture is equally telling. Far from being a global village, racing is like 'The Truman Show' – same faces, same places, same language, same rhythm of life. The scrutiny of Fallon's life and character would naturally increase with his fame and fortune. His inability to see himself as the world outside racing's little village might see him did not make Fallon unique, far from it, but nor did it help his cause when he became one of racing's most wanted sons. On the track, Fallon's forceful riding and escalating warfare with the stewards were beginning to receive attention in roughly equal measure. And the winners were starting to come. Fallon had already finished second in a Classic, on Sapience, in the 1989 St Leger, run at Ayr that year, and his first big handicap winner came four years later when High Premium won the Lincoln at Doncaster for Lynda and Jack Ramsden. For Fallon, this was some compensation for the disappointment of missing Evichstar's win in the same race two years earlier. Evichstar won at 33–1 but Fallon was already too heavy to make the seven stone 12lb weight. Instead, the ride went to Alan Munro, his friend and predecessor as stable jockey to the Ramsdens, who had to put up two pounds overweight.

With the draw favouring the far side, Fallon had High Premium up with the pace most of the way and the pair took the lead with three furlongs left to run, holding on to win by half a length from Michael Stoute's Mizaaya, ridden by Walter Swinburn. Will of Steel, also from the Ramsdens, finished third. It was a bold, strong ride, coming at the start of an association that was to prove the making of both Fallon and, arguably, the trainer too. Although Fallon never won on High Premium again for the Ramsdens, they did team up five years later to win at Leicester when High Premium was trained by Richard Fahey. After winning 13 of his 58 starts on turf, finishing in the places a further 14 times and winning three times on the all-weather, the great old servant was retired at the age of 10. In his last outing, a lady riders race back at Doncaster, the scene of his most famous triumph, he finished seventh.

Most significantly, the victory in such a prestigious early season race gave Fallon a perfect start in his new role at Breckenbrough. 'I enjoy riding for the Ramsdens,' Fallon said in a later interview with John Budden in the *Sporting Life*. 'They are both excellent race-readers who can appreciate the difficulties of the job. I know that there will be no roaring or shouting if things have not gone to plan. They are straight-forward and sensible and I feel confident riding their horses.' The veiled reference to Jimmy Fitzgerald's more volatile temperament was probably intended and might well have been accepted with a wry smile over the breakfast table at Norton Grange.

If Fallon regarded Fitzgerald as his second father, with all the bicker-ing and nonsense that such a complex relationship encompassed, his relationship with Jack Ramsden was based on a different kind of understanding. Fallon admired Ramsden's intelligence and brashness; Ramsden liked the Irishman's modesty and loyalty. 'I don't think they'd ever go out for a meal together, but Jack and Kieren had tremendous respect for each other's abilities,' Andrew Balding recalls. And what they and Lynda liked best was winning horseraces, against the odds, if possible. There was the sense of a guerrilla band about the Breckenbrough runners in their heyday, a sense that the authorities were watching their every move but were never quite smart enough to catch up.

Andrew Balding, an unlikely recruit to the payroll at Sandhutton, arrived in the winter of 1996 just as Fallon was moving in the other direction to find fame and fortune with Henry Cecil. Jimmy Fortune, another young Irishman on the way up, had come to the yard as stable jockey with a strong recommendation from Fallon, but the routine and the unique character of the yard remained untouched. This was a world away from Andrew's privileged upbringing at Kingsclere in Berkshire, where history had been laid down with the bricks and mortar, and training Classic winners was the family business. The facilities at Sandhutton, impressive though they were considering the ramshackle state of the original farmhouse, could have fitted comfortably into the back paddock at Kingsclere, yet young Balding learnt far more than the geography of the local tracks and the art of placing horses in the right races. He learnt to open his mind to new influences. Ramsden was no horseman, but he understood the basic principles of winning and losing in an analytical, mathematical way.

'The only time Jack came into the yard was when he'd come out to empty his wastepaper bin,' Balding recalls. 'Honestly, that was the only time. He wouldn't know one end of a horse from another, by his own admission, but ask anything about a horse's pedigree, what ground the dam liked, the half-sister wanted, the sire's progeny, he would know. He had an incredibly scientific approach to the training and selection of racehorses. There was a story that he'd sat on a horse once, but Lynda was the horsewoman, at her happiest dressed in headscarf and Wellingtons, helping round the yard and choosing the curtains for the lads' accommodation.

'If it was too cold in the morning, Jack wouldn't come out to watch the gallop – he wouldn't come out or he'd drive, and the gallop was no more than five hundred metres from his little office on the side of the house. He'd take the times of the horses and go back to the office again.

He was looking for basic speed and he'd get very excited if something with a middle-distance pedigree did under twenty-two seconds for those two furlongs. There was a time when Jack was even timing the horses round the swimming pool just in case it had any effect. He was always looking for an edge.'

By the time Fallon arrived to replace Alan Munro as stable jockey, the yard was up and running and the bookmakers were beginning to run scared. Often, because of his success, Ramsden was forced to place his bets through other people, notably bookmaker Colin Webster, and, on the odd occasion, Robert Sangster, one of his more high-profile owners. Jack and Lynda were a charming and glamorous addition to the northern racing scene, but they knew how to get horses fit and, most importantly, where to place them, one of the hidden skills of training. Contrary to the established laws of racing, the winners kept coming. At the Lincoln meeting at Doncaster in 1990, Daring Times gave Lynda Ramsden her first big-race win. Perhaps more importantly, having backed the horse from 33–1 down to 9–2 at the post, Jack Ramsden took home a handsome profit of £30,000 from the bookmakers.

Ramsden, one of racing's more intelligent thinkers, was a devotee of speed figures and had very particular views about how his horses – and many of them in the fifty-strong yard were jointly owned with Lynda – should be ridden. All horses were timed on the gallops over the last two furlongs of their work. His views had a profound effect on Fallon in two notable ways. First, Ramsden liked his horses to come from behind, to be doing their best work at the finish, where, he reckoned, most races were won and lost. Second, as an analytical man, brought up to discard rumour and worship facts, he liked the American way of racing, with its emphasis on the unforgiving hands of the clock. His office, like Martin Pipe's sitting room at Pond House, had the facility to show racing from France and, on some occasions, Hong Kong. Ramsden believed that while a good horse is capable of doing a bad time on the gallops, the reverse would not be true for a bad horse, and he developed his own computerised speed figures to support his claims. Fallon once recalled that Ramsden always had a pad of paper in front of him during their conversations and a list of questions. 'There was always a list,' Fallon said at the time. 'He is a shrewd, organised man who rarely gets it wrong.' Jimmy Fitzgerald was a trainer of the old school, brought up with the smell of a racing yard in his nostrils, while Jack Ramsden was an old boy of Stowe public school and a former stockbroker who, with his second wife, Lynda, brought a whiff of expensive cologne and aftershave to the earthy ranks of northern trainers. They were not really northern trainers, not in the accepted sense of the word, but southerners who happened to train in the north.

Ramsden knew exactly what he wanted from his stable jockeys. They had to be precise judges of pace, able to conjure effective late runs out of their mounts in the closing stages of a race, and they had to know to the last inch the location of every finishing post in the land. Ramsden's instructions were always the same – drop them in, give them a chance, get plenty of cover, finish well from two out, do your best. 'Doing your best' was not always the way they looked at it in the stewards' room afterwards. In common with Martin Pipe, the bookmaker's son who revolutionised the training of horses over the jumps and so the thinking of other trainers, Ramsden was forever on the lookout for a loophole.

'There was one classic time when he wanted to run the same horse in two races on the same day, the first and last at Pontefract,' says Balding. 'He was sure he could win both times. There was no rule against him doing it but they found something. He certainly had an anti-establishment streak in him and that seems to be the case with Kieren too, doesn't it?'

On the gallops, the Ramsden horses worked three upsides, in a line – six furlongs round and a stiff two furlongs uphill on the final straight. The gallop was designed to get the riders to judge the pace of the final stretch and develop the delicate art of conserving energy to the end of those tricky two furlongs. Fortune learnt the trick quickly enough, but Fallon was the past master at reeling in the horses who had gone too quickly and too early under less tactically astute work riders. That ability to know exactly where the finishing post is, and how much his horse has left to reach it, is in part down to a jockey's instinct, but on those cold Yorkshire mornings Fallon was refining an innate skill and was smart enough to realise exactly what he was doing.

Ramsden also knew that the quiet young Irishman with the seraphic smile had a steady nerve and a natural confidence in his own ability. Fallon never panicked on the track. He would wait, and then wait some more, until the time was just right. When he moved south to take up a post with Henry Cecil, those qualities were easily exported. And when Hurricane Run was all but last in the Arc in the autumn of 2005 and even John Magnier was beginning to harbour doubts about his jockey's judgement, Fallon's unbreakable belief could be traced all the way back to those days in the north when the money was down and the result *really* mattered. Fallon and Ramsden thrived in each other's company, and the relationship was strong enough to survive the libel case that Jack Ramsden brought against Mirror Group Newspapers, publishers of the *Sporting Life*, in the early months of 1998, nearly three years after the controversial victory of Top Cees in the Chester Cup.

'There was no way Kieren would have brought that case on his own,' says Michael Caulfield. 'I'm sure it was Jack. Kieren hates hassle, loathes it, legal hassle, solicitors, papers, reading stuff, he hates it. He is not one for detail. "This is the goal. How are we going to get there?" That's what he wants to know. If he trusts you, he'll leave it to you. When we had a disciplinary case, you'd say, "Kieren, 11.15 a.m., Portman Square, be there," and that was about it.'

The case, heard in the High Court – Court 13 – kept racing enthralled. The allegation was that the Ramsdens, along with Fallon, had deliberately stopped Top Cees running on its merits in the Swaffham Handicap at Newmarket in order to lengthen its odds for the Chester Cup a few weeks later. This was a trick known to every trainer in the land, and practised by a good few of them, and it is one tacitly encouraged by the handicap system on which the betting industry – and therefore British racing – thrives. It is a game played out between the trainer and the handicapper every day of every week of the year. The principle is that if a trainer can conceal a horse's true ability from the handicapper, one way or another, he might be able to win a few races with his horse and keep his business going for another year. Beating the handicapper is the aim of most trainers. Everyone inside racing knows there is a certain sleight of hand involved and everyone accepts it up to a point. The case with Top Cees reached that point. In an article in the *Sporting Life* the morning after the Chester Cup, the Ramsdens were labelled cheats. The case was not about the ethics of racing, although it prompted a vigorous debate on the matter as a side of racing not always seen by the general public emerged during the trial, but about the particulars of a libel.

Fallon's testimony was central to the success of the case against the *Sporting Life*, but he did not enjoy the experience one bit. He heard of his court victory in the weighing-room at Lingfield and felt only relief at the verdict. He had never wanted to take the action in the first place, not three years after the race. He was now champion jockey and eager to look forward, but he felt an obligation to support the Ramsdens, who had played such a significant part in his success.

Typically, Fallon arrived late for the first morning of the hearing, but the whole case provided a fascinating insight into the workings of one of the most celebrated racing yards in the land and into the mind of the man who, by now, was the foremost rider in the kingdom. Quite what anyone outside racing made of the labyrinthine arguments or the complex language of the turf was another matter. At one point, under questioning from Richard Hartley QC, counsel for the defence, Fallon admitted, 'I'm lost here as well as you are. We're both lost.' Another time, he tapped Ramsden on the arm and asked whether he was a defendant or a plaintiff. Fallon spent five hours in the witness box and, many times, must have wondered why on earth he wasn't back on the racecourse where he belonged. Fallon is not one for details, unless it is the little details required to understand the complexities of a Thoroughbred; nor is he much of a one for questions. The intense interrogation, every word being recorded and every answer analysed, proved to be one of the toughest days of his life, far worse than the usual media attention that his colourful career had already attracted.

It's tempting to recall Caulfield's comments about the Stuart Webster case, and the subsequent six-month ban that could have ended a career still unformed. 'Kieren was very good at taking the emotion out of the whole issue,' said Caulfield. 'I couldn't take sides because it was two jockeys against each other and I had to talk to both. But Kieren was quite cool, never very up or down about it. He knew it was a mistake and he learnt from it. He knew what was coming and he took it.' Fallon's philosophy on life's slings and arrows mirrored that of a true genius of the turf, Lester Piggott, who spent a year in prison for tax evasion without one flicker of emotion or one ounce of self-pity. It was, said Piggott, merely a waste of everyone's time. What Fallon could not know was just how strongly his phlegmatic attitude towards justice and the law, both on and off the track, would be tested in the future.

Fallon proved to be the unlikely trump card in the hands of the prosecution lawyers. Under severe pressure, he remained calm, humble and contrite. When questioned about his disciplinary record, he admitted it was 'appalling'. 'He [Fallon] has a curious manner, dreamy, wide-eyed, as if bemused,' wrote David Ashforth in one of his daily columns from the court in the *Life*. 'There are long, idiosyncratic, pauses even after innocuous questions.' In one of the worst moments for Fallon, the court was told of sixteen different cases of misuse of the whip, including incidents with Rutter and Webster, which he wanted to leave in the past. 'I have a terrible record altogether, you could say probably the worst record of any jockey,' he said. But he gave an interesting explanation for the indiscipline.

'Most [of the incidents] were when I came over from Ireland,' he said. 'In Ireland, jockeys use the whip much more than anywhere else in Europe. My suspensions go back some time. As I have got older and more experienced, I don't use the whip so much. I was suspended only once for the whip last year [1997].' Also highlighted was Fallon's £1,500 fine from the Jockey Club's Disciplinary Committee, imposed in November 1996 for 'deliberately misleading' an earlier enquiry. 'I am suggesting that you did not tell the truth on that occasion,' said Hartley. 'Yes sir, I would agree with that,' admitted Fallon. The jury, it seemed, were impressed by Fallon's openness and by his willingness to admit his mistakes. Fallon's common touch was never so valuable.

The trial provided further insight into the rhythms of life at the Ramsdens' stables and, to outsiders, at least, the Byzantine workings of an industry rarely subject to such forensic examination. Lynda, Court 13 heard, did the horses. Jack pursued his own career as a professional gambler, but made the entries, gave the instructions to the jockeys and generally did what his stockbroker's mind was trained to do, which was master the figures, whether they were on an account – healthy enough, it seemed, given his well-publicised successes on the track and the reluctance of major bookmakers to take his bets – or in the form-book. Only occasionally, over breakfast, the most important meal in racing, did husband and wife discuss the affairs of their own horses, where and how they might run.

Lynda Ramsden, dressed in a new outfit every day for her court appearances (to lift morale, she later said), held the trainer's licence, but Jack was widely presumed to be the power behind the throne. Whatever the exact delegation of duties, no one could deny that their initially ramshackle farmhouse near Thirsk had developed into one of the most formidable training centres in northern racing, responsible for a series of major handicap winners, quite apart from the mercurial Top Cees. Some of the impressive series of developments were paid for by the training successes of Mrs Ramsden. Mostly, one suspects, they were financed by the profits of Jack Ramsden's gambling. The new equine swimming pool was known as the Arbory Street pool after a horse at the centre of a spectacularly successful coup at Leicester in April 1989. Arbory Street opened at 12–1, touched 14–1 and won by three comfortable lengths at 13–2. That, Ramsden said later, was back in the good old days when men were men and bookmakers would take a decent bet.

In court, Ramsden claimed that he could make a profit of between £50,000 and £100,000 in a season backing horses. Only a tenth of his bets, he estimated, involved horses being trained by his wife. The Ramsdens were a golden couple. She grew up in Wetherby with ponies to ride and countryside to explore. After she completed a secretarial course, it was natural that she should use her newly acquired skills working for a trainer in her home town. She helped to exercise the horses and quietly served her apprenticeship as a trainer without anyone really noticing. When she moved to London, she got up at 4.30 a.m. to ride out for John Sutcliffe in Epsom before returning to work in town. It was at Sutcliffe's stables that she first met Jack Ramsden, who was then working as a stockbroker in the City – a 'pretty useless stockbroker', he once admitted. The couple were married in 1977 and set up a small stables, bizarrely, in the Isle of Man. Equally bizarrely, given his subsequent jousts with authority, Jack became an official of the Manx Turf Club and official handicapper. Ten years later, having moved to a rambling old farmhouse at Sandhutton, with its own private bore hole and no obvious potential as a training establishment, Lynda Ramsden took out a training licence and the great, glorious, roller-coaster ride began. It was in the midst of this uniquely colourful operation at Breckenbrough Stables in North Yorkshire that Fallon served another vital part of his apprenticeship, but his appearance in the trial did nothing to lessen his growing reputation as a troublemaker among the establishment and in the eyes of the wider non-racing public.

That the Jockey Club was indeed watching became clear in Court 13 during a critical part of the Top Cees case when it was revealed that Fallon had been sent a letter by the stewards of the Jockey Club, warning him about his riding in the future. Fallon had been cleared of breaking non-trier rules both on the day of the Swaffham at Newmarket and later in a further enquiry into the race at Portman Square, then the Jockey Club's headquarters. The letter read:

> You will be aware that the Stewards of the Jockey Club have reviewed the running of the above race [the Swaffham Handicap] and decided not to instruct the Disciplinary Committee to hold an enquiry into a possible breach of Rule 151 [non-trier's rule] concerning your riding of Top Cees. However, you should not assume from this decision that the Stewards were satisfied with your riding.
>
> In reaching their decision they had particular regard to the problems you encountered in running prior to the furlong pole. However, they considered that once the gaps eventually appeared you failed to ride Top Cees with sufficient effort and therefore, in similar circumstances, an offence under Rule 151 must be a likely outcome.

The letter was signed by Nigel Macfarlane, secretary of the Disciplinary Committee, and sent also to Lynda Ramsden, who promptly threw it in the bin. If Fallon was learning new skills in the saddle at Breckenbrough, he was not learning much about how to influence people in high places or about the importance of cultivating a positive image of himself. The seeds of a conspiracy theory against racing authorities, which dominated Fallon's thinking in the wake of his arrest by the City of London police in 2004, were sown in the soil of North Yorkshire nearly a decade before.

Where it mattered, though, Fallon's career was slowly beginning to gather momentum. His graph of winners showed a steady and healthy rise: 29 in 1991, 45 in 1992 and 60 in 1993. Barring 1994, when he was banned, his numbers rose year on year to a peak of 204 in his second season as champion jockey, also the second of his three successive double hundreds. The extraordinary faith invested in him, in every sense, by Jack Ramsden was paying dividends in the mind of the jockey who was masterminding so many of the successes. When Fallon was summoned to the high table, to Newmarket and the most prestigious job in racing, he had served his apprenticeship well.

At the end of the eighteen-day trial, the plaintiffs – the Ramsdens and Fallon – were awarded libel damages of £195,000 against Mirror Group Newspapers, of which Fallon won £70,000. The Top Cees case, though, would come back to haunt all the participants in different ways. Racing's morality, never its strongest suit, was dragged through the dirt in a very public forum, the *Sporting Life* never recovered financially from the battering, nor from the increasingly savage competition from the *Racing Post*, and the fun went out of the game for the Ramsdens, who sensed that if the verdict in court came down on their side, the judgement of a wider court was not so favourable. Balding, deputed as assistant trainer to mind the shop during the trial, can remember the air of tension in the yard and throughout racing during the trial. In the end, nobody won.

'Jack brought the case because he felt there was a personal vendetta against him,' Balding recalled eight years later. ' "It's only the Ramsdens, we can call them cheats," whereas with some other trainers, people would say, "How clever, what a great coup." The word "cheat" riled him. But the trial had a huge effect on them. I mean, it was fascinating at the time, and my own opinion is that it would have been very difficult for racing if the result had gone the other way. Jack loved the craic, he loved the fun, and after the Top Cees case, it just wasn't so much fun.'

The Ramsdens called their staff into the yard in late summer of 1998 and told them the news that they were quitting at the end of the season. Andrew had already heard as much from Emma Ramsden, the television analyst and commentator who is now married to Jamie Spencer, the 2005 and 2007 champion jockey, and had to pretend to be surprised. It was probably time for him to go anyway, but when he went back south he took two things with him. One was the basic ringcraft of his profession, an experience of new tracks and the art of placing horses in the right races, and the other was a full appreciation of the merits of Kieren Fallon.

'Funnily enough,' he says, 'I can remember very little about the interview I had with Jack when I went for the job. He just said, "We don't take holidays," and that was about it, but I do remember one thing clearly. Jack said how much he was going to miss Kieren and how much money he was going to make backing Henry Cecil's horses the following season, not – and this is the interesting bit – because Kieren was going to be on the phone to him, but because he knew how good a jockey Kieren was and how much he would improve them.'

Soon after Balding returned to Kingsclere to work for his father, Ian, Fallon signed a second retainer with the stable. That arrangement was beneficial for both parties, Cecil not having many runners in mid-range handicaps and the Baldings not having a regular stable jockey. The deal was based solely on performance, Fallon earning three per cent extra on his prize money, and it worked well for two years. Fallon's move from Cecil to Sir Michael Stoute, who campaigned his horses across a wider spectrum of races, curtailed his availability. By then, Martin Dwyer had graduated from stable apprentice at Kingsclere into the role of stable jockey, guiding Casual Look to victory in the 2003 Oaks in Andrew's first season as a trainer.

Elsewhere, the Top Cees case had a profound effect, too. Although not directly involved with it, the Jockey Club could no longer shut its eyes to the wider perception of their sport or retreat back into its quaint and archaic way of government. The accusation of libel was upheld by the court, but racing's integrity took a daily battering in the confines of Court 13. The Jockey Club had to police the sport more effectively and be seen to be doing so. It also knew now what rigorous standards of proof were needed to uphold racing's honour in a court of law. When the betting exchanges challenged the cosy cartels that had been operated for so long by the major bookmakers and refashioned the ancient landscape of the punter, the Jockey Club was already in the process of professionalising its security department and sharpening up its act. Ironically, as news of his victory reached the weighing-room at Lingfield Park, Kieren Fallon was unwittingly laying the trail for another, less rewarding, rendezvous with the courts nearly a decade later.

5

CROSSING THE DIVIDE

'If you're enjoying it, you're relaxed and if you're relaxed, the horses will be relaxed and everything works much better.'

Kieren Fallon

When Kieren Fallon first drove though the gates of Warren Place in Newmarket one February morning in 1997, he was not just entering the kingdom of one of the greatest trainers in the land, he was crossing one of racing's broadest divides. As a northern-based jockey, Fallon was not supposed to be eligible for the job of stable jockey to Henry Cecil. No, the role was traditionally reserved for the top southern boys – Piggott and Eddery – or, in the case of the magical Steve Cauthen, American prodigies. For Cecil, the ten-times champion trainer, to choose Fallon, who was relatively unknown in the south and, at the age of 32, still very inexperienced at the top level, was not just an affirmation of the Irishman's supreme talent but a real condemnation of the standard of jockeyship in the south at that time.

Eddery had captured his eleventh, and last, championship the previous season, but he was now approaching his 44th birthday and his back was beginning to display signs of wear and tear. He had shown how effective and driven he still was, but Cecil was looking for a younger man, a jockey who could fill his boots, and those of Piggott and Cauthen, and take Cecil, whose stable had been deprived of the significant patronage of Sheikh Mohammed, into a new era of independence and prosperity. The only other contender, Frankie Dettori, twice champion and the most flamboyant and recognisable jockey in the land after his 'Magnificent Seven' victories at Ascot the previous autumn, was firmly lodged in the Sheikh's Godolphin camp. Few others matched up to Cecil's stringent standards. It was time to take a gamble.

The announcement, made in August 1996, came as a shock to racing and, most particularly, to the southern press, who had been speculating for some weeks about arrangements at Warren Place for the coming season. 'Kieren Fallon will be the first jockey at Warren Place,' the press statement said. 'Willie Ryan, invaluable to the yard, will continue as a more than capable number two, and Tony McGlone will also be retained again. Pat Eddery will continue to ride when available for the rest of this year. I will do my best to help him become champion jockey. He's been a great friend and a great help to me this year and I hope he will ride for us again in the future if the opportunity arises.'

At the time, eleven months before the controversial defeat of Bosra Sham in the Eclipse, no one knew quite how significant those words would prove to be. Eddery's shadow was never far distant from Fallon in those early months in the job, which did not make life easy for the newcomer.

'Of the more mature young jockeys, he's the most exciting I've seen,' said Cecil. 'I think we get on very well together and I've got a good feeling about it. I wanted someone young because you've got to be thinking about the future. Kieren might have a few rides for me this year, but the retainer doesn't begin until the start of next season. He will be riding for all the owners in my yard.' Cecil further pointed out that he had made Joe Mercer and Steve Cauthen champions in the past and, hopefully, would do the same for Fallon in the future.

From Jack Ramsden came a simple but robust response. 'We're thrilled he's got such a good job. It's thoroughly deserved and we wish him all the luck in the world.' When Manchester United come calling, there's not much point in lesser clubs trying to mount a defence. But the Ramsdens felt genuine pride in the unexpected elevation of their stable rider.

The front page of the *Racing Post* announced the news with the sub-title: 'Surprise move confirms meteoric rise to the top.' Fallon was the slowest burning meteor in racing's constellation, his career taking a marked upward curve only with his move to the Ramsdens when he was in his late twenties. But in one sense it was true – Fallon had not shown real glimpses of his future form until the summer of 1996. After coming close to the century mark in 1995, he was almost certain to break through that significant barrier the next year, but there was a huge difference in the demands of pushing home a host of winners round Beverley and Pontefract and handling the pressure of big days at Newmarket, Epsom and Ascot. The *Post*'s tone was sceptical: 'His [Fallon's] partnership with Cecil is, however, a surprising one. Cecil has a reputation for being laid back but determined; Fallon is a self-confessed hothead who says he still struggles to control his temper on occasions.' At the time, Fallon, who was to become the first retained stable jockey at Warren Place since Cauthen, lay 22 winners behind Eddery in the jockeys' table. The smart money, though, was on Fallon winning the title sooner rather than later with Cecil's 180-strong string behind him.

Even in racing, which is a broad church, Fallon could not have met many people like Henry Richard Amherst Cecil, direct descendant of William Cecil, Lord Burghley, chancellor to Elizabeth I of England, and twin son of the Hon. Henry Cecil and Elizabeth Rohays Burnett, daughter of the 13th baronet of Leys. Few people have understood what makes Henry Cecil tick. Attempts at psycho-analysis – which often begin with the death of his father, who was killed while fighting in north Africa six weeks before Henry and his twin brother, David, were born in January 1943 – have always been doomed to failure. He is almost pathologically disinclined to let anyone into his world. This could be the result of a painfully shy nature, a trait he would share with Fallon, a genuine distrust of fellow human beings or – and this is perhaps the most likely – a genuine distrust of his own talent. An approach for help with this book was firmly rebuffed. 'I am afraid that Henry does not feel he can assist you at this time,' his secretary wrote.

The suspicion was understandable given the messy ending to the relationship with his stable jockey in the summer of 1999. But Cecil has never really found the need to explain himself to journalists, preferring to establish his relationship with the general racing public more directly, through his ability to produce more winners than any other trainer and his particular genius for fulfilling expectations on days when it really mattered. When Light Shift won the Oaks in June 2007, it was Cecil's eighth victory in the race and his 24th English Classic. He has been champion trainer ten times and, most remarkably of all, has saddled 70 Royal Ascot winners. In 1987, numerically his finest year, he broke a 120-year-old record by training 183 winners. A true reflection of the trainer's brilliance lies not in numbers but in names – Ardross, Le Moss, Oh So Sharp, Diminuendo, Bosra Sham, Indian Skimmer, Slip Anchor, Reference Point. These horses did not just win big races, they defined seasons, and in the case of the extraordinary Oh So Sharp, who completed the fillies' Triple Crown in 1985, reshaped the record books.

Frequently, visitors to Warren Place left wondering whether they had just been the victim of an almighty wind-up or merely been in the presence of true eccentricity. Either way, it is a disconcerting feeling. In his heyday, Cecil was so good at his job, he could feign modesty while wearing pink checked trousers and yellow socks, and number collecting toy soldiers and shopping among his hobbies. He owned a clothes shop in the High Street and sold his own fashion line. Winners can make their own rules and through the seventies and eighties, Cecil did a lot of winning. In 11 out of 15 years from 1978 to 1992, he trained more than 100 winners. In 1993, he won his 10th trainers' title with 95 winners.

By the turn of the century, though, the numbers had dwindled, and the squares that Cecil would colour in on a homemade chart to denote his winners just about fitted on an A4 page. In 1999, although he was second in terms of prize money, his tally was just 69; by 2001 it had dropped to 47 and it kept dropping through the early years of the new century. By then, Cecil had suffered a fall from favour almost unparalleled in modern racing history. His own stubbornness, a misplaced sense of invincibility and some lurid tabloid headlines were collectively to blame. Racing, more than any other industry, smells decline and when Cecil turned to look over his shoulder for support in his hour of need, he found no one there. He was even reduced to forming his own racing club as a means of filling the rows of empty boxes, a terrible indignity for a trainer who had never advertised for a horse in his life. 'It seems,' one journalist wrote, 'like the Queen's travel secretary turning bucket shop.' From a stable of almost 200 horses, any one of them a potential Classic winner, he was reduced to barely a handful of horses by the start of the 2004 season, and it wasn't until Light Shift won the 2007 Vodafone Oaks on a glorious day at Epsom that Cecil truly put the dread days of depression and decline behind him and understood the depth of the affection in which he was held by the general racing public. He was quite moved and a little perplexed by the discovery. 'Marvellous, isn't it?' he said in that understated way of his.

In truth, his best days were almost certainly behind him by the time Fallon joined the team in 1997, although the statistics of their brief and explosive partnership barely betrayed the fact. Cecil still had a range of wealthy, powerful owners – Khalid Abdullah, Wafic Said, owner of Bosra Sham and Lady Carla, Fahd Salman and Mahmoud Fustok. But the days of the great owner-breeders – Lord Howard de Walden, Daniel Wildenstein, Jim Joel and Charles St George – were over, and Cecil had not worked hard enough to replace them.

Fallon's arrival was a calculated gamble, prompted not just by Cecil's need to find a younger jockey to rekindle the energy and drive of Cecil's heyday, but one who knew how to handle the high-class Thoroughbreds that routinely clicked out of Warren Place on to the gallops each morning. Cecil, a more ardent student of racing and jockey-ship than he would ever let on, had watched countless tapes of Fallon at work in the north. One above all would have assured him that here was a talent to rank with the best. Even now, a decade and more on, Fallon's coolness aboard Chilly Billy in the Gimcrack at York in August 1994 takes the breath away.

The commentator that day probably still has nightmares about his categoric statement 200 yards from the finish: 'Chilly Billy is making good progress and will be placed.' In that split second, it was no more than the truth. Raceform described Chilly Billy's victory in its time-honoured way: 'hld up and bd, nt clr run over 2f out, switched ins fin fast to ld nr fin' or 'held up and behind, not clear run over two furlongs out, switched inside, finished fast to lead near finish'. Had the normally taciturn race-reader added a postscript 'brllnt rd' (brilliant ride), he would have been forgiven.

This was race-riding from the top drawer. Stop the race at the two-furlong pole and Chilly Billy is still last of the eleven runners, tucked in on the rail in the third rank. Frankie Dettori has seemingly launched the decisive move of the race on David Loder's Fallow down the centre of the track. Moon King leads the chasing group, but in vain. No one spotted Fallon with his white cap aboard Chilly Billy, who had been settled at the back of the field after running very free in the early stages. If Fallon had ever entertained the notion of panic, now would have been an obvious moment, with a rare Group Two at stake and a priceless chance to advertise his own worth to a wider audience. But panic has never been part of Fallon's make-up, neither on the track nor in the boxing ring. As Mick Kinane edged marginally left on Fard, Fallon was given just enough room to unleash his challenge down the rail. Chilly Billy's electric turn of foot did the rest. For a jockey relatively inexperienced on the big occasion, this was a ride of real assurance and nerve. Equally impressive for a trainer of Cecil's stature and sensitivity was that the late charge to victory was achieved without resort to the whip. In winning one of the most competitive juvenile sprints of the season, Chilly Billy was not given a hard race.

Two victories for Fallon at Royal Ascot, on Yeast for Willie Haggas and Dazzle for Michael Stoute, would also have been noted at Warren Place. It would have appealed to Cecil's wry sense of humour that Stoute, according to rumours at the time, was about to sign the Irish-man as his stable jockey. Cecil never needed any excuse to put one across his oldest and fiercest rival. That summer of 1996, Fallon had ridden Dazzle to win the Group Two Cherry Hinton Stakes for Stoute, but the filly failed to spark in the Cheveley Park later in the season and Fallon took the blame. 'Fallon fails to Dazzle' read the headline in the *Sporting Life*.

Inside Warren Place, as the New Year of 1997 turned and the first hesitant steps were walked, trotted and cantered by the new intake of stars, there was genuine curiosity and some anticipation at the arrival of a new and relatively unknown stable jockey.

'We were all waiting for Kieren to come,' said Frank Conlan, Cecil's ebullient and vociferous head lad. 'We'd seen him ride some of Stoute's before, but Henry jumped in first. I knew him anyway, so it wasn't as if a complete stranger was going to be walking in to the yard. What's more, I rated him. Often because they were trained by Henry, our horses would be silly prices in races, but there were many times when one of ours, that you knew wasn't up to much, would win or finish second and the lads in the yard would all be thinking the same – "How on earth did he win on that thing?" He was like Lester, just naturally gifted. No one could compete with Lester. He was an absolute genius, but Kieren came close. He was like Lester in his thought. If he'd got a horse at Ripon and maybe we'd be aiming for a three-and-a-half-grand maiden somewhere, Kieren would have a word with Henry and say, "I think you should go for that seven-grand maiden at Sandown instead. He's capable of winning it." And mostly he'd be right.'

Fallon did not just make an impression on the racetrack – he was smart around the yard as well. While Richard Quinn, Fallon's successor at Warren Place, would drive up to the gallops and ride his two or three lots and then go home, Fallon would throw the keys of his car to one of the stable lads after the final lot and tell him to drive the car back to the yard. The twenty minutes it took for the string to walk back to Warren Place would be a time for joining in the banter with the stable staff and for a private chat with Cecil, who would also ride back on his white hack. Many a plot was hatched during those precious moments on the gallops, according to both Conlan and John Lowe, another of Cecil's regular work riders.

'There was another thing about Kieren,' recalls Frank Conlan. 'Sometimes if you got back to the yard a bit late, Kieren would be sponging his mount down, rugging it up, picking its feet, doing all the chores. He'd talk to the lads and if he said, "Hey, you've got a real good horse here, look after him," the lad would be sky high – "You know what Kieren said about my horse..." He made a point of being very good around the yard because he knew that if things got tough, it could be the stable staff that got you fired. I don't think any rider in the yard ever bought a new whip or a new pair of gloves during the three years Kieren was with us. He was always very generous.'

Fallon needed every ounce of support from the staff inside Warren Place during the early months of the 1997 season as Fallon and Cecil began to form a working relationship. The rhythms and expectations of a Classic-winning yard were very different from those Fallon had known at Norton Grange or with the Ramsdens at Sandhutton. In the spring of a new season, the important thing was always tomorrow, not today, so by the time of the three-day Craven meeting at Newmarket, the first significant Classic pointer, the new partnership was still stuttering into life. More importantly for the destiny of the jockeys' title, Fallon had used the slow start at Warren Place to ride winners at Musselburgh, Hamilton and Ripon. His northern bases were still fortresses. But when Street General took the opening April Maiden Stakes on the first day of the Craven meeting, and Ali-Royal and Dokos prompted a second-day double, the Warren Place team were up and running. Despite a flying start by Frankie Dettori, Fallon had laid down a handsome challenge to the established hierarchy.

On the outside at least, Fallon was still trying to play down the gulf in expectation between north and south, small races and big.

'It's the press, the public, the media who make more of one race than another. From a riding point of view, it's all the same. You know your horse, you know the dangers and you ride your race as you see fit. Once those gates open, you're switched on to riding that race, no matter whether it's a Guineas trial or a seller at Musselburgh.

'When you ride for Henry, he'll always say, "Enjoy yourself," which is right. If you're enjoying it, you're relaxed and if you're relaxed, the horse will be relaxed and everything works better. You've only got to watch Dettori, Eddery, any of the top jockeys, to notice that. It's confidence. If you're tensed up, thinking about what can go wrong, you panic, and if you panic, you make the wrong decisions because nothing works. You can't even think straight. Riding good horses gives you that confidence. They travel on the bridle, they've got gears and you can put them anywhere you want in a race. With the sort of horses I'll be riding now, I can only improve.'

If Fallon thought everything would fall into place once the winners and the confidence had begun to flow, he was mistaken. Privately, this was one of the most contented times of his life. He was building a new house in a village outside Newmarket, his wife and three-year-old daughter, Natalie, were settling in to their new surroundings in a converted Methodist chapel in Newmarket and he had the pick of some of the best Thoroughbreds in the country. It was now up to him to prove himself to owners and the press, who remained sceptical of his ability to hold down such a prestigious job.

Some initial ammunition came the way of the critics on the Friday after the Craven when Sleepytime, the first of Cecil's real Classic hopefuls, emerged to contest the Fred Darling Stakes at Newbury. The market said the well-bred three-year-old could not be beaten, but this was not Fallon's finest hour. Boxed in behind a wall of horses at a critical stage of the race, Fallon could find no way through for Sleepytime, although she looked full of running. Beaten into fourth place on a 4–7 shot might pass relatively unnoticed at Beverley on a wet Monday, but at Newbury on a prominent trials day, the indecision of the new stable jockey at Warren Place produced a few knowing looks in the press room. Cecil's continued confidence in the daughter of Royal Academy only served to sharpen the scrutiny on Fallon.

'In the 1,000 Guineas you will see a different horse,' said the trainer. You will see a better ride, too, he might have added. In both cases, he was right. On Guineas day, Sunday, 4 May, all the breaks that had gone against Fallon at Newbury broke for him when it mattered down the Rowley Mile.

No less than Tiger Woods managing a golf course, race-riding involves working out the percentages. The major difference is that the calculations have to be made against a moving kaleidoscope. A right decision one second might not be the right decision a fraction of a second later. Jamie Spencer, another champion jockey, once spoke of a ride he gave Excellent Art at Royal Ascot in the summer of 2007. It was a carbon copy of a previous ride he had given the highly talented three-year-old in France, but with one significant difference. At Ascot, they won; in France, they lost. Spencer was particularly pleased that he had ridden the horse exactly the same way at Ascot, coming from off the pace, threading his way through horses, to win narrowly. An admirer of Fallon as a race-rider, Spencer had held his nerve under supreme pressure, as Fallon would have done, and he took great personal satisfaction from the fact. In the Pertemps 1,000 Guineas, Fallon was in exactly the same position as Spencer, and he too held his nerve under the severest pressure. Once again, Sleepytime was slowly away and, once again, her rider was tucked behind a wall of horses, on the rail with little room for manoeuvre. Watching from the stands, Cecil must have been cursing beneath his breath as a repeat of Newbury flashed before his eyes. Already that afternoon, Fallon had watched Frankie Dettori reel off the first three races on the card, now he was locked in a pocket and, in the biggest race of his life, about to provide his critics with another pencil-sharpener.

'He didn't panic,' commented John Francome at the time. 'Fallon knew he had to squeeze, sit and suffer. That's exactly what he did.'

Part of Fallon's confidence was derived from the filly beneath him. Later, he would talk of the spectacular piece of work Sleepytime had done in a gallop before the Guineas. But now, angled out three off the rail, she needed every volt of that electric current as Dazzle and Oh Nellie duelled for the lead well into the final furlong. The speed with which Sleepytime cut down the gap spoke of a high-class filly trained to the moment. By the line, Sleepytime and Fallon had four lengths to spare over the 50–1 shot, Oh Nellie, trained by Neville Callaghan – four lengths and counting. Dazzle found no extra and faded into third ahead of Pas de Reponse, the Criquette Head-trained favourite.

'I've been looking forward to this since February when I started with Mr Cecil,' blurted Fallon into the Channel 4 microphone. 'It's all been worth it.'

The season had only just begun. Within the hour, Fallon had matched Dettori's three-timer with victories on Cyrano's Lad, who led all the way down the six furlongs, and Valedictory for Henry Cecil in the sixth race on the card. There was much to celebrate – a first Classic winner, but, more importantly, a bit of breathing space.

'Kieren is a very hard worker,' said Cecil in the winner's enclosure. 'He's shown that he is a Group One jockey, which is all we need.'

It was not quite that simple. The feeling was still widespread that Fallon had taken unnecessary risks in bringing Sleepytime home, that the filly with the skinny frame of a catwalk model, had helped him out of a crisis of her jockey's making. The southern press did not yet subscribe to the view that Fallon had proved himself a Classic-winning jockey, whatever the record books said.

Next off the Warren Place production line and into the Classic fray came Reams of Verse, who had finished sixth to Sleepytime in the Guineas under Pat Eddery. A mile was too sharp for the chestnut daughter of Nureyev, but a further two furlongs in the Musidora Stakes at York would reveal more about her ability to tackle the tougher test of the Oaks at Epsom. Reams of Verse went off a strong favourite at 11–10 and never gave a moment's doubt to any one of her backers, winning by eleven lengths, and although nothing in her breeding suggested that a mile and four furlongs at Epsom would be to her liking, the formbook said otherwise. Reams of Verse was imposed as hot favourite for the fillies' Classic at the beginning of June.

Fallon was beginning to discover the relentless pleasure and pressure of riding for a stable with potential Classic winners in every nook and cranny, but he was also setting a strong pace in the championship. A trip to Hamilton at the end of the York meeting in May for just a single winner showed the depth of his desire to be the champion. To his credit, Cecil proved to be more relaxed about his stable jockey's relentless work load than Stoute a few seasons later. To Fallon, winning the title was the ultimate prize. If he could do so riding nice horses and big winners, so much the better.

The next real test of Fallon's nerve came at Epsom in early June. Epsom was not a track that Fallon knew well, and it was one that took some knowing. Later in his career, Fallon rode it better than anyone since Lester Piggott. The previous year on Oaks day, when Pat Eddery had guided Lady Carla to victory for Henry Cecil, Fallon had been otherwise engaged at a humdrum meeting at Catterick. Now, in his first Oaks ride, he was sitting on the odds-on favourite, trained by an acknowledged master of the Classic, ready to race around one of the most awkward tracks in the kingdom. He had already been bailed out by the Italian authorities, who had softened a ten-day ban so that he could ride at Epsom and Royal Ascot.

Around him in the weighing-room were a posse of old hands, quite ready to exploit the inexperience of the new hotshot at Warren Place. John Reid, Pat Eddery, Mick Kinane, Ray Cochrane and Michael Roberts all knew their way round Epsom and not one of them was inclined to give Fallon one inch of the downland. A Classic victory was at stake and, besides, if they could make life difficult for a man of Fallon's talent now, they might save themselves a lot of problems later on. Everyone knew that the relationship between Fallon and Cecil was still in its formative stage. Other winds blew through the Downs on the unsettled afternoon of 6 June 1997.

Understandably, Fallon had chosen to ride Reams of Verse over stable companion, Yashmak, who had overcome a disappointing start to her three-year-old campaign in the 1,000 Guineas to win her trial at Newbury with real authority. The field that day was not top class, but a nine-length victory and a strong staying pedigree had prompted a few to suggest that the stable jockey had made the wrong choice. In reality, there was no choice to be made. If Reams of Verse stayed, she won. That was certainly Cecil's firm belief and Fallon was not far behind in his confidence.

Also in the field for the Oaks was Ebadiyla, inexperienced but undeniably talented and trained by John Oxx, who would not go for the Oaks just for the sake of it, particularly not with the Aga Khan's first runner in a British Classic since his Aliysa had been so controversially disqualified eight years before. Ebadiyla had been beaten two short heads in a Derby trial at Leopardstown, form that put her right in contention for a place, at the very least, at Epsom. But little could shake the confidence of punters on the day. Reams of Verse was sent off 5–6 favourite ahead of Yashmak at 6–1 to give Prince Khalid Abdullah two chances of winning his first Oaks, with Ebadiyla at 15–2.

Fallon would not relish a replay of the video of his first Epsom Classic win. He rode like a novice caught in the headlights, outridden and out-thought first by Kinane on his stablemate Yashmak, and then, most forcefully, by Jimmy Fortune on the unfancied French challenger, Gazelle Royale.

'Mick tightened me up and then Jimmy shut the door just as I was about to make my move,' explained Fallon to Cecil afterwards. 'I thought Jimmy had stolen the race off me, but my filly pulled out something extra and is as tough as they come.'

The margin of victory, a comfortable one and a half lengths, was a tribute to Reams of Verse's evident superiority on the day. Stopped twice just as she was gaining momentum, Reams of Verse would have won by half the length of the straight had Fallon taken the easier option and been more decisive. Welcome, his fellow riders were saying, to the big wide world of race-riding. Cecil's face, caught on camera at the finish, was a picture, a mixture of relief, disbelief and slight disgust. Even without binoculars, he knew that Reams of Verse had been given a harder race than she needed and that her jockey had shown an uncomfortably rough edge. 'Uninspired', one writer termed Fallon's ride. He would have acknowledged the criticism himself. Fortune received a two-day ban for careless riding. Fallon gained a priceless education in the art of riding Epsom. His second British Classic was in the record books and no one could argue with that. Cecil, though, was still unconvinced about the big-race temperament of his new stable jockey.

The early summer in British racing has a neat rhythm to it. Hot on the heels of the first four Classics comes Royal Ascot, always the first date in Cecil's diary. Here was another test of consistency for Fallon, who had a book of rides of almost unprecedented quality going into the four-day meeting and was odds-on favourite to win the jockeys' title. On the eve of the Royal meeting, Fallon gave a rundown of his potential winners – Bosra Sham, 'an unbelievable turn of foot'; Sleepytime, 'she's a lovely stamp of a horse now'; Lady Carla, last year's Oaks winner, 'everyone is very happy with her'; Ali-Royal, 'at his peak at the minute'; Shaheen, 'worked brilliantly the other morning'.

Bosra Sham duly won the Prince of Wales's Stakes on the opening day, putting up an extraordinary performance to win by eight lengths, but Sleepytime proved disappointing in the Coronation Stakes and Lady

Carla finished last but one in the Hardwicke Stakes on Friday, a huge letdown for the stable. Yashmak and Canon Can gave Fallon and Cecil two more winners, but it wasn't quite the return they had been anticipating. Surprisingly, Cecil accused Mick Kinane of waging a vendetta against Fallon on the track, an allegation unsupported by the evidence of the races or the interpretation of the stewards at the course. Cecil was particularly incensed by what he called 'blatant interference' to Lady Carla and Canon Can. 'These kind of incidents happen all the time,' said Kinane coolly, but the inference was not liable to endear Fallon to any of his colleagues in the weighing-room, or ease his own peace of mind. If the pressure was not obviously getting to the rider, it seemed to be playing tricks with the trainer. Cecil was only trying to help, but Fallon was quite capable of looking after himself in the rough and tumble of the psychological battle in the weighing-room. Kinane has never been Fallon's best mate, by any stretch of the imagination, but he was too wise to be drawn into a duel with his younger countryman. 'Racing,' Kinane was fond of saying, with a twitch of those bushy eyebrows, 'is not an "after you" sport.'

The real test of Cecil's commitment to Fallon was yet to come. In early July, Bosra Sham, the runaway Royal Ascot winner and one of Cecil's all-time favourite horses, was due a sterner test in the Eclipse at Sandown. Fallon had the ride in a field of five, which included the Derby winner, Benny the Dip, trained by John Gosden, and the brilliant five-year-old, Pilsudski, from Michael Stoute's Freemason Lodge stable. Fallon has never accepted publicly that his ride in the Eclipse on Bosra Sham, which was quickly nicknamed 'Bosra Shambles', was entirely his fault. Three things worked against him. One was that he had been asked to hold up the filly in the early part of the race, so was never in the ideal position. The second was that the other jockeys, he believed, were riding to stop him, which is much easier in a small field, and third, he was unlucky in meeting the kink in the running rail just as Bosra Sham was making her run up the inside. By the time he had put on the brakes and pulled the favourite out of the pocket, the race was over. Fallon and, depending on how you interpret his blazing criticism at the time, Cecil were never convinced that the loss of momentum was necessarily the turning point in the race, but it did not help, either on the course or off it, where the demise of the flashy upstart from the north was being widely predicted.

Fallon's timing was impeccable – impeccably bad. He needed every big winner he could get, not because Cecil was losing faith, although there was a suggestion that he might be, but because he needed to buy time and space to grow into a job way beyond his experience. He was learning as he went along, which is always a tough method of education. Fallon could have chosen any other horse in the yard on which to make such a mistake. But, of course, this was Kieren so it had to be Bosra Sham, Cecil's sentimental favourite, the horse recently described by the trainer as the best he had ever trained.

The claim puzzled racing experts at the time and it seems no less strange now. On her day, Bosra Sham was brilliant – she had won a Guineas, demolished the field in the Prince of Wales's at Royal Ascot and, on the morning of the Eclipse, had been beaten just once in eight starts. But better than Oh So Sharp, winner of the fillies' Triple Crown, or Indian Skimmer, Slip Anchor, Reference Point or Diminuendo? There was more to it than that. Bosra Sham had helped Cecil to recover after the traumatic split from Sheikh Mohammed in the autumn of 1995 when, at a stroke, Warren Place lost forty of its best horses. Cecil knew better than anyone that to replace Thoroughbreds of such impeccable breeding could take years. But Bosra Sham had ended her two-year-old career as winter favourite for the 1,000 Guineas and all was right with the world.

The seeds of Cecil's subsequent decline can be traced back to the split, which was ostensibly caused by Cecil's failure to tell the Sheikh of an injury to his prized colt, Mark of Esteem. However, Cecil's private life, his divorce from Julie Cecil, daughter of Noel Murless, the former master of Warren Place, and subsequent marriage to Natalie Payne, a young stable girl, came under scrutiny. Natalie Cecil was determined to have her way round the yard as well as in the house, and several senior staff, including Frank Conlan, were unsettled by the emotional currents eddying through the yard. But Cecil's infatuation with Natalie was not the key reason for the split. The Sheikh perhaps felt that Cecil was not just losing his touch, but taking his own patronage for granted. Both signposts were pointing in the same direction. He would take his training operation in house, where he had more control. Natalie's outspoken criticism of the Sheikh's initial removal of Mark of Esteem from the yard was certainly, in the mind of one of the chief paymasters of British racing, a symbol of disrespect, but the Sheikh is too pragmatic a man and Cecil too good a trainer for a relatively minor spark to cause such a bonfire of the vanities.

Opinions within racing were immediately divided as the Arab domination of British racing came under scrutiny for the first time amid fears for the future of the old owner-breeders, many of whom, including Lord Howard de Walden, a former senior steward of the Jockey Club, were long-standing supporters of Cecil's. The smaller set-ups could not compete with the limitless resources of the Maktoum family.

'I don't like to criticise those who are beating me,' said Bill Gredley, a leading owner-breeder, who had drastically reduced his operation in recent years, 'but it's like the same football team keep on winning all the time.' The view was echoed down some stately old corridors in the aftermath of the split between Cecil and the Sheikh, not least because, earlier in 1995, news had been announced that Dubai, fast becoming the epicentre of world racing, would stage the $4m Dubai World Cup, billed as the richest horserace in the international calendar. Changes were afoot; the establishment was being roused from its slumber. Bosra Sham was a symbol that nothing had changed, that Cecil, the ten-times champion trainer, was still at the height of his powers and that great horses transcended the petty politics of the sport.

Like so many fillies, Bosra Sham was fragile. Races had to be chosen carefully and, because they were so precious, used to full advantage. Who knows how many more times Cecil would be able to bring Bosra Sham to the peak of condition for a given afternoon? On the morning of the race, Ron Cox, the *Guardian*'s highly respected racing writer, sounded a prescient warning to his readers: 'Top jockey though he undoubtedly is, Kieren Fallon got away with a poor ride on Reams of Verse in the Oaks. He didn't on two occasions on Sleepytime this season and one hopes he doesn't ask the impossible of

Bosra Sham.' Small fields, he added, have a habit of producing surprise results.

The result was not so much of a surprise – Pilsudski was a seasoned campaigner, blessed with a good cruising speed and reserves of professionalism. He knew his job just as surely as the man on board. This was a very different task from the Prince of Wales's at Ascot, but no one would hear of defeat for Bosra Sham, which was a credit to the public's faith in Cecil and dangerous territory for the rider in the eye of the hype. The severity of the criticism heaped upon the head of the luckless Fallon in defeat reflected disappointment as well as failed investment.

Had Fallon ridden the race the following day, certainly the following year, he would have had the confidence to take it by the scruff of the neck before it was too late, but with Cecil's advice about switching her off ringing in his ears, Fallon took up a position on the inside following Benny the Dip and waited. Ordinarily, in a five-runner race, gaps will come. At least, that was the presumption made by both Fallon and Cecil as they previewed the race. But as Pilsudski came to challenge Benny the Dip, Michael Hills brought Sasuru through on the outside, cutting off an obvious escape route for Fallon and Bosra Sham. Fallon, though, thought he had room up the rail as Willie Ryan just eased out a fraction, but the gap disappeared just as swiftly. Fallon had to check and by the time he had switched Bosra Sham around the field and launched a run down the outside, Pilsudski had stolen a three-length lead, which proved irretrievable for the hot favourite. She did not even finish second, failing by a short head to beat Benny the Dip.

Fallon had some explaining to do and his trainer was in no mood to listen to excuses. 'Getting caught in a pocket in a five-horse field is, on the face of it, inexcusable, but while jockey error could not be denied, those who said the move cost Bosra Sham the race should possibly think again,' wrote the highly respected John Karter in the *Sunday Times*. Reactions elsewhere were less forgiving. Cecil refused to talk to the press after the race; nor had he cooled down much a day later.

'She's had a hard race for no reason and I don't think she will be able to run again until York in August,' he said. 'I have never had her better than she was on Saturday, but she never had a chance. It would have been far better if she had stayed at home. I'm not going to blame anyone, but anyone who didn't see what happened in the Eclipse would be better off watching theatre. The whole thing was appalling.'

Fallon knew exactly where he had gone wrong. Once Willie Ryan had declared his intention of making the race a two-furlong burn-up, Fallon should have made the running himself. The general consensus from rider to trainer was that Bosra Sham would have won by six lengths in those circumstances. Fallon had been selected for his ability to make courageous decisions swiftly, so why didn't he make the move? The answer can be found in the relationship between jockey and trainer, which is as complex a partnership as any in sport. This is Michael Stoute, Fallon's next employer, on the subject.

'I never like to give my jockey too many instructions. You want your jockey full of confidence. Sometimes I told Kieren nothing at all, particularly at Epsom, where he knew what to do. You don't want him being tied down, thinking, "I've got to do this or be here," in a race. You've got to tell them they're the best, now go out and show it.'

Stoute understood Fallon's mentality better than Cecil did, which might have had more to do with the move in the summer of 1999 than many people presume. Stoute and Fallon saw something they recognised in each other, but then Stoute was benefiting from the experience Fallon had gained at Warren Place. Cecil should have taken as much of the blame for the Bosra Shambles as his jockey, and he certainly should not have heaped more pressure on Fallon at a delicate time in their working lives. A quiet word after school would have done.

The fall-out from Fallon's ride on Bosra Sham was out of all proportion to the severity of the mistake. But when Cecil, who had earlier issued a statement saying that 'it is in the best interest of the fillies [Bosra Sham and Lady Carla] if Kieren Fallon is replaced', reacted angrily to further press questions about the issue in the winner's enclosure at Newmarket, there was a general air of bemusement. Cecil himself had fanned the flames and now that Wafic Said, the owner of the two Classic-winning fillies, had removed the stable jockey from the rides, the press seemed to be the ones in the firing line. Fallon acted with the utmost dignity throughout the week, feigning nonchalance about his removal

82

from Bosra Sham and Lady Carla, and acknowledging that his boss's confidence in him might have been a bit shaken after the Eclipse.

'I remember Kieren came back to the yard after Bosra Sham got beat and apologised personally,' said Frank Conlan. '"I'm sorry, I fucked up," he said. He thought he had the pace to get through on the rail and he was blocked. It's unusual for a jockey to come into the yard and admit that he was wrong. In fact, I never knew it before. At the time, we did think he was on a knife edge with the boss. We had owners saying, "Well, I don't want him on mine," and it didn't happen. But believe me, Kieren won far more races he shouldn't have done than the other way round.'

One of Fallon's great strengths as a jockey, and great weaknesses as a person, is that he cares nothing for tomorrow. For Fallon, tomorrow never comes. It's the child in him, the country lad who played endlessly in the woods when he should have been at school, who boxed and hurled against boys twice his size without thinking, who believed that authority, wherever it was, would never quite catch up with him. In the early months of his time at Warren Place, the thumping reality of tomorrow began to hit home. Cecil was under pressure from important owners to sever his links with his patently inexperienced new stable jockey. Fallon had messed up a big race in full view of a public and an industry sceptical more of his character than his talent. Inside, he now knew where he stood. This was very different from the routine bollockings from Jimmy Fitzgerald on a Monday morning, or the very particular routines of the Ramsdens at Sandhutton. No one noticed those. Fallon was outside his comfort zone now, and on the day after the Bosra Shambles, it was not a comfortable place. Reassurance came from his old mentors, Fitzgerald and the Ramsdens, from old friends, too, but Fallon needed to work out the right way forward on his own. When he wanted protection from his trainer, he had found none. Fallon does not forget these things.

The fragility of his position was expressed most forcefully, as ever, in the markets. From 7–4 favourite to win his first jockeys' title, he was eased dramatically to 7–2 behind both Frankie Dettori and Pat Eddery.

'Maybe Henry Cecil's confidence in me is not as great as it was,' he said. 'I hope to change all that by the end of the year.'

The change came rather sooner than that. Fallon's reaction to being cornered is always to come out fighting and never was that defiance, the edge that danger brings to his riding, more apparent than in the week after the Eclipse.

Still, by nightfall on 8 July, the odds-makers seemed to have a point. Three ahead of Eddery and two ahead of Dettori going into the first day of the July meeting at Newmarket, Dettori banged in three winners to Fallon's one to close the gap. Eddery was also on the board. Justification of sorts for the Irishman came as Dushyantor beat only one home in the Princess of Wales's Stakes. Lady Carla was quite clearly far from being the Classic-winning filly of the year before and trailed home a forlorn last under Willie Ryan, who had replaced Fallon by orders of the owner, Wafic Said.

The following day, though, Fallon exacted considerable vengeance for the indignities of the past few days as he won the opening maiden on Light Programme for Cecil, and followed up with three more winners – Bold Fact in the Group Three July Stakes, Memorise and, perhaps most appropriately, Daggers Drawn – in the afternoon. In total, Fallon rode eleven winners in the week after Sandown, ten of them for Cecil.

By early August, when Brough Scott caught up with the prospective new champion during a five-day suspension, Fallon had passed the century mark and had opened up a lead of fourteen over Eddery and Dettori. Scott found Fallon, Julie and daughter Natalie still in a chaos of boxes and unopened tea chests in the little converted Methodist chapel, his first home in Newmarket. 'I must try and get myself organised,' was Fallon's forlorn cry as he surveyed the ragged scene. 'His friend Tony gets him to the races in the red Saab six days a week, his long-serving agent, Dave Pollington, fixes the rides – over five hundred in the last five months. You get the impression there isn't much time for anything else,' Scott wrote in the *Sunday Telegraph*. 'We were a long way from the glamour lifestyle of his peers.' He had bought a small house, Fallon later confessed, because he was uncertain how long he would survive in the south.

Scott had accompanied Fallon to Brighton on the previous Wednesday, part of a double shift that floundered when the evening meeting at Epsom was abandoned because of waterlogging. The Brighton road had been blocked by running water and Fallon had turned up only just in time to take his first ride on a filly for Mick Channon. It was a strange ride to be taking anyway. Shalabella had finished plum last in both her races and her only hope seemed to be an appreciable drop in class for the opener at one of Britain's most picturesque and quixotic racetracks. There was no fairytale ending to the story. Shalabella finished third, but Scott was struck by the energy and inventiveness of the ride, later recounted by Fallon. Not content with just pushing his mount into a steady third, which would have pleased the connections no end, Fallon had done something different. He had switched the filly to the outside, switching his whip at the same time, so startling Shalabella into action that she might have surprised everyone even further by coming second had the horse on her inside not tightened her up inside the final furlong. The point, well made, was that we were all looking in the wrong place for Fallon's true talent. Yes, he was learning to ride the big races more consistently, which was the hallmark of the great jockeys, but the real Fallon was best spotted on lesser tracks riding horses that would see Newmarket or Ascot only in their dreams.

'It was an obscure incident,' wrote Scott of the ride on Shalabella, 'yet the big-eyed enthusiasm with which Fallon related it showed why it is he, rather than even Eddery or Dettori, whom the ordinary trainer seeks.'

Fallon admitted at the time that he needed to calm down, 'to ride smoother' on the big days, and would never achieve the 'beautiful poise' of Dettori, but he believed that he was improving every day. 'I promise you I can get better,' he said. That, by the way, was a lifetime best for Shalabella, her only placing in six starts.

John Lowe, an old friend of Fallon's from his days in the north, was working at Cecil's when Fallon arrived in Newmarket. Lowe is an impassioned talker and a shrewd observer of the racing scene. He had known Fallon for a decade, spent day after day with him in India, but would never confess to being a social colleague. They were professional colleagues, who travelled together to the races constantly during Fallon's early days in the south. Lowe, purposefully, kept his distance and for that reason was trusted to give Fallon solid advice, not the advice he wanted to hear.

'If he got a suspension, which he did quite a lot, he'd often ask me to look at the video and see if I thought it was worth him appealing,' Lowe recalled. '"Lowey, I know you'll tell me the truth," he'd say. I didn't want to be his mate by going to dinner with him.

'What was interesting about Kieren's arrival at Henry's was that he wanted to be there more often than Henry's other stable jockeys. Mostly with Henry, the stable jockey would just come and ride work. Fallon wanted really to know about the horses. Sometimes with Henry, you'd say something and he wouldn't seem to be listening. Then, two days later, he'd say, "John, let's drop that horse out in the gallop this morning," and you'd be thinking, "I said that last weekend." He'd think about it, like my old governor, Bill Watts. Maybe Lester had that sort of input, but no one else before Kieren had really begun to tell Henry how horses might be ridden, or how they might be trained. Before he came, Henry wouldn't tend to have horses coming from off the pace. You'd always sit in the first two. It's totally different. Kieren messed up on Bosra Sham and it took Henry a long time to forgive him for that. Bosra Sham was one of his favourite racehorses and unless you worked in the yard and saw what delicate feet she had, you wouldn't have known how difficult it was to get that horse on the racetrack, let alone winning big races. But, after that, Kieren came to the July meeting and you can ask anyone in the yard, he was electric that week.'

If you were charting the many twists and turns in the contrary career path of Kieren Fallon, the week of the Newmarket July meeting in 1997 would feature prominently in the geography. After the four-timer at Newmarket, one of the major meetings of the summer, the rising chatter about Fallon's future at Warren Place was stilled. Moreover, the sense that the Irishman was too much of a hothead to be a consistent rider on the big days was replaced by the notion that here was a unique talent. Four winners could not sway the balance of opinion so suddenly, but the tide that had been running against Fallon since his arrival in the south did start to turn.

Lowe firmly believes that the jump from north to south did not affect Fallon's psyche for one moment, but the events of the first half of the 1997 season, and Fallon's own comments on the furore, suggest a different view.

'It was as much of a surprise to Kieren as to everyone else that he should be wanted by Henry Cecil,' said Lowe. 'I was surprised. I thought Kieren would make it as a jockey from the first day I saw him ride, and I knew he thought he'd make it. But number one jockey to Henry Cecil? Henry very rarely took on a jockey without knowing all about him, so he must have seen something in Kieren that he liked. Kieren, remember, had already been involved in some controversy. Henry never missed a thing.

'The move didn't seem to affect Kieren. He was in there straight away in the Classics. You have to have self-confidence to do that, know that you're good at your job and make sure that if you do make a mistake, you don't make the same one again. If a trainer's had a go at you, you're thinking better not do that again, better go round the outside or what-ever. Fallon would never do that. He always took the brave way, and whether it was luck or that he made his own luck, things invariably opened up for him.'

For every Bosra Sham, there were a host of winners, 202 of them in all – including six on the all-weather – as Fallon simply carried all before him in the second half of the season, riding 41 winners in September alone. Big winners such as Ali-Royal in the Sussex Stakes at Goodwood garnished the year, but Fallon's real constituency remained at Hamilton and Brighton on afternoons when only the betting-shop dweller really noticed. By Sunday, 9 November, racing had a new champion, Fallon had accumulated almost £2 million in prize money and punters from Hamilton to Folkestone were hailing a trusted new ally. A £1 level stake placed on each one of Fallon's 909 turf rides would have yielded a profit of £118.23. Only two other jockeys in the top 50 – Carl Lowther and Olivier Peslier – showed a profit of any sort. Given that Fallon was riding for Cecil, whose horses, as Frank Conlan noted, often went off at unattractively short prices, this was a staggering achievement.

In Raceform's review of the season, Richard Onslow wrote: 'Kieren Fallon, whose conduct throughout the season was exemplary, fully deserved his first jockeys' championship'. Timeform paid the new champion a rather fuller compliment: 'Fallon partnered a winner on all but two turf tracks and rides far more alive than most jockeys to the wide variety of course and draw biases. Front running has so far played little part in his success. His typical ride sees him taking up a good position in the pack, seizing the initiative at the most opportune time and using his strength in the finish. He was willing to concede publicly style marks to Dettori but he cuts a powerful figure in the saddle next to most. His six-month ban in 1994 now reads like a turning point.' Shrewd judges would claim the same for his ride on Bosra Sham in the Eclipse.

The journey from the Curragh to champion jockey had taken Kieren Fallon nearly sixteen years. He had changed from Kieran to Kieren in the process and defied his volatile temperament and every single one of his critics. In his former stable jockey's moment of triumph, Jack Ramsden was asked for his reaction: 'This year, I knew his riding would not be a problem, but I admit I feared his conduct would.' It was a telling remark, and one that summed up Fallon's mercurial past and foretold his stormy future. In those precious first few months as the new champion, Fallon was able to look down and survey the valley below. He had climbed a long road, but the summit still seemed a long way distant, and yet, perhaps for the first time since his childhood in Crusheen, Fallon was content. You don't need to ask him, just look at the photographs from that time – the relaxed, smiling face and the deep blue eyes alive and confident.

In an interview a few days before the end of the season, the full extent of his insecurity at the move south became apparent. Fallon was still unable to work out why he, of all jockeys, had been chosen by Cecil. He considered himself more of a horseman than a jockey, referring back to the days with Charlie Swan at Kevin Prendergast's when Fallon proved the master of breaking the difficult horses.

'Horses, particularly fillies, are sensitive animals,' he said. 'They need to be understood not bullied.'

The same could easily have been said of the rider. More significantly,

The fresh-faced claimer: Fallon in 1988, the year he moved to the North of England. *(George Selwyn)*

Fallon had to wait nearly a year for his first winner, a nervous chestnut called Piccadilly Lord at Navan on 19 June 1984. 'Kieren rode him beautifully, very naturally,' recalled the late Gabriel Curren, Prendergast's stable jockey. *(Pat Healy)*

Below Distinctively upright in the saddle, Fallon thrusts Eric Alston's Stack Rock to victory in July 1991. Stack Rock won seven races for Fallon over three seasons. *(George Selwyn)*

Left High Premium (nearside) wins the Lincoln at Doncaster in March 1993, the first of many big handicap victories for Fallon and trainer Lynda Ramsden. *(PA Photos)*

Below Last of the eleven runners with two furlongs to go, Fallon coolly steers Chilly Billy through a gap on the rail to land his first major prize in August 1994. A month later, after pulling Stuart Webster off his horse at Beverley, Fallon's season was over. *(George Selwyn)*

Below The brilliant, quirky and infamous Top Cees romps home in the Chester Cup in 1995, a controversial victory which prompted the Ramsdens and Fallon to prosecute a celebrated and successful libel case against the *Sporting Life* three years later. *(George Selwyn)*

Fallon with Sleepytime after the 1000 Guineas, May 1997. A first Classic winner for the unknown northern rider silenced the criticism, but only temporarily. *(PA Photos)*

Reams of Verse, the overwhelming favourite, sweeps down the outside to win the 1997 Oaks under strong driving from Fallon. Fallon became a master of Epsom, but not that day. 'Uninspired' was one of the politer descriptions of the ride. *(Getty Images)*

Cecil's favourite: Bosra Sham slams her field in the Prince of Wales's Stakes at Royal Ascot, June 1997. Three weeks later, after the filly's defeat in the Eclipse, Fallon was roundly criticised by his own trainer. He responded by riding eleven winners in a week, ten for Cecil. *(PA Photos)*

Fallon at the Breeders' Cup in 1998, the champion at the end of a long season. *(George Selwyn)*

Calm before the storm: Oath completes an Epsom Classic double in June 1999, 24 hours after Wince's Oaks victory, and brings Fallon the first of his three Derbies. Rarely demonstrative in the moment of triumph, Fallon's face betrays only relief. By the end of the following month, he was out of a job. *(Getty Images/PA Photos)*

The strain shows on the faces of both Cecil and Fallon at Goodwood after the announcement of their split 'for personal reasons'. Fallon never rode for Cecil again, but did not have to wait long for alternative employment. *(PA Photos)*

Back as a freelance, Fallon completes his third successive double century of winners on Alva Glen at Nottingham in late October 1999. Only Fred Archer and Sir Gordon Richards had matched the feat, but, at the end of another controversial season, the three times champion was not in the mood to smile. *(Getty Images)*

At ease: Fallon and Stoute formed a strong alliance through five seasons at Freemason Lodge, marked equally by controversy and success. Fallon admired his trainer's loyalty; Stoute respected Fallon's judgement. Both liked winning most of all. *(Racingfotos.com)*

Ecstasy and agony: the brilliant but temperamental King's Best wins the 2000 Guineas at Newmarket in May 2000 for Fallon and Stoute. Six weeks later, Fallon's career was threatened by a horrific fall on the second day of the Royal meeting. Injuries to his left shoulder required an eight-hour operation and months of rehabilitation. *(Getty Images/George Selwyn)*

Nine months after his fall, Fallon returns to ride Wintertide (nearside) on the all-weather at Wolverhampton. He won three more titles and two more Derbies, but the pain from his left shoulder was ever present. *(Getty Images)*

Fallon emerges from the jockeys' quarters at the racetrack in Macau. Always a willing traveller, Fallon rode winter seasons in India, Hong Kong and Dubai and served an influential apprenticeship on the west coast of America while completing his six-month suspension in the winter of 1994/95. *(George Selwyn)*

he had also thought of himself as a small-time rider. He had bought a small house in Newmarket because he feared that the job might not last long. Like everyone else, Fallon was only just beginning to come to terms with the extent of his own talent.

6

BITTER AND STOUTE

'To fly in Concorde, now wouldn't that be something for somebody like me who has come from nowhere.'

Kieren Fallon on his ambition in life

Fallon could reflect on his first season with Henry Cecil with some satisfaction. He had come through a baptism of fire and become the champion jockey, a seemingly impossible objective when he had first arrived in the north of England back in 1988. If his constituency was still the humdrum tracks on midweek afternoons, he had learnt to become a more consistent and calmer rider on the big occasion. A winter in Hong Kong had also proved beneficial to his education as a rider. His time there would later form part of a 'Panorama' investigation into corruption in racing, but when he returned to take up his post at Warren Place for the second season, he was close to being the complete champion. Now all he had to do was behave like a champion.

Fallon, acutely aware of his background and reluctant to shed any association with it, found that hard. Unlike his counterpart in jump racing, Tony McCoy, who also comes from a tough rural background – McCoy from the north, Fallon from the south – Fallon the champion was easy prey for racing's hangers-on. If they came with an Irish accent and a hard-luck story, Fallon was also easy money. His judgement of people was much worse than his judgement of horses, as he himself has acknowledged privately.

When Tony McCoy was once asked about the nature of being a champion, he said he had one simple rule – if in doubt, trust no one. He was a much younger champion than Fallon, but he swiftly realised two things. Firstly, he understood that his very being, the whole definition of his life in the saddle, lay in riding more winners than anyone else. Whether that meant he was better than everyone else was a matter for others to debate but no one could argue with the numbers. Only half jokingly, he refers to Sir Gordon Richards and his 26 titles, and he will look at you with a mixture of contempt and bewilderment if you suggest that a day will come when he might not be champion. McCoy's ability to ride more winners than anyone else year after year is a product of an iron will, total self-belief and an absolute ruthlessness. Like Fallon, he battles his weight and the fear of failure with equal passion. McCoy truly believes that he could wake up one morning and never ride another winner. He always treats his last winner as potentially his very last, and the insecurity drives him on to greater and greater glory.

The second thing he realised was that to ride every day, every week of the year, he needed to surround himself with the right people. Very early in his career, he recognised that to stay as champion, to resist the burn-out that seemed his only rival, he needed to pare his life down, like his body, to the bones. He had the best agent in the business in Dave Roberts, a personal assistant in Gee Bradburne (née Armytage) who acted as PR officer, travel agent, business manager and factotum, and a driver to get him to the races. That was the McCoy team. It helped that McCoy is a natural ascetic, a non-drinker, non-smoker, a man blissfully happy in his own company and utterly dedicated to the cause of winning.

At the races, McCoy is business-like, more talkative and relaxed in his latter years, certainly, but still monastic in his habits. He is the master of the jog trot, the little run that jockeys adopt when they don't want anyone to bother them on the way in to the weighing-room. Conversations with McCoy on the racetrack are, generally, brief and to the point. Fallon has much of the same drive, but only a fraction of the self-discipline and none of the inner confidence.

McCoy is, like Fallon, proud of his roots, rightly proud of his family and grateful to the people who have helped him on the way up, but the rest he has worked out for himself and he is pretty proud of that, too. He knew instinctively that being the champion brought distractions and he set up an effective defence to cope with the demands. Fallon patently did not. A steady stream of visitors would attend him at the races, not so much on the big days, but at lesser meetings an assortment of friends and hangers-on would invariably vie for his attention. McCoy's loyalty to old friends from his days with Jim Bolger is unbreakable and, among the ranks of the jockeys, his best friends are also well chosen, solid citizens including Carl Llewellyn, Mick Fitzgerald and Ruby Walsh.

Being a champion is a lonely way of life and to stay there requires determination, which Fallon has in abundance, and a rigid discipline, which he does not. Fallon was careless in his choice of company and if that was not so much of a problem on the way up, it was a problem when he reached the top and became not just the champion, but the representative of his sport. It was very definitely a problem when the betting exchanges arrived and loose talk could be deemed conspiracy.

'A.P. is one of the smartest athletes I've ever come across,' said Michael Caulfield. 'He realised that's the only way to survive in the game. Kieren is resilient and tough, but he surrounded himself with people who wanted a bit of mischief in life and he was easily led. Bad people are clever people, too. Kieren is a recognisable personality type – one who attracts danger, who mixes in dangerous environments, so dangerous people will find him. It's unpredictable, high-octane stuff. It's "Jeezus, how do we get out of this one?" The pattern is very familiar since he arrived in England. The golden rule is to surround yourself with good people. I've told many jockeys there are two clubs to join. One is exclusive and costs a fortune. It's the boring club – you do your job and you go home in the evening quietly. The other is easier, more fun, more mischievous. You never know what's going on next. Go down that road and you're inviting trouble. Kieren was at his best when he was riding seven days a week, Sunday to Sunday, two meetings a day, and going to bed knackered.' A natural generosity of spirit and a deep-rooted insecurity compounded the vulnerability.

'If you needed some money and Kieren had twenty quid on him, he'd give you nineteen of it,' recalled Charlie Swan, who also understood the potential pitfalls. 'When I was riding, God, the number of people who would ring me and you might say the trip's not right or the ground's not right or whatever. It doesn't mean you're going to stop a horse, it's just an opinion. You might tell a friend that, jeez, I can't see this thing winning. I had a call on the gallops the other morning, someone asking would I have a winner that day at Clonmel. I didn't know the guy at all. I might have said, "Got no bloody chance," and it might have been an odds-on shot and then he'd have laid it to lose – where do you draw the line? With Kieren, there's a touch of naïvete. He's a bit shy, Kieren, but he's a nice fella. Anyone can come up and speak to him.'

At the start of the 1998 season, Fallon was contemplating life as the champion. With the backing of a stable as powerful as Cecil's, his northern bases well covered and the support of a host of smaller trainers all around the country, the title seemed locked away for however long Fallon and his body could stand the pace. Fallon's hunger was his greatest asset. He gave equal attention to unlocking the talent of the lowliest selling plater and the potential Classic winner. He found the former as much of a challenge as the latter, which made him a coveted commodity among the smaller yards and with the punters in the high-street betting shops. If Fallon couldn't find a way to win on it, the horse was probably incapable of winning. Either way, it was a useful piece of information for trainer and investor. 'Fallon,' wrote Simon Barnes in *The Times*, 'is a cast-iron certainty to ride his guts out in a thousand-quid seller in a night meeting on his tenth ride of the day. Fallon gives his all every time. Dettori may be the man for all seasons, but Fallon is the jockey for all seasons.'

On a horse, Fallon could be as forceful as any rider in the pack, but the key to his riding was compromise and persuasion. No one was better at switching off a horse, relaxing it so that the minimal amount of energy was used in the early part of the race. Then, slowly but surely, he would increase the momentum until the horse was giving its all without really knowing it. The deception, only slowly understood by the wider racing community, was that Fallon would often be the first to start pushing away at his mount and the last to go for the whip. Riding on a long rein, using his prodigious upper body strength, legs clamped to withers, torso upright, head down, a low, intimidating whistle advertising his challenge, Fallon did not just win races he should have lost, he brought a new dimension to the art of race-riding.

An interview in the *Racing Post* with Tom O'Ryan, his old friend from their days together at Norton Grange, in the spring of 1998 finds a champion in full command of his kingdom. He has learnt from his mistakes, he says, has become less self-conscious about his own style of riding and more confident in his own temperament both on and off the track.

'I used to look at Pat Eddery,' Fallon told O'Ryan, one of the few journalists he trusted. 'You'd see him get buried in a race but you'd never see him come back in, throw his tack around or lose his head. He'd just go again and ride in the next race, with not a bother on him. And I'd be thinking, "Oh, if that was me." I did some silly things over the years, which I would never dream of doing today. I don't know why but I had completely the wrong attitude. Getting the job with Henry Cecil when I did was a godsend. If I'd got it a few years ago, when I was in the wrong frame of mind, it would have been so much harder for me to make it work.' Eddery would catch up with the transgressor sooner or later on the track, but not by pulling him off his horse in full view of the stewards. Fallon, too, was learning the art of gentle intimidation.

Only slowly did Fallon reveal to O'Ryan the extent of his vulnerability over the move to the south, and how much he had been influenced by the pressure thrust upon him by others. 'Although I won the Guineas and Oaks, I didn't get the same sort of thrill as I would if I won them now. The pressure didn't allow me to enjoy it as much as I should have done at the time. I just wanted to get on to the next day. It was only when the season finished that I felt good about it. Deep down, I knew it had to work for me, and that if it didn't work for Henry Cecil, it wouldn't work for anyone else and I'd probably be finished. It would have been very difficult for me to go back north and pick up the pieces. I remember Mark Birch saying to me years ago that riding down south you were a little fish in a big pond. That was always in the back of my mind.'

He was, he added, much more confident about making decisions in the saddle now, not wondering first how they would look to his boss, and then how they might look to everyone else. He was also confident enough as the champion to explain in precise detail his philosophy and technique of race-riding, giving a particular insight to Sue Montgomery, whom Fallon knew to be a knowledgeable and conscientious journalist. 'I just like being on a horse, whether it's riding work or just riding in the country,' he said. 'But when you're racing, you get the ultimate feeling, the rhythm and flow of a race, getting deep into your horse, getting him to stretch, becoming one with him.' This was Fallon at his most poetic, but also at his most analytical. 'I like to throw them their heads, on the buckle end of the rein. I ride the horse, you see, not just its head. You use your legs and your body to keep a horse balanced, not your hands. Some jockeys just push the reins and when you see that, you know they could be getting so much more from that horse. Willie Carson is always criticising me for not getting hold of their heads, but to me that's gagging them, stopping the forward movement. He says I'd look the part better if I did, but I'd rather be in the winner's enclosure.' It was a neat and deadly rebuff to the BBC's expert analyst. Fallon was finding his feet in the south and finding his voice. He no longer cared whether he looked as smooth as Frankie Dettori. He was riding more winners.

The season proved a personal triumph for Fallon and, in a different way from the previous season, for Cecil. There were no Classic winners and fewer Group winners but the trainer topped the 100-winner mark for only the second time in six seasons and finished second in the trainers' championship. Much of the quality in Warren Place that year was just below top class. Most stables in the land would have been delighted with a total of eight Group winners and 13 Listed winners, but, for Warren Place, that was a below par return. The big guns failed to fire effectively on the big days and although Dr Fong beat Desert Prince in a protracted duel for the St James's Palace Stakes to bring Cecil his 64th Royal Ascot winner, Jibe disappointed in the 1,000 Guineas and Midnight Line, second in the Musidora at York and a strong favourite for the Oaks, could not match the closing speed of Shahtoush, the first-ever runner at Epsom for promising young Irish trainer, Aidan O'Brien. Sadian, beaten by a neck in the Lingfield Derby trial, but still a 25–1 shot, ran in accordance with his odds to finish in mid-field as High-Rise brought Luca Cumani a second Derby. One bright light was the rapid improvement of Royal Anthem, who kept his unbeaten three-year-old record by winning the Group Two Hardwicke Stakes on the final day of the Royal meeting; another was the juvenile debut of Wince, who finished a promising third to Blue Melody at Epsom. Almost a year later the same horse provided Fallon with his second victory in the 1,000 Guineas.

Surprisingly installed as 7–2 favourite for the King George, ahead of the far more experienced Swain and High-Rise, Royal Anthem ran a cracking race on his Group One debut and lost nothing in defeat by those two horses after Fallon had, to the surprise of some, turned the race into a test of stamina by kicking on early in the straight. Whether that had anything to do with his subsequent replacement for the Breeders' Cup at Churchill Downs at the end of October is a matter of debate, but the American Gary Stevens won the Canadian International on Royal Anthem and, much to Fallon's annoyance, was preferred for the ride in the Breeders' Cup, too.

Fallon, though, was at his imperious best the length and breadth of Britain, on just those sort of two-meeting days that Simon Barnes had described. During late July and into early August, he was virtually unstoppable. Eight winners at Glorious Goodwood were followed by a four-timer at Newcastle, two more at Haydock and a treble at Yarmouth. Victory in the Ebor on Cecil's filly, Tuning, closed an old sore. It was the race Fallon felt he should have won when he was jocked off Sapience by Pat Eddery nearly a decade earlier. Despite suffering a series of bans, Fallon had opened up a gap of nearly fifty on Dettori by early September, effectively wrapping up the defence of his title two months before the end of the season.

There were also glimpses of promise for the following year as the eyes of the top trainers turned to their crop of two-year-olds and every-one tried to identify favourites for the 1999 Classics. Enrique's victory in the Tattersall Stakes at Newmarket prompted an unusual bout of hyperbole from his jockey. 'He's the kind of horse that can shorten the winter,' said Fallon. With the highly rated Lujain, trained by David Loder, and Aidan O'Brien's Stravinsky also juveniles of distinct promise, the cognoscenti looked forward to the showdown in the Dewhurst, the race that traditionally determines the favourite for the 2,000 Guineas. Cecil and Fallon felt confident that, in Enrique, they had a genuine challenger for the honour. But, come the day, the sound of punctured reputations filled the air over Newmarket. Lujain, Stravinsky and Enrique all failed to fire as Mujahid, a well-beaten favourite in the Gimcrack earlier in the season, and Auction House fought out the finish. Even John Dunlop, trainer of the winner, Mujahid, could barely believe the result.

In the final week of the season, at Musselburgh, Fallon rode his 200th winner to join Dettori, Sir Gordon Richards and Fred Archer in riding consecutive double centuries. By nightfall, Fallon had stretched his tally to 202; by the end of the season he had ridden 204 winners (from 972 rides), 185 on the turf, bowing to second-placed Dettori only in terms of total prize money. Interestingly, only 57 winners – and 212 rides – had been provided by Cecil, which was a tribute to the universal demand for the champion's services outside his stable, and the shrewd shepherding of his rides by his agent, Dave Pollington. Cecil had promised to make Fallon the champion and had been as good as his word, but now it was quite conceivable that Fallon would stay as champion, with or without the services of Henry Cecil. The theory would be put to the test sooner than many people thought.

Fallon returned for work at Warren Place as usual in the early weeks of February 1999 after a highly successful and lucrative spell riding in Hong Kong, where his skill at getting the best out of disillusioned old horses paid particular dividends. As usual, he could survey the inmates at Warren Place and anticipate another summer of success. In one corner stood Ballet Master, fluent winner of a maiden at Yarmouth and a potential Derby prospect; in another, Royal Anthem, winner of four from five as a three-year-old and bigger and stronger a year on. Bionic was there, too, a daughter of the brilliant Zafonic, who rendered Fallon speechless after hacking up in her maiden at Goodwood. Despite his defeat in the Dewhurst, Enrique was expected to carry Cecil's standard into at least one Classic. Shiva, Killer Instinct and Chester House also caught the eye of the stable jockey. Yes, this was going to be a great season. And as usual, Fallon lined up the pretenders to his title without truly believing that anyone was prepared to work harder, travel more miles or ride more winners than he was over the coming months. Richard Quinn, he believed, would be his main challenger. 'Who knows?' he asked. 'By mid-season, I might be chasing, not being chased.' Some chance! To add to the brief glimpse of contentment in his often turbulent life, Fallon's wife Julie was expecting twins in June. Fallon just hoped they would not arrive on Derby day.

No one quite anticipated the dominance that Cecil and Fallon would exert over the Classics, nor the spectacular falling-out that would end the partnership in high summer. That he should win three of the first four Classics, add a first Irish Classic to his growing list of triumphs and be out of a job by mid-August was beyond the scope of even Fallon's chequered life history. Perhaps the move to Newmarket and the almost unbroken run of success was too good to be true. Certainly, the course of Fallon's career suggests he is never more dangerous than when things appear to be going well. Wince, a replacement for the injured Bionic, won the 1,000 Guineas after a ride of calculating confidence by Fallon. It was not a particularly distinguished Guineas field, nor did Wince prove to be a particularly distinguished winner, but the filly landed a massive gamble on the day, which was unusual for one of Cecil's horses. Opening at 8–1, Wince had touched 4–1 by the off, a reflection of the confidence in both Fallon and Cecil on Classic days. Had Enrique not been baulked marginally as he began to make his run in the 2,000 Guineas, the pair would have completed a rare Classic double, but Frankie Dettori, controlling the pace from the front on Island Sands, rode a copybook race, stretching into a decisive lead before Fallon and Enrique had recovered their momentum. Instead of congratulating himself for his calm and patience aboard Wince, Fallon was still berating himself for getting caught out twenty-four hours earlier. The obsession with defeat rather than victory is another trait he shares with McCoy.

A month later, there was no need for any such recriminations, except for the defeat of Royal Anthem in the Coronation Cup, which made Fallon wonder if he had gone for home too soon. He was still kicking himself later that evening, long after Ramruma, another filly off the Warren Place production line, had spreadeagled the field to give Cecil his sixth Oaks win. Remembering his experience on Reams of Verse two years earlier and with Cecil's instructions ringing in his ears, Fallon had no hesitation in letting the daughter of Diesis stretch for home fully three furlongs out. Zahrat Dubai, the Godolphin-trained favourite, chased hard, but was overhauled for second inside the final furlong by the outsider, Noushkey, at 33–1. Victory brought Cecil his third Guineas-Oaks double in four years, after Bosra Sham and Lady Carla in 1996 and Sleepytime and Reams of Verse the following year. Fallon flew back home to Newmarket knowing that he had a live chance of completing the Oaks-Derby double on Oath the following afternoon.

That evening, Fallon recalled an earlier conversation with Frank Conlan, Cecil's head lad. 'In the yard, they knew when I went quiet at the end of a gallop I was on a good one,' said Conlan. 'I was often thinking, "I wonder what price I could get on this one." I rode Ramruma one time on the Racecourse side [one of the Newmarket gallops] with two other potential Oaks fillies and they never saw me. I went very quiet. I was on a different planet. Kieren knew it, too, because I told him.'

Back at Warren Place, they knew Oath was good because he had won the Dee Stakes doing cartwheels, but with Godolphin's potential wonderhorse, Dubai Millennium, Beat All from Michael Stoute and Luca Cumani's Daliapour in a strong field, there was no shortage of contenders on an overcast day. Much of the conversation at the breakfast table that morning concerned the preliminaries, always lengthy at the Derby and always noisy. Highly strung three-year-olds have rarely experienced such a raucous atmosphere and Cecil's prime concern was that Oath should not get overly wound up in the parade ring or going down to the start, when the horses have to thread their way through packed crowds.

Fallon decided to break the parade and not worry about the inevitable fine. He is a fan of the American way of ponying horses to the start, but, in the absence of any company, he uses the precious time better than any other jockey. On the way to the start of the one mile and four furlong Derby course, way off across the Downs, it is quite possible to expend needless energy, particularly on a hot summer's day, and lose the race before it has begun. It's like lighting a firecracker and watching the fuse burn down. Fallon broke the parade and took his mount down gently. He wanted to arrive last to minimise the time spent circling at the back of the stalls.

Drawn on the inside, the other concern that morning was how to get a good position to the top of Tattenham Corner without using up Oath's finishing speed. Go too fast to hold the inside position as the field tracks over to the inside rail and you risk expending too much energy at the top of the hill. Go too slowly and you risk being shuffled to the back of the field. Fallon timed it just right and although Oath did not travel down the hill as well as either jockey or trainer expected, they arrived at the bottom with Daliapour, the horse Fallon had identified as the main danger, in their sights. A couple of slaps down the neck to keep Oath balanced and Fallon was ideally positioned to cover the move when Gerald Mosse slipped Daliapour clear of the field at the two-furlong pole. Fallon asked Oath to quicken and the response was immediate. The pair ranged alongside Daliapour for the final duel. 'A dozen strides and it was all over,' wrote Sue Montgomery in the *Independent on Sunday*. At the line, Oath had a comfortable length and a half of daylight back to Daliapour with Beat All under Michael Stoute's new American rider, Gary Stevens, staying on into third.

Fallon did not indulge in any unnecessary histrionics on the line. Instead, a broad grin spread over his face as he savoured his first Derby success, on only his fourth ride in the race. A 22nd Classic win for Cecil beat the all-comers record for the twentieth century set by Alec Taylor between the wars. Fallon gave the obligatory press conference, rode in the next race at Epsom and was back in Newmarket to ride Brightest Star, a promising three-year-old maiden, into third in the closing race of the evening meeting.

The following day he travelled to Chantilly to ride Royal Rebel for Mark Johnston in the Prix du Jockey-Club, the French Derby. Fallon and Royal Rebel watched from a respectful distance as the great Montjeu swept home to win by four lengths. Oath was not in Montjeu's class, but he had been good enough on his day at Epsom. It was his only day. A morning gallop just before the Irish Derby was so appalling that Cecil had no alternative but to withdraw him. Conlan still laughs at the memory of that gallop.

'I rode a lead horse, a sixty-five handicapper, over seven furlongs and Kieren was pushing at Oath like crazy and swearing at me to pull my horse up because he knew there was a photographer about. He said, "This one's not going to the Irish Derby, is he?" He knew the writing was on the wall. I never thought Oath was a real Derby horse, but Kieren rode a cracking race on him, as he did on Ramruma.'

Six weeks later, Oath and Daliapour finished second last and last in Daylami's King George. Shortly afterwards, Oath was sent off to stud, his career cut short by a leg injury, a star for barely a day.

Royal Ascot brought more disappointment than delight. Endorsement won the Queen's Vase and Pythios the Britannia Stakes, but Chester House and Killer Instinct were beaten and, most surprising of all, so was Royal Anthem, by the 12–1 Fruits of Love, in the Hardwicke. Cecil was convinced Royal Anthem did not stay the mile and a half and told journalists that, after a break, the colt would revert to ten furlongs in the Juddmonte International at York in August. He did and won, but by the Ebor meeting, the partnership between the most prolific Classic trainer of the twentieth century and the most successful jockey of the age had ended amid acrimony, scandal and bewilderment in a way only racing can contrive.

In Newmarket, nothing stays secret for long. The trick is to sift out the truth from the rumour. On the outside, the relationship between Fallon and Cecil, initially hesitant and uncertain, had blossomed into a strong working partnership. The plasterer's son from County Clare and Cecil were never going to be dinner companions, but they had begun to understand each other over the matter of their horses, which was all that counted.

Inside the yard, though, all was not well. Paddy Rudkin, one of Cecil's most trusted lieutenants during the endless years of success, had gone and Frank Conlan was certainly not as enamoured as his boss with the new mistress of Warren Place, Natalie Cecil. Mrs Julie Cecil, the daughter of Noel Murless, a trainer greater even than Henry Cecil, had every wife and mother in the land applauding her when she calmly packed up her husband's things in a suitcase on being told the news of his new love, and parked them outside the door of their house. By then, the whole nation was tuned in to the riveting soap opera, news of which had broken over racing during the week of Glorious Goodwood, the most elegant meeting of the English high summer. Faced with the long and often newsless weeks of late July and August, the press could hardly believe their luck. This was the racing story from heaven, except that, as ever, there were real lives involved and real futures at stake, Fallon's not least.

On the Sunday before Goodwood, 25 July, the *News of the World* carried allegations about Natalie and a friendship with a top-class jockey that had become more than a friendship. The unnamed jockey was widely rumoured to be Kieren Fallon. Fallon swiftly denied any involvement as he has continued to do ever since. Frank Conlan says that Fallon couldn't stand Natalie any more than anyone else could in the yard at Warren Place, but the story, already careering out of control by the time the racing actually began at Goodwood, was given added momentum by the news that Fallon had been precipitately sacked as the stable jockey at Warren Place for 'personal reasons'. Fallon would, Cecil announced, ride his horses for the rest of the week and in Deauville on Sunday. 'He will, I know, keep himself fit and well and ride to his full ability...after that, our association will be permanently terminated.'

On the Thursday, Fallon gave an interview to the BBC, in which he attacked the 'parasites' of the press. Shortly afterwards, he provided hard evidence of his ability to switch off from the outside world by giving a quite masterful exhibition of race-riding on Cecil's Selfish in the opening Listed Oak Tree Stakes. Even Cecil had to admit that it was a brilliant ride and, on his way back to the winner's enclosure, to reflect on the consequences of his decision. Under the full gaze of the media spotlight, news reporters mingling with the racing writers and gossip columnists, Cecil had saddled Enrique in the Sussex Stakes the previous day, but the horse had not read the script properly and faded into fifth behind Godolphin's Aljabr.

Neither man could wait to get away from the full glare and retreat behind racing's high walls. Natalie Cecil had issued her own statement that same Thursday: 'After several months of ill health and personal difficulties, I became close to a married man who appeared to show me kindness and companionship. This was no more than a strong friendship, but, unfortunately, on one occasion this went beyond friendship. The friendship was ended soon after. I am most upset that a private conversation with the one person I thought I could trust has become public knowledge and I deeply regret the hurt and embarrassment the publicity has caused to those close to me, including, in particular, my husband and family.'

This did nothing to damp down the fever of speculation surrounding Fallon, who had his own wife and young family to consider. Fallon released a statement through his solicitor: 'Mr Fallon has not been directly informed by Mr Cecil that he has been dismissed, nor has he been given any reason for his dismissal. Mr Fallon understands that Mrs Cecil has recently been quoted in the national press to the effect that she has had a relationship with a top jockey. For the avoidance of doubt, Mr Fallon would like to make it clear that he is not the top jockey involved. Mr Fallon is very much saddened by the recent termination of his successful partnership with Henry Cecil.'

Endorsement, the last runner for Cecil and Fallon, dribbled home sixth in the Prix de Pomone at Deauville on the first day of August. Cecil did not travel to watch the sad finale. On his first day back in the ranks of the freelances, Fallon went to Ripon, saying that he had always preferred riding in the north anyway. At the same time, Stuart Webster announced his retirement and Gary Stevens, who, just a month or so earlier, had professed his undying love for English racing, announced that he would be leaving Michael Stoute's and returning to the States to ride for Prince Fahd Salman's Thoroughbred Corporation. Fallon's luck was holding.

Instead of speeding up the hill to Warren Place, Fallon had only to turn down the Bury Road to find Freemason Lodge, the home of

Sir Michael Stoute. It was like leaving Arsenal to play for Manchester United and having both teams in the same parish. Fallon's career, widely presumed to be close to termination after the messy split with Cecil, barely missed a beat. Luck? Good planning? Stoute had long coveted the intelligent horsemanship of the man from County Clare and had made tentative moves in Fallon's direction before Cecil had jumped in to offer him the plum job at Warren Place. Racing returned to its normal beat, its moral code dictated as much by winning and losing as by right and wrong. Racing has a Nelsonian ability to turn a blind eye to human faults, and Fallon has exploited that tendency to the full over his career. He was still the best jockey in the land, by a considerable distance, and therefore worthy of full employment for the following season, no questions asked. If by hiring Fallon, a trainer could steal an extra yard on the rest of his rivals, it was a risk worth taking. The law of the turf, understood by trainers and jockeys since the turn of the seventeenth century, demanded it.

Fallon was not just swapping offices by moving from Warren Place to Freemason Lodge – he was trading characters and culture. Cecil and Stoute shared a special talent that might loosely – and to the embarrassment of both – be termed 'genius', plus a short fuse and a ruthless competitive streak, but they had little else in common. Cecil had arrived in racing almost by a process of elimination, armed with a dilettante's air and a decent pedigree, having served his time with Lord Boyd-Rochfort and Noel Murless; Stoute had arrived on the doorstep of Pat Rohan in Malton, a 19-year-old all the way from Barbados, where he was born, carrying an address and a dream. As a youngster, Stoute's curiosity had been roused by the island's Garrison Savannah racecourse, where he spent a deal of time, but the leap he took in coming to England was considerably bolder than the one over the wall that separated his home from the racetrack.

Rohan had forgotten Stoute was coming and had gone to the sales. So when Stoute knocked on the door, it was answered by Rohan's mother-in-law.

'Where have you come from?' she asked.

'Barbados,' said Stoute.

'Well then, you'd better come in and have a cup of tea because you've come a long way.'

Stoute tells the story with accompanying guffaws and still wonders what would have happened if he'd have said Bradford instead of Barbados, or been successful in his interview for a commentator's job with the BBC, a job filled by Julian Wilson. As it was, his education into the ways of racing in England had begun. Rohan took him in and put him under the wing of Bobby O'Ryan, his head lad, the father of the award-winning racing writer, Tom O'Ryan. O'Ryan taught the young Stoute about horses and Stoute listened and learnt. Much later, on the Christmas Day after Bobby's wife died, Stoute made a point of ringing his old friend, just for a chat.

'We were big pals, Bobby and I,' Stoute once recalled. 'You can talk to people and learn, but I was actually working with Bobby in the yard. He'd say, "Hey, come and have a look at this," and the next day I'd say, "What do you think of this?" That's the best way, when you're working together.'

Stoute's passion for racing is equalled only by his passion for cricket. The captaincy of the Newmarket Trainers XI has marked the height of his cricketing ambitions, but there seems no obvious boundary to his appetite for winning on the racetrack. Deep into the fourth decade of his career as a trainer, he has still failed to master the art of tolerating fools, or to embrace the idea of inviting others into his world. Journalists are a particular pest. Stoute's overriding belief is that training is a private business and that the only number that really matters to owners will be found in the winners' column. In the springtime when the horses are all good and the mood relaxed, Stoute can be a forthright and informative interviewee, but once the season is in full swing, a growled answer down the phone will be the sum of communication. It is a fault he is willing to admit and has no intention of correcting.

With his contacts in the north still working, and from the evidence of his own eyes, Stoute had clocked Fallon's ability a long time ago.

'He rode for me up there,' Stoute said, when, after two years, he had agreed to be interviewed for this book. 'I knew him more by voice than sight, but he always had a very good input. He might ring you a couple of days after riding one and say, "You know, I think I got that filly of yours wrong the other day." He wasn't frightened of admitting he'd made a mistake and he wasn't frightened of telling you his opinion.'

Long before Fallon arrived in the south, Stoute was established as one of the sport's powerhouses, one of the rare private trainers who could compete with the big battalions of Coolmore and Godolphin. He had a formidable array of backers, including Lord Weinstock and the Aga Khan, who had only recently returned to British racing after the disqualification of Aliysa from the Oaks. Stoute would refer to his better-bred horses as the 'lollipops' and said that when the lollipops were more evenly distributed among the trainers, it would probably be time to go to watch some more cricket. But, in several conversations over a number of years, he has never given the impression that the time was close. Stoute would test his continuing appetite for the fray each spring, his favourite time of the year. If he felt the thrill of anticipation as he watched the ranks of well-bred Thoroughbreds clicking out of his yard each morning, if the dreams began to form, he was ready for another season.

'I suppose I never contemplated not doing this,' he said. 'The most important aspect for owners is success. Even if they think you're a bit boring, or don't communicate with them as well as some others they employ, if you win races for them, you'll probably hang in there. If you're not ambitious, you're not competitive. If losing doesn't matter, you won't be successful. I don't have any difficulty in that area. Godolphin? Little Aidan? I want to beat them all.'

For both Fallon and Stoute, the timing of the split with Cecil was perfect. Fallon was looking for another team to join; Stoute had a vacancy for a stable jockey. If there was any hesitation in replacing one troubled Irishman in Walter Swinburn with another in Fallon, it was overridden by the performances Stoute noted every day on the racetrack. Nevertheless, the parallels were uncomfortable. Fighting an eternal battle with his weight and his nerves, Swinburn had been forced for his own peace of mind to take a year's sabbatical through 1997, just over a year after suffering a life-threatening fall in Hong Kong, which left him in intensive care for ten days. Swinburn had returned, seemingly fit and well, to ride three winners in a day for Stoute at the Royal meeting in 1998, but soon afterwards he slid from view again, trying one more comeback before announcing his retirement from the saddle.

Stoute's relationship with Swinburn was very different from the one he would forge with Fallon. Swinburn had arrived at Freemason Lodge as an 18-year-old prodigy with a proper racing background and talent to spare. He was nicknamed 'the Choirboy' for his fresh-faced good looks. Stoute always maintained that Swinburn had the best hands, meaning the gentlest hands, of any horseman he ever knew. 'The jockey you'd really like would have Walter's hands and my strength,' Fallon once told Stoute.

Fallon came to Stoute as the reigning champion and, at the age of 35, a rider at the peak of his powers. He had always known how to coax and cajole the best out of handicappers round lesser tracks, but his two and a half years with Henry Cecil had taught him the art of riding top-class horses consistently. Once Fallon became available, there was no need for overtures. Fallon was hired.

'Sir Michael is a trainer I have always liked and admired,' cooed Fallon. 'He likes his horses to be ridden in the way I like to ride them. If you had asked me five or six years ago what job I wanted above all others, it would have been to ride for Sir Michael.' That might have been news to Henry Cecil, but Fallon has a tendency to speak with an appealing, if frustrating, disregard for yesterday or tomorrow. A few days earlier, he had said he preferred riding in the north. The day before that he had said he wanted his riding to do the talking.

The first horse Fallon rode as a freelance in August 1999 was Water Echo at Ripon for Stoute. The even-money favourite could finish no better than third. His first winner came the following day on Ogilia in a maiden at Bath for Ian Balding, his second retained stable. He completed a double two races later for Milton Bradley. There was barely a hiccough in his chase for the championship and by early September, having ridden ten winners in three days, five in one day at Lingfield, Fallon was more than fifty clear in the title race. Later that month, he was confirmed as Stoute's stable jockey for the following season, as if any confirmation was really needed.

Viewed cynically, it was all too neat to be true. Either, as Mrs John Lowe used to tell her husband, Fallon was the luckiest jockey on the planet or the smartest. While Cecil's career went into steep decline in the years following Fallon's departure, Stoute was still on the crest of his profession. At the time, his five trainers' titles had been spread over sixteen years, the last of them in 1997, but Stoute was the fighter to Cecil's elegant boxer and in that sense a much closer emotional fit with his new stable jockey.

Fallon still had some loose ends to tidy up. His ride on Grangeville to win the Ayr Gold Cup was a gem, a ride not of tactical finesse but sheer bloody-minded tenacity. Sent for home fully three furlongs out, with a field of competitive handicap sprinters at his heels, Ian Balding's game four-year-old would simply not be passed under Fallon's strong and rhythmic driving. One by one the challengers loomed and one by one they were repelled. 'The man in the saddle once again may have made the difference,' commented Raceform. It was particularly sweet for Balding, who had insisted that Fallon honour his retainer with the Kingsclere team and not switch to Astonished, the French-trained favourite. Astonished finished well down the field on the day.

A month later came another emotional victory for the Balding family at Newmarket when their faithful old Top Cees defied his nine years and fragile legs to win the Tote Cesarewitch, one of the toughest of the late-season handicaps. 'It's as good as riding a Classic winner,' said Fallon. Top Cees had been found a home at Kingsclere after his time with the Ramsdens at Sandhutton and, although running in the name of the father, was effectively trained by the son, Andrew Balding. There was barely a dry eye in the house as Top Cees, one of the great warriors of the turf, returned to the winner's enclosure in triumph, prefacing the ecstatic reception accorded Sergeant Cecil some years later. The public love grand old stayers and Top Cees, on the flat or over the jumps, had more than earned his share of public affection. 'I always like a horse that gives his all,' Fallon had once said, before adding a strange tailpiece to the thought, 'especially if he doesn't win.'

That the notion of the gallant loser should penetrate the psyche of an obsessive winner is a surprise in itself, but Fallon had a soft spot for the downtrodden trier in life because, deep down, he saw himself in there. Fallon knew when a horse was giving its all and, whatever the standard of the race, admired that nobility of effort. Top Cees was whimsical, but he was wholehearted when it mattered. He would be right there in Fallon's top ten favourite racehorses.

Fallon completed his third consecutive double century of winners on Stoute's Alva Glen at Nottingham, ending a sequence of nineteen consecutive losers. As he came back into the winner's enclosure on a cold and wet October day, he felt more relief than delight. He was certainly not much inclined to smile for the photographers, who had been gathering every day for a week or so to record the moment. It had been that sort of year.

Still, there was much to look forward to in life, the progress of his new twins, Cieren and Brittany, for one thing. Despite everything, despite all the nonsense – because of all the nonsense perhaps – he was still the champion. But this was a different champion from the one who took the title two years previously. The toll was beginning to tell on his body and his mind, and although his weight was stable for almost the first time in his riding life, sticking to a strict regime still required every ounce of his will. Alcohol is one of the most tried and trusted methods of alleviating hunger for jockeys and, during his days in the north, Fallon had been a willing participant in the drinking culture. There is no way of monitoring his slide into greater dependency other than to look at the most accurate gauge of his well being – the winners' column in the *Racing Post*. No jockey who was on a bottle of vodka a day, as Fallon once claimed, could sustain the consistency of performance that brought him three consecutive double centuries through the late nineties, but the relatively mediocre returns of 166 and 149 in 2001 and 2002 were certainly at the heart of Fallon's decision to seek help from a rehabilitation clinic in the winter of 2002. The social drinker, the man who had a drink on the way home and another when he got home, was in danger of stepping into a darker world. His work was suffering and that would inevitably have had an impact at home, too. It is no coincidence that the season after his trip to the clinic in Cahir produced 221 winners, a career best.

In hindsight, Fallon needed a rest at the end of 1999. Instead, another spell in Hong Kong beckoned in the winter. Stoute was always on at him about slowing down, but the master of Freemason Lodge was hardly one to talk, as Fallon pointed out. The difference of opinion was not going to ruin a budding relationship. With his new stable jockey in place, Stoute was relishing the chance to regain his trainers' title from Godolphin. It did not take long for the new pairing to strike at the start of the 2000 season nor for Stoute to appreciate what it meant to have the champion on his side every day of the week.

King's Best was a colt of talent, temperament and charisma. Everyone knew he had ability, but a tendency to boil over in the preliminaries and not settle in his races had already cost him the Dewhurst as a two-year-old and was in grave danger of ruining his Classic season. Stoute and Fallon went to work, learning all that needed to be known about the workings of a fragile mind. Fallon rode King's Best every morning; Stoute watched intently. By Guineas day, Fallon knew enough about the colt to ride him with an almost unworldly confidence.

'At halfway, Kieren had got pushed to the back of the field and I was starting to plan his next race because he seemed in such a hopeless position,' Stoute recalled. 'But King's Best was a very good horse and Kieren kept calm. Had he pulled him round the field, he wouldn't have got the splits he did and he wouldn't have won. The horse got him out of trouble but Kieren showed great calmness, great nerve. I didn't have much big-race experience with Kieren, but I knew he was a very calm operator, which is what you need.'

Once released into the open by Fallon, King's Best accelerated through the field to record an ultimately comfortable victory. Stoute had planned the day with almost military precision and Fallon had instilled his own coolness into a horse on the verge of boiling over.

Given his awesome burst of acceleration and the casual defeat of a horse as strong as Giant's Causeway, it was no surprise that King's Best was installed as favourite for the Derby. Stoute, meticulous as ever, took his colt to Sandown on a bank holiday to get him used to the crowds and the noise, but two days before Derby day came the news that dampened the whole week. King's Best had pulled a muscle and would not run. Fallon rode a brilliantly judged race on Daliapour in the Coronation Cup to win by three-quarters of a length. He dictated the pace from the front, holding off the persistent challenge of Fantastic Light, who had earlier in the season won the Dubai Sheema Classic for Stoute before being transferred to Godolphin. But the defection of King's Best took the gloss off the Derby for the crowd as well as for Stoute. In the absence of the Guineas winner, the Aga Khan's Sinndar proved a worthy champion, but it was not quite the same. King's Best ran once more, pulling up lame in the Irish Derby. His career had blazed and died in the space of a few seconds down the Rowley Mile, leaving a trail just long enough to win a Classic.

However, Stoute and Fallon were already proving themselves a formidable alliance. Next stop, Royal Ascot.

7

BACK DOWN TO EARTH

'My God was he determined, just so determined to get back.'

Dr Dennis Smith, on course medical officer at Royal Ascot

There are those who will swear that, in the summer of 2000, Kieren Fallon was at the zenith of his powers. He had been champion for the past three seasons, becoming the first jockey since Sir Gordon Richards, fifty years before him, to ride more than 200 winners in three successive years, and he was already on course for a fourth championship and a fourth double century. Nevertheless, at one of the most prestigious meetings of the year, he still wanted to show off the quality of his jockeyship to a wider public. This was not arrogance, merely the lust for performance demanded by the leading tenor at La Scala or the solo violinist at the Royal Albert Hall. Jump jockeys define their season by the Cheltenham Festival and, although there are plenty of good prizes on offer throughout the summer months, flat jockeys have the same sense of occasion, experience the same relief, the same joy and the same loneliness at Royal Ascot, racing's most conspicuous garden party. Just one winner will do.

By the end of the first day of the meeting, Fallon had ridden two – Kalanisi in the Queen Anne Stakes, the first race on the card, and Dalampour in the Queen's Vase, both for Michael Stoute. By late afternoon on the second of the four days, he had ridden two more, Caribbean Monarch winning the Royal Hunt Cup with a vintage late charge, and Celtic Silence completing the double half an hour later in the Chesham Stakes for Mark Johnston. The title for leading rider at the meeting was already in safe keeping as Fallon went out for the Ascot Stakes, a long-distance handicap and traditionally the last race on the Wednesday card.

By the track, Dr Dennis Smith was preparing to complete his final duties of the day. The son of an equine vet, he had been chief medical officer at Royal Windsor since 1986 and on secondment to Royal Ascot for the last five years. When he was a junior doctor in Accident and Emergency at Epsom Hospital, he had occasionally ridden out for Ron Smyth, and he'd hunted enough in the army to know what being hit by half a ton of horse can do to the toughest of bodies. For a long-distance race such as the Ascot Handicap, Dr Smith was detailed to look after the start and then make his way to the finishing straight. Two other doctors were on the course following the race, while a third stayed in the grandstand to co-ordinate ambulance movements and operational requirements and to look after the jockeys on their return to the weighing-room.

The race was just reaching its decisive phase coming off the final bend when Prairie Falcon slipped and fell. In a field of twenty-four horses tightly bunched and racing hard, there was no room for manoeuvre, even if any of the jockeys following Michael Hills had anticipated the incident. One moment Fallon was in the saddle starting to pump his mount into a challenging position round the bend, the next he had been hurled into the lush Ascot turf. Around him, Hills and Alan Daly, whose mount Natural Eight had also been brought down, were sitting up, cursing and checking for damage. Fallon lay ominously still.

Dennis Smith was not closest to the fall, but one of his colleagues had been delayed in getting through to the scene. He arrived less than a minute after the jockeys had hit the ground.

'Kieren was lying very still and obviously in pain,' Dr Smith recalled. 'A rear hoof of a horse behind had clipped him on the left shoulder as he fell. He was talking to us and he was saying there was a pain in his shoulder. Two paramedics were with me, so we removed his silks and body protector. I gave him some opiates to dull the pain as he was lying on the track. Then I had another look at his shoulder and I could see an imprint on his skin. I was very concerned about it because it was beginning to swell.'

Dr Smith's concern took two forms. Firstly, he travelled in the ambulance with Fallon, something he wouldn't usually do, and secondly, he called a golfing friend of his, Charles Litchfield, who was consultant for the A&E department at Wexham Park Hospital in Slough. Litchfield had just finished his shift, but knew Smith would not ring him unless it was an emergency, so he turned his car round to head back to work.

'I just felt we couldn't hang around,' Dr Smith said. 'The shoulder was probably filling up with blood, he could have had circulation problems, it could have been haemorrhaging, which could in turn have had serious repercussions on his shoulder and his nerve.'

Fallon knew that something was seriously wrong. He knew from the tone of the doctor's voice and from the dull weakness of his left arm. All he wanted to know was that he would be able to ride again. Smith reassured him, but deep down was not so sure. When the ambulance reached the hospital, Dr Smith stayed on, talking all the time to help Fallon's morale.

'It's important for people to feel they can cope with the pain and the uncertainty,' he added. 'But Kieren was a tough nut. There was a seventy-five per cent chance this guy was in trouble with his future racing career – I mean guiding a racehorse round a bend at high speed. I was distinctly depressed about the prospects, but, my God, was he determined, just so determined to get back.'

Fallon was transferred to Stanmore into the care of Professor Rolfe Birch, head of the Peripheral Nerve Injury Unit. He could have been in no better hands. Professor Birch was one of the foremost neurological specialists in the land. For nearly thirty years, he had been studying in the field of nerve injuries, furthering the research on nerve repairs initially begun by the Medical Research Council during the Second World War. If anyone could save Fallon's career, he was the man.

An account of the operation and the recovery was printed in the *British Journal of Sports Medicine* a year later under the title: 'Rupture of axillary (circumflex) nerve and artery in a champion jockey.' Fallon is not named, but the significant point is that his injury, a near severing of the nerves that control the movement of the arm and down to the fingers, was considered sufficiently severe – and the operation to implant new nerves sufficiently unusual – to warrant a special report. 'Early diagnosis of a nerve rupture or significant nerve injury is essential for prompt surgical intervention and optimal management,' the *Journal* records. In other words, Fallon's eventual recovery was due not just to the skill of the surgeon, nor to the jockey's own iron will, but to all the medics and consultants who had so swiftly diagnosed the extent of the injury and identified the right course of treatment.

'The surgery is what saved him,' says Dr Smith. 'But it's partly down to luck. Credit should go to the whole medical team. My part was just to get him into the right hands quickly.'

When Dr Smith called Fallon's room following his operation, the champion was in pain but watching the rest of Royal Ascot on television. He had a vested interest in the outcome. By the end of the meeting, he was still leading rider. His wife, Julie, collected the trophy on his behalf.

No one could be sure how successful the surgery had been until the bruising on the shoulder had started to ease several weeks after the operation. Birch once compared the nerve to an electronic cable 'with thousands and thousands of wires within it', which only hints at the complexity of the graft he had just performed. Slowly, Fallon began to recover movement in his fingers, a sure sign that the nerves were functioning normally again. Birch told Fallon that the new nerve had taken and that he would be able to ride again, although it might take a year to heal properly. Fallon, like all jockeys given such a depressing deadline, divided the time in half and vowed to be back for the first day of the 2001 season. But not even Fallon had appreciated the extent of the pain and frustration caused by his rehabilitation – the long nights spent lying awake, his shoulder aching, or pacing the room downstairs, trying to spot the fractional differences in the feel of his left hand, the extra iota of strength in his left arm and the added fraction of flexibility in his shoulder joint.

This was a process of recovery known only too well by Slade Callaghan, a Barbados-born jockey now earning his living at Woodbine Park in

Canada. The only connection at the time between Fallon and Callaghan was that the latter once rode for Sir Michael Stoute's father. Now they were united in their appreciation of what it takes to come back. If anything, Callaghan's recovery from an horrific fall at Garrison Savannah in the late eighties is even more remarkable than Fallon's more than a decade later.

'I was sixteen when it happened and I was told by the neurosurgeon that I would never ride again,' Callaghan remembers. 'I was lucky in one sense. My nerve was completely severed in my arm so I had no pain. But when the guy told me I'd never ride again, I just told my mother, "Man, he's crazy." '

Callaghan was hurt in August and back a year later. A few months after he was told his young career was over, he was riding ponies with one hand on the reins. For Fallon, it was the extent and complexity of the recovery that was important.

'I used to practise trying to get feeling in my fingers,' Callaghan recalls. 'I'd try to pick up marbles and paper clips off the floor. It was just about impossible. I couldn't feel them. I still can't bend the top joint of my thumb and I have no feeling in the tips of my index and middle fingers. Other muscles compensate. You know, it's amazing what the body and the mind can do.'

Callaghan has ridden against Fallon a couple of times since Fallon's recovery. They compare scars, Fallon's a long winding road – actually, Fallon likes to compare it to the River Shannon – from the top of the left breast, round the armpit and down into the forearm; Callaghan's, in his own words, 'bigger and better'. Callaghan has never fully recovered the strength in his left bicep, while Fallon's shoulders and arms are no different in size or muscle tone. The similarities start at the neck and work upwards. Neither Callaghan nor Fallon were about to be denied their childhood calling by the dictates of medical science.

'I had no doubt whatsoever that I'd get back,' says Callaghan. 'I won on my first ride back, on a horse called Amazing Grace, but, in truth, it took me a good two years to get back to where I was before in terms of strength.'

Fallon, more than twice Callaghan's age at the time of their respective injuries, would have taken heart from the simple courage of the

Barbadian and from the source of his tenacity. Callaghan's father was full-blown Irish. But the road to recovery was still daunting for a jockey who had brought adversity on himself a few times but had never before been subject to such an uncontrollable spin of fortune's wheel. Quietly, many good judges had written off the champion on the perfectly logical grounds that, even if he managed to ride again, he could never replicate the all-action rhythms of his championship years. Fallon could finesse a horse with the best of them, but his stock-in-trade, the style that made him such a favourite with the punters, was the driving use of the upper body and the pumping arms. Surely, that action could not have survived the surgeon's knife. And then there was the mind. In the saddle, Fallon brooked no argument. He held a psychological sway over the weighing-room that, at times, enforced on his rivals a subconscious acceptance of defeat.

'A certain number of the younger and less experienced jockeys would have been intimidated by Kieren,' said Philip Robinson, one of the most experienced heads in the weighing-room. 'Some of the boys have an element of respect for certain people and they'd rather give way than upset them. Kieren was one of those people it was best not to upset. It could work both ways. If Kieren came looming up on your outside and he wanted to tuck in, some might give him some room, but Kieren was often on one of the best horses so sometimes it was smart to let him tuck in and then follow him. I always found Kieren a fair rider. I enjoyed riding against him.'

The question now was whether the champion's vulnerability was open to exploitation.

In August, six weeks after his fall, Fallon took Julie and the children to Barbados. The trip was organised and encouraged by Stoute, who knew that his stable jockey's impatience was near breaking point already. Fallon later made plain his gratitude to Stoute not just for keeping his job open through the remainder of the 2000 season but for his active support in the complex process of physical and mental rehabilitation. This was not a purely philanthropic gesture, though Stoute is a generous enough man. Fallon was an important part of his team, a key player in the decision-making, and he wanted his jockey back fit and strong. There is a resonance to the story that would echo through Fallon's guilty conscience a few years later when Coolmore came calling and the loyalty was not reciprocated.

'When I was at a low ebb,' Fallon said at the time, 'Stoutey said, "Look, there's a place in Barbados. Take Julie and the kids out there and give yourselves a break."'

It was not just a holiday. Stoute had contacted Jacqueline King, the physio for the West Indies cricket team, to work on restoring strength to Fallon's shoulder and arm. King, who has a clinic in Belleville in the St Michael parish, had also helped with Slade Callaghan's rehabilitation, so knew the extent of the injury and of the pain.

'He didn't particularly like me on day one,' King recalls. 'On a scale of zero to five in terms of strength, he was a half when he arrived and a four when he left. On a scale of zero to ten in terms of pain, he was a seven. He did suffer pain. When he came to me he had some movement already in his arm, but there was still a lot of stiffness.'

Under King's expert supervision, Fallon began to expand the range of his movement. He shouldered weights on pulleys, lifted five-pound dumbbells, did exercises for his hands and fingers, and flexion exercises to build strength back into his biceps and his forearms. He also swam every day and enjoyed the warmth of the Caribbean sunshine. Damaged nerves repair naturally at a millimetre a month. Fallon, at the age of 35, did not have that much time. Six years on, King remembers Fallon's charm and optimism, also his faith.

'Someone had told him that there was this woman in Barbados who would make him better,' she says. 'So he was very positive about what I could do. That helped.'

Mostly, though, Jacqui King remembers Fallon's determination and his absolute refusal to contemplate failure.

'He had the mindset of the athlete,' she says. 'The first question is, "How long will I be out?" It's not just the financial aspect – when they're not out there, they're losing money. It's the excitement, the thrill and the adrenalin rush. Kieren came here with the right attitude. If a patient comes here depressed or pessimistic, you have to change that way of thinking. I didn't have to do that with him. He said early on, "Whatever you have to do, you do," so he took the pain. I had the sense of a tough man, very tough, very focused on what he wanted to do. He wanted to be back up there and he wanted to be back up there yesterday.'

The first justification of King's optimism came at the end of September when her patient rode out at Freemason Lodge for the first time. In December, the first winner came, in Dubai, 'a runaway job' that Fallon didn't count. He worked on his rehab every day, sometimes at the rehabilitation centre in Lilleshall, mostly at home, lifting weights, clenching and unclenching his fist, picking up paper clips from the floor. He went to America for a fortnight to make sure the clock in his head was still working. Stoute advised him to be cautious, which was important. Fallon wanted to ride three lots every morning. Stoute held him back. 'I want you for next season, not for now,' said the trainer. When motivation began to flag, Fallon switched on the television and watched Kevin Darley win his title. Darley was a personal friend and a decent jockey, but Fallon did not regard him as an equal on the racetrack. The suggestion by Darley's agent that his man should have got the job at Stoute's before Fallon added a flicker of anger to the cause. Fallon pinned the quote to his wall and read it every day. 'If I had been Kevin or his agent, I would have said something different,' Fallon said in an interview. Darley duly won the title and Fallon vowed to win it back the following year.

Fallon's return gave the start of the flat season, always a time of hope and promise for jockeys, trainers and press, an intriguing storyline in 2001, one at least to counter the depressing images of foot and mouth disease, which was sweeping Britain's countryside. Could this jockey possibly be the same one who walked out of the Ascot weighing-room at 5.15 p.m. on 21 June 2000? The consensus among those who did not know their man was against it. Those close to Fallon, and a corps of bookmakers who had been burned too often by the Irishman, were less didactic. Fallon was odds-on to regain his title. Paul Haigh recounted a good story in a piece he did with Fallon in the spring in Dubai.

'Can you ever see yourself winding up horses the way you used to?' Haigh asked. 'Can you ever be quite as strong as you were?'

Even the writer admitted that this was a brute of a question.

'No way, no way at all,' replied Fallon, looking wistfully into the distance. 'But I tell you, if that 4–7 about me winning the championship ever goes to 7–4, sell everything you've got and stick the money down.' If his timing was as devastating on the track, the championship was already back in safe keeping.

It was not just Kevin Darley who fancied his chances of giving Fallon a run for his money in the race for the title. Richard Quinn, Fallon's successor at Warren Place and forever the bridesmaid in terms of the jockeys' championship, had announced his candidacy by stacking up a few early winners. When Fallon stepped outside the door of the weighing-room on Tuesday, 27 March 2001 for the Henry Royce Maiden Stakes, the fourth race on an ordinary all-weather card at Wolverhampton, the circumstances could not have been more different from his last ride, 279 days earlier. A sparse crowd was curious to witness the return of their champion in a race over one mile and four furlongs worth a mere £2,926 to the winner. The significance of the day was not in the result of the race – defeat by a head on a horse called Wintertide, trained by Richard Fahey – nor in the inevitable inquisition that followed his return, but in the fact that Fallon was back doing what he loved best.

The day before, he had faced an altogether more daunting test – a thorough and searching examination of his physical health by Dr Michael Turner, the Jockey Club's chief medical adviser and a notoriously hard man to dupe. It was, Fallon admitted, the stiffest test he had endured since he had started riding again.

'They stuck a big needle into my shoulder and tested muscle reaction and the nerves in my shoulder with electric shocks that nearly lifted you off the ground. If there were any signs then that everything had not healed, they would have found them.'

Reviewing Fallon's untypically timid effort on Wintertide at Wolverhampton, the critics were quick to suggest that the three-times champion would never be the same. In their defence, there was some justification for the call, but Fallon was so incensed by the criticism that he fired a swift riposte in an interview.

'I know there are critics out there and I'm going to prove them wrong,' he told O'Ryan. 'There were some people writing me off before

I'd sat on a horse again, and others are criticising me now. It's typical of how some people think in this game. The shoulder is fine now and it will get better and better.'

The previous day, Fallon had been cautious with his assessment of his ambitions for the season. The Derby was his priority, he told reporters. Twenty-four hours later, in typically contradictory fashion, came the real truth. 'The only way I won't be champion again this season is if I have another injury,' he said. The quote was printed as the page headline in the *Racing Post* just for the record. But three more rides, at Nottingham on Wednesday, produced no winners, and the more he protested his fitness, the more people doubted it.

March turned to April, and Fallon rode at Southwell, Lingfield, Nottingham again and back to Southwell. The miles were going on the clock, but there was still no sign of a winner. Fallon fretted and strove harder, telling himself that he was riding bad horses in poor races and that as soon as the ground dried out and some of Stoute's superstars stretched their expensive legs, his luck would change. He wanted desperately to have at least a semblance of his confidence back for the first big meeting of the year at Newmarket in April, but confidence does not come from finishing down the field on the all-weather.

On the Friday, the day before the Grand National, Folkestone was abandoned due to waterlogging. Fallon headed north to Musselburgh and a meeting transferred from Hamilton. While the nation was intent on watching Red Marauder win an extraordinary Grand National, run in a bog and completed safely by only four of the forty runners, Fallon finally sealed his comeback on Regal Song in the Scottish Racing is Fun for Everyone Handicap, the second race on the card at Musselburgh. It was a busy, forceful, ride, typical Fallon in other words, and when he followed up on Lennel for Denys Smith in the last race of the day, the relief poured off Fallon and spread through racing.

'Kieren was brilliant,' said Tim Etherington, trainer of Regal Song. 'Perhaps it helps a jockey like him to have a few people knocking him because it makes him even more determined.'

No one could be in any doubt about Fallon's intentions now. In its way, this was his finest hour.

8

THE KING OF EPSOM

'It is vulgar to win the Derby two years running.'

Lord Weinstock

Lester Piggott won the Derby twice in a row, with Empery in 1976 and The Minstrel in 1977, but by the time North Light had followed Kris Kin into the tiny, quaint circle of turf known as the winner's enclosure at Epsom, Fallon had proved himself the modern master of Epsom Downs. No one could quite bring themselves to make the ultimate claim – Piggott, after all, won nine Derbies and Fallon a mere three – but Fallon was coming close, both on the track, where he knew every bump, rise and turn of the most extraordinary and exhilarating mile and a half in racing, and in the betting ring, which danced to his tune with equal spirit. The plunge on Kris Kin to win the 2003 Derby was certainly reminiscent of Piggott in his pomp, a sweeping surge of belief that defied the logic of the formbook and mocked the vagaries of horse and human.

For years, the Derby belonged to Lester, financially and emotionally. Every five-bob punter in the land waited until Lester had selected his Derby horse, because it narrowed down the odds of getting it wrong on the day. Lester, in turn, loved the increasingly frenetic game of cat and mouse as the press monitored his every monosyllable for hidden meaning and the bookmakers trembled at the prospect of another

Lester-inspired pounding. 'God's in his heaven, Lester's won the Derby and all's right with the world,' as Tony Morris, the *Sporting Life* journalist, wrote in June 1983 after Teenoso had added a ninth Derby to Lester's tally. With Fallon, the feeling was different. He had won his Derby, on Oath for Henry Cecil, but his worth on Derby day stemmed more from the understanding that he was, by some distance, the best jockey in the land and that, around the switchback contours of Epsom, he could make a difference between winning and losing. Only Dettori could match Fallon for popularity and he was cast in another role on Derby day. If Fallon was Lester, Dettori was Gordon Richards, who had to wait until his very last Derby to win the race just once.

The instincts of the betting public – and for the Derby and the Grand National that constitutes most of the population – were more finely attuned to the demands of those two very particular races than many experts were prepared to admit. Despite Lester's oft-stated belief that the best way to win the Derby was to get on the best horse, there was rather more to the art than the Long Fellow was prepared to allow. To celebrate the fiftieth anniversary of Piggott's first Derby winner, on Never Say Die in 1954, a pictorial history of Lester's Derbies was published under the expert guidance of Sean Magee. Magee had the unenviable task of persuading Piggott to describe each one of his Derby winners and then committing the maestro's notoriously short sentences to paper. He did so brilliantly; but the real artistry emerges from the photographs and, in particular, from the photographs routinely taken as the field swept round Tattenham Corner and into the long Epsom straight. Turn to each one and there is Lester's unmistakable figure perched just behind the leaders, alert and ready to pounce. If a horse has the ability, he will win from there. Even in 1954, on a 33–1 outsider, he is poised, fifth, just off the rails but not too wide, his body curled low, his arms pushing, gathering Never Say Die for the surge home. On Crepello, he is sixth, one rank closer to the rails this time but utterly in command as befits a 6–4 favourite. Only on Nijinsky in 1970 is he in the front rank at the bottom of the hill, and only on Roberto in 1972 does he look anything less than comfortable with his position. On Teenoso, he is captured with his head turned as if in earnest conversation with the jockey on his outside, Brian Rouse on Neorion. Rouse would have known right then that his vague hopes of Derby glory were about to be extinguished. To emerge from the Derby pack so consistently placed involved precise calculation, a measure of bullying, untold courage and a huge amount of tactical skill, but Piggott managed it time after time. Fallon had the same calculating mind, the same balance and, above all, the same confidence, and the punter knew it.

Fallon later claimed that he had loved Epsom since riding a winner there for Guy Harwood as an apprentice. The facts are lost in the mists, but Fallon would not have known Epsom or the Derby half as well as Lester in the early days. His win on Oath was only his fourth ride in the race. What mattered was that Fallon instinctively rose to the challenge of the course because he saw it as the ultimate test of his horsemanship and because he felt utterly confident about his ability to ride it better than anyone else.

'Epsom has always been a lucky track for me and I like to think that I'm more confident there than at any other track,' he once said. 'People say that I love Pontefract, but I don't. I hate riding Pontefract, but I love Epsom. If you like a track, you feel good on it, and things will usually happen for you. Riding is no different from playing golf – if you feel confident, you will play well. It's like Frankie when he goes to Ascot. It's as if he knows he's going to ride a winner there. You get excited and it helps your horse. That's how I feel about Epsom.'

Piggott might have put it more tersely, but his genius flowed from the same well of self-belief. Above all, Piggott, Fallon and Walter Swinburn, another acknowledged master of the track, were not daunted by the demands of Epsom or the frenzied atmosphere of a day once described by a Victorian aristocrat as a cross between a 'Cockney carnival and suburban saturnalia'.

Kris Kin's success, while down to the Fallon factor in the eyes of the bookmakers, was no less a tribute to the skills of Michael Stoute. Preparing a horse for Derby day is one of the most challenging tasks in training.

'I can't stress too much what a tiny arrow-slit of opportunity the

Derby is – you get one shot, round a Disney ride of a racecourse, with a pubescent horse who is still learning his trade,' explained journalist and broadcaster Alastair Down. It's like preparing a wayward teenager to run in the Olympics. Empery was trained by Maurice Zilber in Chantilly; The Minstrel by the incomparable Vincent O'Brien in County Tipperary. They happened to be ridden by the same jockey. The successive victories of Kris Kin and North Light were all the more remarkable because they were trained by the same man. To thread the eye of the needle once is hard enough, but to do so twice in two years is close to miraculous.

Stoute, no less than his jockey, was a man at the pinnacle of his profession. Meticulous to the point of obsession, inquisitive, open-minded, energetic, competitive to the point of ruthlessness, blessed with infinite patience where horses were concerned and none at all with the press, Stoute knew that he needed all the help he could muster in keeping the growing powerhouses of Coolmore and Godolphin at bay. He would never admit it, but the arrival of Fallon gave his long and illustrious career a new lease of life. It was not just the Irishman's drive and energy that lifted the whole yard, it was his uncanny ability to anticipate the long-term futures of the Thoroughbreds he rode each morning on the Newmarket gallops and, where horses were concerned, his powers of communication.

'I enjoy having an input from the stable jockey,' Stoute said. 'The feedback is so important because we work together. It's a professional relationship and it took time to build up at first. Kieren's a shy man but he loves talking horses. He's happiest on a horse. That's what he's best at.'

Fallon also sensed that in Stoute he had found a man who would listen to him and trust him unquestioningly, neither of which he had necessarily felt at Warren Place. Like Cecil, Stoute did things his way, but in making subtle judgements about the potential of high-class horses, four eyes were definitely better than two. Fallon was a jockey with a trainer's mind. Although his relationship with Fallon developed into a genuine friendship, Stoute stood by his man through some seriously rough times not out of emotional attachment but sheer pragmatism.

Frank Conlan had the privilege of watching both Cecil and Stoute, the two foremost English-based trainers of their generation, from close quarters.

'I was with Cecil for sixteen years, then with Stouty for seven years from 1985 to 1991 as head man before I went back as travelling head man to Henry's. Henry is soft in his manner, he's a gentleman, but he doesn't suffer fools, believe me. Henry is more laid back than Stoute. He had a Midas touch. He could look at a horse and he'd know. Stoute is an absolute perfectionist. He would look around every horse, every night, check them himself. Henry would come and meet me in the yard and maybe look at one or two.

'With Stoute, everything was worked out to the second on the gallops. You'd walk around for forty-five minutes as a warm-up, like an Olympic athlete, and you'd get a right bollocking if you let one canter even for fifty yards. You'd be out for two hours with Stoute, about forty-five minutes with Cecil.'

According to Walter Swinburn, Stoute's stable jockey for a decade, Stoute would time the gallops with the precision of an Olympic coach, not clocking the gallop itself but co-ordinating the movements of all his string so that each one worked to an exact schedule. Exercise began the moment the horse was saddled and ended when it was unsaddled. Every step in between was choreographed.

'Henry liked his horses to walk slow everywhere,' said Conlan. 'The colts were bigger and stronger than the fillies, so he made them walk slower so the fillies weren't jig-jogging trying to catch up. It's like me walking next to you. I'd have to run to match your stride. Stoute would have his blow-out [final work-out] on Thursday if the horse was running on Saturday and an easy day Friday. Henry would blow him out Friday if he was running on Saturday. Cecil would allow no water in the box from eleven if he was running at five. Stoute would say leave it in. Stoute had two head men over at his other yard and three at Freemason. Henry liked to have one head man overall. Which one is right?'

There were other differences of method. Cecil preferred his horses to work-out fully over their distance, while Stoute wanted something kept in reserve for the next day.

'If you were working over seven furlongs with Stouty, he liked you to draw up with the leader at the four-furlong pole and then sit together to seven furlongs,' Conlan explained. 'If you came too soon and he asked you at the end if everything was OK and you said yes, he'd rip you for disobeying instructions. If you said the horse was pulling a bit and went a bit earlier than you wanted, he would say, "Right. OK." He gave his instructions and liked them carried out. Henry would give me or whoever was on the lead horse more responsibility for setting the pace. Mind you, Henry could go barmy too. He'd say, "If you want to ruin some horses, go and ruin someone else's," and he wouldn't let go of it, either. He'd be on at you all morning. But he wouldn't lose it quite as often as Stoute.'

Both trainers could nurture Classic winners on the gallops, one of the tests of the master trainer, but by producing Golan to win a King George on his seasonal reappearance, in the high summer of 2002, Stoute completed a much more difficult trick. So did his jockey. Golan did not have a lot to spare, so Fallon had to take the shortest route, conserving his energy and waiting for the gaps to open.

Yet Kris Kin almost fooled the pair of them. 'He was one of those delightful surprises,' said Stoute. 'Usually horses disappoint you. He was just the opposite. I remember I was at the Breeders' Cup when he won his maiden at Doncaster and I thought I'd misheard the call. He was very laid back. He showed you nothing on the gallops. He wouldn't have been in the top twenty in the pecking order midway through his two-year-old career.'

The son of US stallion Kris S had made an inauspicious debut at Newmarket in early October in a maiden. Fallon had ridden the winner, Desert Star, for Stoute, which showed exactly what the pair thought of Kris Kin's chances. Under Johnny Murtagh, Kris Kin finished 15th out of 26, but three weeks later, defied his work on the Newmarket gallops to win his maiden at Doncaster quite cosily. With Fallon elsewhere, Fergal Lynch took the ride. 'A host of inexperienced horses racing on soft ground, the outcome hardly convinced that you were watching potentially decent sorts,' commented the *Racing Post*.

If the trainer could not fathom the extent of his horse's ability, what chance did anyone else have? Kris Kin was still being underestimated by pretty well everyone, including Fallon, during spring training at Freemason Lodge. However, despite the negative feedback from his jockey and the evidence of his own eyes, Stoute still had an inkling that the compact chestnut had more to offer. An entry in the Dee Stakes, one of the most significant Derby trials, seemed optimistic even for a trainer of Stoute's capabilities.

Fallon had begged to get off his stable ride in favour of the hot favourite, Big Bad Bob, trained by John Dunlop. Although not wanting to set a precedent, Stoute did not think this was a principle worth defending at odds of 20–1 on Kris Kin and 4–6 on Big Bad Bob in a field of four. It might have been politic, given the rift that had developed between Fallon and Saeed Suhail, the owner of Kris Kin, midway through the 2002 season, for Fallon to have taken the stable ride in the Dee. But diplomacy had never played much of a part in his life before and it was not about to now when an obvious Group winner was at stake. Stoute held his tongue and allowed Fallon to ride against him. Fergal Lynch kept the ride on Kris Kin. A few minutes later, Stoute did not know whether to feel ebullient or thoroughly embarrassed as Kris Kin moved smoothly through the small field to bring Lynch his first Group win. Lynch celebrated his triumph so extravagantly he was not ready for Kris Kin's jink after the winning post and was deposited on his backside on the Chester turf. So Stoute had an unlikely Derby prospect on his hands, except for one small fact – Kris Kin had been taken out of the Derby the previous autumn.

Stoute had a dilemma. He had a horse with Derby-winning form and no place in the race. It was not the size of the supplementary fee of £90,000 that mattered most, but the dread of getting it wrong twice, once by taking the horse out, the second time by putting him back in. 'It doesn't look too good,' Stoute said. 'Your head is on the block a bit.'

To add to a precariously balanced equation, unease with Fallon's riding had spread, initially from the Aga Khan, who had been a significant factor in the termination of Fallon's retainer in November 2001, then to other owners, notably to Saeed Suhail and Sheikh Maktoum al Maktoum in the middle of the following season. Retainers in racing are coveted, but rare. Only the top stables can afford to employ a jockey on an exclusive basis. Fallon's retainer was paid by the major owners, which meant that the Aga Khan and Sheikh Maktoum had a significant say in the size and length of any contract. The Aga Khan did not want Fallon riding his horses. Why?

Fallon's volatile past would not have helped, nor his inconsistent riding during the 2001 season, which only served to heighten the belief that his injury had left a permanent scar on the mind as well as the body. Stoute, aware of time's ability to heal both, advised Fallon to take his medicine and get on with the job of riding for him as a freelance. As owners pay the bills, the trainer has little say in the matter. He is just another hired hand.

When Fallon's retainer with Stoute was cancelled, it was widely presumed that the Irishman had lost his second high-profile job in three years. Stoute, who liked the continuity of thought and deed provided by a stable jockey, but, as he tells you with delight, has won several trainers' championships without one, did not want to find himself light of forty top-class horses as Henry Cecil had done a few years earlier with the defection of Sheikh Mohammed. Neither, though, did he want to lose the services of the best big-race jockey in the kingdom and a natural educator of horses. Peter Reynolds, the manager of the Weinstock family's Ballymacoll Stud, long-time supporters of the stable, had a stock reply for everyone who asked about the secret of Stoute's longevity. 'Infinite patience,' he would say. Fallon too had an instinct for keeping a horse for another day and so he and Stoute formed an instinctive and invaluable partnership. Stoute walked the tightrope; Fallon lowered his profile.

There was another problem. Fallon had never ridden Kris Kin on the racetrack, could not get a tune out of him on the gallops and so was little help in assessing the potential of the easy winner of the Dee Stakes. All these complex calculations had to be balanced by Stoute and Joe Mercer, the amiable former champion jockey who was now the racing manager for both Suhail and the Sheikh. But this was the Derby and if Kris Kin could reproduce his Chester form, or even improve on it, then £90,000 was a small price to pay. Kris Kin was supplemented for the race. He could have stayed in it for £1,100.

Even from a distance, the Derby field looked strong, yet all the main contenders had glaring faults. Refuse to Bend, the Guineas winner, was by no means guaranteed to stay a mile and a half and if the old adage was true – if you're still deciding on your Derby horse two weeks before the race, you haven't got a Derby horse – Aidan O'Brien, who had won the previous two Derbies with Galileo and High Chaparral, did not have a Derby horse. Brian Boru was his favoured option. The huge question marks over the horse's temperament and form were largely obscured by O'Brien's imperious Derby record. Norse Dancer looked a definite danger after his excellent run in the Guineas and, like Kris Kin, had been supplemented, and any horse wearing the colours of the Aga Khan and trained by John Oxx had to be respected. Alamshar had won the Derrinstown Stud Stakes in Ireland, one of the most informative trials, but there was no outstanding horse in the field, no Galileo or High Chaparral. So for Stoute, entering Kris Kin was a gamble worth taking.

Stoute worked with renewed vigour at this unexpected project. Like Fallon, he was never better than when under pressure and he felt under pressure. 'We'd taken him out of the Derby because we thought a) he wasn't going to be good enough, and b) Epsom wouldn't be his place. Kieren had ridden him on the gallops and his work could be appalling. I was trying to protect the owners. Then he travelled round Chester for fun and dumped Fergal after the winning post. Kris Kin was a tough little horse, but we needed to be in the first three to get our money back, so the pressure was on, both me and Kieren. And Derby day was Kris Kin's day.'

A few years later, when he had established himself as the king of Epsom, Fallon gave an insight into the particular travails of riding a course that rises and falls the height of Nelson's column. He divided the mile and four furlong course into four parts – the start, the hill, Tattenham Corner and the straight. No horse in any Derby field will ever have experienced anything like the extraordinary contours of Epsom Downs. Trying to guess whether they will enjoy the event is half the battle. It is generally a matter of calculated guesswork. For a human, running down a steep hill requires balance and, to do it at full speed, a certain amount of confidence and bravery. For half a ton of horse, careering downhill, surrounded by a host of other charging three-year-olds, all on the margins of control, requires real athleticism and vast courage. All horses reach the bottom somehow, but some enjoy the experience and some don't. Some arrive like a child tumbling down a hill and some, often the more compact, physically aware horses, come down it on rails.

'Coming down the hill isn't as bad as people think,' Fallon once explained. 'If your horse is travelling well and you've got a good hold of its head, it's a piece of cake really. But all the time you're also thinking about being where you want to be when you turn the corner and go down the straight.'

Swinburn, a consummate rider of Epsom, always believed that more races were won and lost at the top of the hill than the bottom of it. The trick was to get a good position by the top of the hill, in touch with the leaders, preferably near the rail, without expending too much precious energy in the process. Two other potential pitfalls could trap the unwary, according to Fallon. One was to get pushed too wide coming out of Tattenham Corner, and the other was hitting the front too soon. It is a mighty long way down the Epsom straight at the best of times, let alone when the Derby is the prize, and the camber will press tiring horses further into the course towards the rails. Frank Conlan tells the story of Walter Swinburn being driven to Epsom by his father, Wally Snr. Young Walter slept all the way, announced on getting out of the car that he had better go and win a Derby, duly did so on Shergar and slept all the way home. Fallon's ability to stay calm was never more apparent than on Derby day. Stoute's overt confidence helped, too.

'Remember Daliapour,' Stoute told his jockey in the parade ring. 'You gave that a great ride round here.' Daliapour had won the Coronation Cup three years earlier.

Kris Kin was widely available at 14–1 in the betting shops that June morning. By the off, he was barely 6–1. The extent of the coup took the bookmakers by surprise because it was not an orchestrated gamble by a known gambling yard, nor was the confidence in any way justified by the formbook. The market was sure to be dominated by the three

Irish contenders – Brian Boru, O'Brien's number one, Refuse to Bend and Alamshar – but the money kept coming for Kris Kin in a steady flow, and bewilderment soon began to turn to panic in the ring.

'This was a betting-shop gamble,' said the Ladbrokes spokesman, Mike Dillon. 'Fallon is God in the betting shops.'

Stoute still regards Fallon's ride on Kris Kin as one of the great Derby rides. He said so on the day and he has had no reason to change his opinion with time. The public saw The Great Gatsby and Pat Eddery almost steal a Derby on the jockey's last ride in the race. The outsider of the O'Brien quartet was slipped into the lead by the eleven-times champion in an inspired move that almost worked. By the furlong pole, Eddery was still bumping and pushing away and The Great Gatsby, Eddery's pink silks twinkling in the sun, showed no sign of stopping. For a moment it seemed not only that O'Brien would walk away with his third successive Derby but that he would get the one-two as Ballestrini, under Jamie Spencer, loomed to challenge his stablemate. On the outside, Norse Dancer and Alamshar were racing each other into contention. The least noticeable of the challengers was Kris Kin, who had been driven along from the bottom of Tattenham Corner and thrust into the race with the long, rhythmic, bobbing style that was Fallon's trademark.

It takes several replays of the race to realise exactly how much ground Kris Kin made up down the Epsom straight, but he was eighth or ninth coming round the home turn and still fifth a furlong from home. Had there been a horse with a real turn of foot in the field, he might have stretched too far clear, even for Kris Kin. But there wasn't. Fallon set about the task of reeling in the leaders. He burst Kris Kin up the inside off Tattenham Corner and then angled him out three wide halfway down the straight to catch the daylight. Powered by the piston-like motion of the man on his back, Kris Kin had little option but to keep galloping until the result became inevitable. Freeze frame the tableau of the 224th Derby a furlong from home and every punter in the land could have told you the outcome without knowing. Fallon to win, like McCoy, like Tiger Woods leading into the last day of the Open and Roger Federer in a Wimbledon final. Sometimes the beauty of sport lies in its predictability. By the line, Kris Kin was not just a head clear but a length, a clear-cut result that had seemed impossible a second or two earlier. As usual, Fallon did not indulge in any histrionics at the finish. A private smile of satisfaction creased his face. Cocooned in their own little world for the two minutes and 33 seconds of the race, this was a moment for him and his horse.

Stoute, not a man to praise lightly, called the ride one of the greatest in Derby history in the post-race press conference. But he was not talking about the way Fallon and Kris Kin had timed their run up the straight. In truth, by the bottom of Tattenham Hill, the pair had little option but to go for it. Stoute was talking about the complexities of the debate being waged from the moment stall number four opened and Kris Kin was pitched into a race completely beyond his understanding. Kris Kin did not seem to enjoy his experience one bit, but Fallon was not in the mood for compromise. Long before the top of the hill, Fallon could be seen pushing away at his mount to try to hold his position on the inside, a critical moment in the race, demanding resilience from horse and rider.

'Kris Kin didn't learn a lot on winning his maiden at Doncaster because it was a straight track, and he didn't learn a lot at Chester because it was only a four-runner field,' Stoute explained. 'So he came to Epsom very inexperienced. Coming down the hill you can see him holding back, wondering what was going on. "Hey, you've pitched me in here," he's thinking. He was a bit timid. It took talent combined with courage to gather him together, but Kieren wouldn't let him lose his place. He kept at him and so when the split came in the straight, he was through it and away.'

Kris Kin never won another race, although he was a highly respectable third in the King George in July. He was not, in the assessment of Stoute or the handicappers, who make a living out of rating the ability of Thoroughbreds, a great Derby winner. But, for two minutes and 33 seconds, he was a great horse. The best horse in the race, by the admission of his rider, Johnny Murtagh, was Alamshar, who went on to prove himself by winning the Irish Derby and the King George for the Aga Khan. But the emptying satchels of the bookmakers told a different story. Fallon, the punters believed, could have won on anything that day. Stoute had particular reason to be pleased that he had stuck by his stable jockey during some dark hours. For, although he knew his parish well enough to understand that hiring Fallon was a calculated gamble, off the horse rather than on it, he had not quite anticipated the diplomatic tightrope he would need to walk to protect his jockey.

The pair enjoyed plenty of big-race success in 2001 and 2002. A year after King's Best, Golan won the 2,000 Guineas (and finished second to Galileo in the Derby, although Fallon was suspended) and the following year the King George; Medicean won the Lockinge, the Queen Anne Stakes and the Eclipse in one inspired sweep, the latter under a particularly forceful ride from Fallon; Independence took the Sun Chariot; Islington, beaten in her first two starts as a two-year-old, emerged as a high-class three-year-old, winning the Musidora at York, the Nassau Stakes at Goodwood and the Yorkshire Oaks back at York. Only in the Oaks did Islington disappoint, but she was still fresh enough to finish a gallant fifth to Marienbard in the Arc and third in the Breeders' Cup Filly and Mare Turf at Arlington. Fallon won back his title in 2001, as he so desperately wanted, but it was a close-run thing – a scrap with the holder, Kevin Darley, that lasted right through to the last days of the season. Fallon's tally for the 2001 season was a mere 166 (including all-weather), his strike rate (percentage of winners to rides) was under 17 per cent. He was working as hard, with nearly 1,000 rides in the season, but the rewards were less than he had expected. The days of the double century seemed to be gone.

As the 2001 season drew to a close in the usual welter of maidens, Fallon could be found at Newmarket, putting a brave face on the announcement that he would not be Stoute's stable jockey next season. The blistering criticism by the now late Lord Carnarvon was still ringing in his ears. The Queen's racing manager had taken exception to Fallon's ride on Flight of Fancy at York and had told the press of his misgivings. Fallon's gentle response was to wonder when it last was that the noble lord had ridden competitively, which was not quite the tug of the forelock expected from one of the Queen's jockeys.

However, you did not have to walk far that bleak autumn day to find support for the subject of a growing crescendo of whispers.

'All of a sudden, everyone is pointing a finger at Kieren,' said Gerard Butler, a bright young trainer and a regular employer of Fallon. 'They seem to forget the brilliant rides he has given horses this year. He does flirt with the bad-boy image he had a while ago, but Kieren has never taken a backward step in his life, no matter what has happened to him. He's had to raise himself from the dead and he's done that, and he's now on the verge of winning the championship again this year. A lot of guys would have taken the easy way out and gone round with a sulky look on their face, saying, "Look what's happened to me." That's not Kieren. He's back.' Butler emphasised the point by recalling a race at Ascot in late September on Beauchamp Pilot. 'He never gave up, pushing, pushing, pumping and, boom, he won on the line by a neck. No one would have won on him that day except Kieren.'

The following season was no less of a personal struggle for Fallon. His numbers dropped again – 149 winners from fewer than 800 rides was enough to win a fifth title, but Richard Hughes, his pursuer, would not have been within hailing distance in a normal season. Fallon was unhappy with himself and with his riding. Although he trusted Stoute implicitly, he had to win back the confidence of some of his owners. Stoute wanted Fallon to slow down. Fallon wanted to speed up again, to return to the days of plenty, while, instinctively, knowing how much the two-meetings-a-day regime would take out of him. He was 37 now and had to pace himself through tomorrow.

Yet it was still a surprise to Stoute when Fallon came to him towards the end of the 2002 season and asked for his advice. Increasingly concerned about the way his life was going, Fallon was thinking of checking himself into a rehabilitation clinic to receive treatment for alcohol abuse. Actually, Fallon had made the decision already, but Stoute's support was vital to the process of reform, which would not last just for the twenty-eight days of his treatment but, as any recovering alcoholic will tell you, for a lifetime. Fallon had found out about the Aiseiri Treatment Centre in Cahir from a friend. The Aiseiri did not just treat the person for alcohol or any drug-related dependency, it went deeper than that, to the root cause of the problem. Equally important, given Fallon's allergic reaction to authority, it did so without relying on a long list of rules.

In a revealing interview with David Walsh in the *Sunday Times*, Fallon spoke more openly about himself and his way of life than at any time in his career. Was he an alcoholic?

'How do you define an alcoholic?' he asked Walsh. 'We imagine the alcoholic as the guy with the wine bottle in a brown paper bag sleeping on the bench. You can drink once a month and be an alcoholic, you can be a binge alcoholic or a social alcoholic, many different kinds. I was a serious social drinker, a few drinks after racing, a few in the house that night, and eventually it started to tell on me. But I've never had a craving for a drink. Does that make me an alcoholic? I don't know. I do know I have a problem with alcohol.'

John Lowe, for one, was surprised at the admission. He knew about Kieren's generosity and that Kieren would always be the one to put his hand in his pocket for the drinks on the way back from racing. He knew about the problems he had with his weight, which were no different from a vast percentage of other jockeys, and how alcohol was an easy way to dull the hunger, but he would never have defined his friend as an alcoholic.

'When we were in India one time, all he could drink was milk because of his ulcers,' Lowe said. 'That [ulcer trouble] was brought on by the wasting. Cash Asmussen was the same. Most jockeys who had trouble with weight did what the American jockeys did, which was to bring food back up again. Flipping, they call it. Kieren did that, most jockeys did that. They thought it was easy. They could eat what they wanted then.

'The drink culture started when Steve Cauthen arrived. Steve would bring champagne into the weighing-room. In the north, somebody would bring the drinks in the car and we'd all have a few beers on the way home. But there was a strict rule – whoever was driving didn't drink. Maybe Kieren going into rehab stemmed back to another time in India. We were only racing two days a week, the rest of the time we were sitting around with a beer, being taken out by owners or someone. I had a wife who said when I'd had enough. Other jockeys didn't have that. But somewhere he realised that if he carried on the way he was going, if he didn't go to Ireland and get dried out, he wouldn't be able to continue race-riding, and you had to take your hat off to him for that. He did it, no one else did.'

In the interview with Walsh, Fallon admitted that the search for an easy way to beat the weight problem was a way of life for all jockeys. It came with the territory – flipping, diuretics, one pill to kill the appetite, another to keep you mentally sharp. Very few jockeys will admit to having problems with their weight for fear of losing rides, and studies carried out in the UK to assess the extent of the problem – the last of them was conducted by Michael Caulfield in 2002 – have been hampered by lack of information. Fallon had only to look across the Atlantic to the chequered history of high-profile jockeys he rode against regularly in America to know the next stop on the line beyond taking pills. Pat Day, Pat Valenzuela, Steve Cauthen, Jerry Bailey all battled various demons in their fight to survive in a sport once memorably described by Chris Antley, the Kentucky Derby-winning jockey who died of a drug overdose at the age of 36, as a 'game of "what have you done for me lately", like in the last seven minutes?'

Day, who fought cocaine and alcohol addiction early in his career before becoming a born-again Christian, once spoke of needing an outlet for the emotions and insecurity generated by winning or losing eight times every afternoon of the week. 'We need something to calm us down,' he said. 'We have a great way of validating our actions, regardless of whether they're right, wrong or indifferent.' Looking for a place to hide, as Kent Desormeaux, another top-class American rider, put it.

In the winter of 2002, cloistered in his retreat under the care of Sister Eileen Fahey, who founded the Aiseiri Clinic in 1983, Fallon would have identified with those sentiments. He had been on the treadmill, spring, summer, autumn and winter, for more than a decade and he'd loved pretty well every minute of it, but he needed the world to stop spinning for a month or two so that he could clear his head and point his life back in the right direction. His aim had been to reach the top, but no one had told him what to do when he got there.

Stoute was delighted at the honesty and so were his owners. Instead of going to Barbados on the traditional end-of-term holiday – or Newmarket on Sea as the island became known each January – Fallon took himself away to an unpretentious country house located in quiet grounds deep in the heart of the Tipperary countryside, where the prevailing motto was 'The Courage to Change' and the inmates came from every walk of life, their stories linked by an invisible frailty.

Fallon found he was no different from the rest, a familiar face, yes, but no different. Here, the pressure came not from having to win, from having to 'outwit the other bastards' on the racetrack day after day, in Fallon's own inimitable phrase, but from having to look straight into the mirror and to like the face looking back. That was much harder.

'I knew if I didn't change my ways,' he told David Walsh, 'I was going to miss seeing our kids grow up. You come home late in the evening, you've had a few drinks on the way home, you're tired and don't have much time for the kids, and you're actually thinking about having another drink. What I've seen is the misery – the misery of the life I've had, the stupid things I was doing. Everything should have been so much better.'

The problem for Fallon was that he was at his most fulfilled when he was riding two meetings a day every day, and riding a ton of winners. How then to reconcile the new, relaxed, post-Aiseiri Fallon with the old workaholic? Fallon's answer came soon enough. In 2003, besides taking the 1,000 Guineas on Russian Rhythm and the Derby on Kris Kin, he carried all before him on virtually every track in the land. By the close of the season, Darryll Holland, his nearest pursuer in the jockeys' title, was so distant, he might have been riding in another country. On turf alone, Fallon's tally of 207 winners outstripped any other season, while his strike rate of 21 per cent, from 948 rides, was back to its pre-injury reading. Add in the all-weather and Fallon reached 221 winners, a total beaten only by Frankie Dettori and Sir Gordon Richards in the previous 100 years. To cap a memorable season, Stoute won his seventh trainers' title and Islington, given a superb ride by Fallon, became the first English-trained winner of a Breeders' Cup race in California. Fallon had changed; redemption was complete. For now.

By the start of the 2004 Derby meeting, a big black cloud had formed over the champion's head, this one stormier than any of the others. The case of Ballinger Ridge is the subject of a later chapter, but when the *News of the World* lured Fallon into giving tips – one of which forecast Ballinger Ridge's defeat by Rye – to two fake sheikhs, and then blazed the headline 'Mr Fixer' over its front page a few days later, even Fallon loyalists threw up their hands in despair. 'You want to scream at him, with him, for him,' as Tom O'Ryan wrote.

Yet again, Stoute stayed firm in his support, and Epsom proved Fallon's playground. First, the brilliant Ouija Board, trained by Ed Dunlop in Newmarket, swept the famous black colours (with one white button) of Lord Derby into the winner's circle after the Oaks, and then, twenty-four hours later, the late Lord Weinstock's North Light franked the domination of Fallon and Stoute in the Derby. It was Fallon's third win and Stoute's fourth, their second in succession, and it was every bit as straightforward in planning and execution as Kris Kin's had been perverse.

'I was really confident with North Light on Derby day,' recalled Stoute. 'He was beaten the shortest of short heads the first time out, and then won his maiden at Goodwood, and the Dante at York. He was bigger and scopier than Kris Kin, but he was very consistent in his work, so much easier to evaluate. I also knew I could get him fitter than he was for the Dante, and he stayed well in that. We felt we only had to beat the Godolphin horse, Snow Ridge, who'd run a brilliant Derby trial in the Guineas, and he was beaten coming down the hill.'

Fallon still earned his riding fee, more for his work before the start as North Light became uncharacteristically flustered by the claustrophobic atmosphere in the paddock and the raucous expanse of humanity spread across the Downs. Fallon was concerned that North Light would run his race before the start. So he held him and held him and talked to him and soothed him on the long reverse journey down the course to the start. Once the race started, if a leaf had been missing from the Lester Piggott book of Derby rides – and the great man was the guest of honour – then it could easily have been found in Fallon's pocket. North Light was in the front rank, behind the pacemaker, Meath, in the first half of the race and was released for home fully three furlongs out, so confident was his jockey that nothing would come to find him. Remarkably, the form of the Dante – North Light, Rule of Law, Let the Lion Roar – was replicated at Epsom, North Light winning by a length and a half and returning the pale blue silks of the Weinstock family to the winner's enclosure twenty-five years after the supercharged victory of Troy. Just let him flow and be positive had been Stoute's message to his troubled jockey that morning. Fallon knew all along what to do. 'That was just smooth, so smooth,' he said. The knowledge that Godolphin had chosen to buy Snow Ridge in preference to North Light, both products of Weinstock's Ballymacoll Stud, in a desperate bid to find that elusive Derby winner only heightened the sense of satisfaction within Freemason Lodge.

Two more Classic winners – the first of them a stroll on the brilliant Ouija Board – to add to his growing collection, and two more winners on the card by nightfall, confirmed Fallon's mastery of the grand old course. Typically, just a few weeks later, Fallon's impossibly erratic riding at Glorious Goodwood tried even Stoute's patience. Stoute held his fire until Favourable Terms had won the Nassau by a short head after a lengthy stewards' enquiry. 'That was a good ride,' said Stoute pointedly, 'but some of the others weren't so good. I'll let you work out which ones.' Somehow, Fallon lost an undercard handicap on Peeress, who would later go on to claim two Group Ones. A public rebuke would have been a last resort for Stoute, who had stayed firm through injury, rehabilitation and splits with several of his major owners. He may have been the King of Epsom, but the new, reformed Fallon was starting to look vulnerable.

9

THE LOOK –
'PANORAMA' AND BEYOND

'I don't know if it [Fallon's look] scared the TV man, but it sure as hell scared me.'

Paul Haigh, *Racing Post* journalist

When the much-publicised and boldly titled 'Panorama' programme, 'The Corruption of Racing', was aired in the autumn of 2002, Kieren Fallon was about to become champion jockey for the fifth time. He was, indisputably, the dominant rider of his time, second to Frankie Dettori in terms of image and ebullience, but very much the Italian's equal on the track in big races, and his master in the day-to-day combat of the jockeys' championship. The one blip in the almost unbroken period of Fallon's hegemony had been caused by ill luck.

Many jockeys would not have recovered at all from the shoulder injury he suffered at Royal Ascot, let alone returned to the top, but Fallon had faced down the challenge and proved his doubters wrong again. Fallon showed extraordinary courage and will to overcome physical injury, embracing the daily step-by-step ritual of reaching a target – being able to move a finger, stretch out an arm, shake hands, lift a pencil, lift weights, get back in the saddle – and absorbing all the punishment and pain of recovery. But his shoulder was still giving him a lot more pain than he allowed anyone to see and his drinking was becoming a problem. He was neither as focused nor as sharp in his work as he had been before the accident. The fact that the winners were not flowing as readily as in his previous championship seasons was a sure sign that all was not well with the champion.

On the track, Fallon was involved in a protracted battle with fellow Irishman Richard Hughes to defend his title. Hughes, at five feet nine one of the tallest jockeys in the weighing-room, had always struggled with his weight and he knew that a chance to win the title might not come his way again. That he was as close as he was to Fallon in the autumn of the season was as much a surprise to him as to the champion.

'To be honest,' he said at the time, 'I was poodling away, riding a few winners and all of a sudden, I thought, "God, I'm awful close here." So for the past few weeks now, it's been on my mind, which makes it mentally draining.'

The 29-year-old Hughes, son of Dessie Hughes, the great Irish horseman, was not presumed to be a champion in waiting, yet he had ridden like a demon all summer, his rake-thin frame curled precariously above his mounts in a style reminiscent of Lester Piggott, his hero.

The pair, Hughes and Fallon, were old friends from their riding days together in India. Fallon, in fact, had been instrumental in persuading Hughes to cross the Irish Sea and take his chances in England. The move had paid off as Hughes established himself as one of the stable jockeys in the powerful yard of Richard Hannon. He'd also been smart enough to marry the boss's daughter.

One chill October day on the Knavesmire in York, Hughes was huddled inside a dark overcoat, warding off not only the wind but a touch of flu. It had not been a good week. Fallon had ridden a four-timer at Pontefract on Monday morning, a characteristic response to the troubles heaped on him by 'Panorama' the evening before, when Hughes had calculated on his rival getting a single winner at best.

'I don't think any other jockey in the world would have won on a couple of them,' he said. 'But that's Kieren.'

Exhausted, a ghost, pale and ill, Hughes nevertheless spoke with spirit about the title chase, about his rival and the mentality required of a champion. The title chase was beginning to take its toll on Hughes's state of mind. In the past few weeks he had been banned for seven days for aiming a blow with his whip at a fellow jockey, Shane Kelly, at Yarmouth, got into a slanging match with trainer Terry Mills over the riding of Tillerman, and shouted at the stewards at Doncaster after receiving another ban. By October, a mild sense of frustration had curdled into a full-scale conspiracy theory. Someone, he believed, was out to get him. With Fallon as the beneficiary, it was hardly a plausible theory, but long hours of wasting, followed by long hours of fasting had shredded all logical thought. And he wasn't the champion.

'It doesn't matter if I win or not because no one expects me to win,' he said. 'I'm still climbing the ladder, Kieren's trying to stay up there and that's the bloody hard bit. When you're on top, you want to stay on top, and when you drop down, it's a bit of a killer.'

A treble for Fallon on the following Saturday at York effectively sealed a fifth title for the champion. It had been surprisingly hard earned. Ten days later, Fallon knew he had enough of a cushion to fly to Chicago a full three days before the Breeders' Cup meeting at Arlington to prepare for rides on Islington and Golan.

'Winning the jockeys' title will always be the number-one aim for me,' he told journalists on arrival. 'That's every year. It doesn't change. But if I could win a title and my first Breeders' Cup, that would be some achievement.'

Fallon had been preoccupied with the dog days of the season when 'Panorama' was aired on 6 October. The thrust of the programme was that racing was 'institutionally corrupt' and that the Jockey Club, a self-elected oligarchy, out of touch with the needs of a fast-moving, multi-million pound industry, was not policing its sport effectively. The programme was stylish, well put together and brilliantly advertised, and, as expected, it had racing running round in ever-decreasing circles. Racing insiders – jockeys, trainers and journalists – predictably tried to hide under the carpet, falling back on two tired old arguments: a) no one outside racing knows how racing works, and b) it's always been this way, so why change now. Fallon was the catch. The producers knew that, in Fallon, they had a name that the ordinary racing fan respected and a face that non-racing people might recognise. If

Fallon, the champion jockey, one of the Queen's jockeys and one of the sport's figureheads, could be implicated in the corruption, their thesis would gain a new credibility. Their hook was a confidential report compiled by the Hong Kong Jockey Club and sent to the security department of the Jockey Club.

During the investigation, Fallon had been ambushed by reporter Andy Davies on his way from the weighing-room to the paddock at York races. He was wearing the Queen's colours. Davies did not have much time. The distance from the end of the walk from the weighing-room across to the entrance to the paddock is no more than fifty yards and he had a tough question to ask about Fallon's time in Hong Kong.

'Panorama' was basing its claims of corruption on the evidence of the former head of Jockey Club security, Roger Buffham, an old friend of producer Stephen Scott. They had once tried to set up a sting together to expose race-fixing at Hamilton Park, without success, but once Buffham had been dismissed by the Jockey Club, Scott saw his opportunity to investigate the state of racing through the eyes of an insider. The plan had two advantages. One was that Buffham might be feeling ready to talk after his bruising departure from the Jockey Club; the other was that he knew his beat. Either way, having a whistle-blowing insider to tell the story made for good television. One of the documents that Buffham had taken with him when he left Jockey Club headquarters was a copy of the HKJC's report. Kieren Fallon had been contracted to ride in Hong Kong for the 1998–99 and 1999–2000 seasons.

Hong Kong is a racing world apart, not a sport but a business. Some, including Derby-winning jockey Alan Munro, love the way of life and the way of racing. Munro, who won the Derby on Generous in 1991, had based himself in Hong Kong for a decade, learnt martial arts and made a healthy living, far better than he could have earned driving thousands of miles around England. Others, such as Derby-winning trainer Peter Chapple-Hyam, hate the claustrophobic nature of the racing, the endless chit-chat with owners, the night-time phone calls from irate owners who want to know why their horse hasn't won, and the abiding sense that someone is watching your every move. After a chastening few years, trying to coax miracles out of bad horses, Chapple-Hyam returned to Newmarket to start anew. He never looked back or, at least, he never looked east again.

However, the prospect of earning good prize money for racing twice a week, and enjoying a celebrity lifestyle along the way, was more appealing to most riders than a winter on the all-weather at Southwell. Hong Kong was as much a cultural and stylistic melting pot on the track as it was on the streets. Riders from Australia, America and South Africa mixed with the top riders from Europe and, almost subconsciously, were influenced by the confluence of riding styles. Dettori, for example, who had begun riding with his stirrups under the ball of his foot in the traditional English way, began to copy the US style, with just the toes in the irons, which was also common to many of the riders in Hong Kong. Fallon, too, was a voracious learner and a ready traveller.

The HKJC is similar to the Jockey Club in its remit and constitution but a hundred times more powerful. In Hong Kong, the organisers of racing hold a position of political, social and economic influence unparalleled by any other governing body in sport. They license the riders and the trainers, they hold the gaming monopoly in the territory and, with the help of the Independent Commission against Corruption, set up initially to investigate corruption in the HK Police Force, they police the sport. They also finance educational trusts, hospitals, orphanages and charities. They are the Levy Board, the Tote, the big bookmakers and the Jockey Club all rolled into one. Nothing much happens inside the hugely profitable sport of racing without the knowledge or sanction of the HKJC.

More than £6 billion is wagered on horses by the racing-mad population of Hong Kong, offering plenty of scope and incentive for corruption. In 1986, the exposure of the Shanghai Syndicate revealed just how easily trainers and jockeys could be controlled by businessmen. The organiser of the Syndicate was fined £400,000 and given a two-year suspended sentence. Five jockeys were jailed. That was the law of business. Just two years before Fallon had been granted licences to ride in Hong Kong, the police had cordoned off the weighing-room at Sha Tin during racing one Sunday evening and arrested a number of prominent racing people including trainers and jockeys. In 1999, Stanley Chin, a champion apprentice, was convicted on two charges of conspiracy to cheat after attempting to bribe eleven apprentices to lose a race, and served a three-year sentence. In February 2002, Robbie Fradd and John Egan were among twenty people arrested on charges of race-fixing and illegal bookmaking. Egan is still wanted in connection with the charges and has never been back to ride in Hong Kong, while Fradd was cleared. More recently, Chris Munce, a top-class Australian jockey with more than forty Group One races to his name, was sentenced to thirty months in jail for passing on information for money. Having arranged to serve his time in a jail in Sydney, he was due for release on parole at the end of 2008. The sentence shocked racing.

The substance of the five-page report by the HKJC on the UK champion jockey has never been fully revealed. Fallon has always denied the allegations and he brought successful libel actions against both the *News of the World*, who published the leaked document, and Roger Buffham, who did the leaking. The HKJC was embarrassed by the publication of a private report and took a firm step away from involvement in the controversy and from any suggestion that Fallon would be unwelcome in Hong Kong in future. Fallon, though, never did ride on contract in Hong Kong again.

Fallon's reaction to the intrusion of the press was unfortunate. When Andy Davies asked him for a reaction to the investigation in Hong Kong, Fallon's cold, hard gaze, the look he reserved exclusively for pushy news reporters and bullying photographers, betrayed anger and a little fear. A smile would have been the better option. The stare turned racing people to stone. The champion with the famously short fuse seemed a spark away from launching himself at the reporter and cameraman. The image became one of the abiding memories of the programme, a symbol of defiance within racing, of fragility elsewhere.

'Kieren Fallon is another who will not have increased the membership of his fan club,' wrote Paul Haigh in the *Racing Post*. 'The look of pure malevolence he bestowed on the unfortunate Davies has already passed into legend. I don't know if it scared the TV man, but it sure as hell scared me.'

The programme was made more dramatic by the background inter-vention, ironically, of the BBC's own racing expert, former champion jockey Willie Carson. 'I tried to save you,' Carson is heard to say to Graham Bradley off camera, which only compounded the view of a sport in an advanced stage of paranoia. Well aware of what was coming, more aware certainly than the Jockey Club, Fallon and his solicitor, Christopher Stewart-Moore, started High Court proceedings against Buffham twenty-four hours before the programme was due to be aired. A libel writ had already been issued to the *News of the World*, who had published similar allegations based on the leaked report, in July. 'The report concerned makes various statements concerning Mr Fallon, which are extremely defamatory and damaging to Mr Fallon's reputation.'

Although both libel actions were eventually successful, the damage to Fallon's reputation was less easily repaired. Fallon repeatedly referred to the pressure hanging over him after his arrest in September 2004, but, in reality, the pressure had started to build more than two years before that with the exposé in the *News of the World.*

Fallon's turbulent past was one thing, but he was racing's front-of-house now, the perennial champion, at a time when the betting exchanges were enfranchising a wider betting public and the integrity of the sport was becoming an increasing cause for concern. Racing did not just have to be clean, it had to be seen to be clean. In such a frenetic climate, when horses could be laid to lose and every punter could be a bookmaker via the exchanges, Fallon was an easy target.

Alerted initially to the need to tighten up its security in the wake of the Top Cees case four years earlier, in which Fallon and the Ramsdens had won substantial damages from the *Sporting Life*, the Jockey Club were already starting to reorganise their structures to cope with the new betting landscape. The process was in motion at the time of the 'Panorama' programme, but, as ever, the wheels were turning slowly, and when, in the programme, the new head of security, Jeremy Phipps, was secretly filmed agreeing with Buffham over lunch in a wine bar that the members of the Jockey Club did not have the backbone to clean up the sport and were 'fucking ignorant', the governing body of a highly serious and lucrative sport became a laughing stock.

Unfortunately for Fallon, the most recognisable human face of a sport in crisis was not that of Jimmy Fitzgerald or Gay Kelleway, the two trainers confronted and accused in the programme of having 'no lose' accounts with a major bookmaker, nor of Dermot Browne, who had admitted in court that he had doped more than twenty horses over two months on behalf of drug dealer Brian Wright, but the taut and angry face of the then four-times champion jockey. Browne, a former jockey, had already been disqualified for ten years and was later banned for a further twenty. Jump jockey Graham Bradley was warned off the following month for eight years, reduced to five on appeal, for passing on privileged information to Brian Wright. These cases were already under investigation by the Jockey Club. The link between Fallon and various allegations, however tenuous, threaded through the remainder of the Irishman's career and, according to those closest to him, and to Fallon himself, fuelled his descent into personal crisis.

The sport of racing has thrived on scandal. It is part of the attraction of the track, but punters want to know that, in a mug's game, they are not being taken for complete fools. They want a straight run for their money. If the champion jockey, one of the most respected and prolific jockeys of all time, one of their greatest allies against the bookmakers, was in the frame, surely the sport must be rotten from top to bottom? Four million viewers, the fifth largest audience since the BBC's flagship investigative programme had been moved from its traditional slot on Monday evening to late on Sunday, tuned in to find out. Regardless of the criticism levelled by racing insiders at the substance of the programme, some but not all of it justified, it looked bad – bad for racing, bad for the Jockey Club and bad for Fallon. No one could envisage just how bad it would prove to be for the long-term future of one of racing's most recognisable and popular figures. The question of whether Fallon, the champion, was a fit and proper person to ride in the UK, a question put to Roger Buffham in the programme and answered in the negative, hung like a dark cloud over Fallon's career for the next five years.

There were great times ahead for Fallon – another championship, two successive Derby victories on Kris Kin and North Light, Breeders' Cup wins on Islington and Ouija Board, more Classic success for

Coolmore, and Arc wins on Hurricane Run, arguably the finest ride of his life, and on Dylan Thomas. But his personal life, always a roller-coaster, was now plunging into an abyss. The continued success merely disguised the speed of the descent. With his behaviour increasingly erratic, Fallon at last did something he had very rarely done in his life. The winter of 2002 was when he faced up to his demons and, with the public support of Michael Stoute, admitted himself to the Aiseiri Addiction Treatment Centre in Cahir, County Tipperary.

10

THE MYSTERY OF
BALLINGER RIDGE

'This was not Fallon's finest hour.'

Racing Post race-reader

Some horses leave a legacy of sporting brilliance – Sir Ivor, Nijinsky, Brigadier Gerard. The record books will tell you the names. Some horses, such as Devon Loch and Crisp, become famous for losing. Racing has a third category – those horses remembered merely for being in the wrong place at the wrong time. Into that select number, at Lingfield Park on Tuesday, 2 March 2004, galloped a little known five-year-old, Ballinger Ridge. The race, ironically, was sponsored by Bet Direct, one of the new online betting companies that had utterly reshaped the landscape of the betting industry and the complex network of information, rumour and speculation around which racing's carousel turns. The first prize for the Maiden Auction Stakes, the third race on the all-weather card, was worth a princely £1,463 to the winner, but it was not the prize money that invested Ballinger Ridge's participation with such significance for trainer Andrew Balding. After eighteen races, the bay gelding had yet to reach the winner's enclosure, but nevertheless, the likeable young master of Kingsclere was sure there was a race some-where that Ballinger Ridge could win. This low-grade median auction stakes, held on a nondescript afternoon on the all-weather, was surely going to be the one. This was the day when the patience of owners Paul and Hazel Barber would be rewarded. After all, they had recruited the services of Kieren Fallon to their cause. If anyone could find the key to victory for the hapless Ballinger Ridge, it was the six-times champion.

Also taking a special interest in the race was John Maxse, then the chief press officer of the Jockey Club. Maxse had received a call from Paul Scotney, the head of security, who had been alerted to some suspicious betting patterns on the race. Scotney wanted Maxse to record the race and also to watch it carefully, which he did in his office back at Portman Square.

The reason for the Jockey Club's sensitivity was wrapped up in the increasingly bitter turf war between the new betting exchanges and the old bookmakers being played out in the corridors of power. The potential reward for the winners was incalculable, and the Jockey Club were caught in the crossfire. For the benefit of racing's fragile integrity, the racing authorities badly needed a horse that had drifted on the betting exchanges – and Ballinger Ridge had gone from 2–1 to 4 – to defy the betting patterns and win.

So when Ballinger Ridge entered the straight ten lengths clear of the odds-on favourite, Rye, who was being strongly driven by his jockey, Chris Catlin, Maxse began to smile. Here was another piece of evidence to counter the rumours of wholesale corruption in racing. Balding too was smiling because trainers take as much satisfaction from winning with a bad horse as they do from winning with a good one, particularly when the owners are personal friends and loyal supporters. At last, good old Ballinger Ridge was going to win. Maxse was on the phone directly to Scotney, telling him the good news. 'He's well clear, nothing can stop him now,' he said.

Only slowly did it dawn on all of them that Rye, trained by Jamie Osborne, was closing fast and that Fallon appeared to have suddenly stopped riding Ballinger Ridge. The *Racing Post*'s race-reader put it thus the following morning:

Kieren Fallon set out under instruction to make all on Ballinger Ridge and looked in control turning into the straight, at which point Rye was ten lengths down and being vigorously ridden. Fallon had glanced round at the furlong pole and shook up his mount and then had a longer look behind just inside the final furlong, after which he started to ease down his mount. But in the last hundred yards he got back to work on the blinkered Ballinger Ridge only to be caught by Rye in the last stride.

In the end-of-season *Form Guide*, Lee McKenzie substantiated the verdict, but was not so polite.

> Still travelling easily turning in, he [Ballinger Ridge] was shaken up over a furlong out and the race looked his, but at the furlong pole Fallon looked over his right shoulder and, appearing not to notice that the favourite was making inroads, briefly eased his mount. Taking another look shortly afterwards, Fallon became aware of the danger but was a shade slow to galvanise the gelding who, his momentum lost, was touched off. This was not Fallon's finest hour.

Luckily for the jockey, Lingfield is rarely thronged with punters on a midweek afternoon, but there were enough jeers for Fallon to feel the unforgiving mood of the track and, by extension, the stewards and racing. The fact that Betfair, the leading online betting exchange, had alerted Jockey Club security to suspicious betting patterns prior to the race meant that the matter was automatically referred back to Portman Square rather than being dealt with on the day by the Lingfield stewards. Fallon knew his fate anyway – later confirmed as a twenty-one-day ban for not riding out his horse for the best placing – but the implications of the manner of his defeat were to reverberate through the sport and deep into the jockey's psyche long after the scorn of disappointed punters and the inevitable splutterings of John McCririck, racing's self-appointed moral guardian, had died away. The defeat of Ballinger Ridge was to form a central part of the case brought against Fallon by the City of London Police more than three years later.

Fallon's strongest defender both on the day and subsequently was Andrew Balding.

'It was a few weeks before the Dubai Carnival and the Dubai World

Cup, and Kieren wanted to get a couple of winners on the board before he went out there,' Balding recalled. 'We decided that as Ballinger Ridge was a frontrunner with a number of runs under his belt, we'd let him bowl along at the front, take the race by the scruff of the neck, and hope to catch the favourite a bit green. With luck, we'd have the race won by halfway.'

Balding watched the race on a television monitor in the betting office at the back of the main stand at Lingfield and was about to turn away to greet his horse in the winner's enclosure when he saw Fallon stop riding for a few strides.

'On a horse like him, if you sit up for a few seconds, he'll drop the lot on you. Coming in, I remember it well, Kieren said, "Shit, did that look bad?" I said, "Yes, it looked awful." Then Kieren said, "Shit, I'm going to get banned for the World Cup." At no stage was there anything other than he'd made a genuine error and he'd be banned for the big race. There was absolutely no way he was thinking of anything else. When he was getting off the horse, he said again, "Shit, it's the World Cup coming up," which meant, "Help me out here." '

Balding told the stewards that he was happy with all but the last fifty yards of Fallon's ride and that there was a reason why Ballinger Ridge remained a maiden after nineteen starts.

'I tried to help Kieren out. I said that Ballinger Ridge hangs, which he did, and that he's not an easy ride, which is all true. Everything should be taken in perspective. People make mistakes and this was a two-grand banded race. Whether it's Kieren or an apprentice, it's not going to change the result if I jump up and down. He's going to ride for me again, and against me, and you're not going to fall out over a two-grand race in which, in my opinion, he made a total error of judgement. If he's riding a thousand races a year, there's going to be one fuck-up. It just happened to be on my horse.'

The problem for Fallon was that the language of racing, the cosy collusion instinctively understood by officials, trainers, jockeys and journalists for centuries, was changing. In the good old days, an error by a jockey, even one of Fallon's status, would have made no more than the odd line or two in the national press. These things happen, chaps.

Now where's the rule book. But, by the time the Sunday newspapers had hit the stands, this was no longer just a parochial racing matter. Fallon stood accused of a crime far worse than dropping his hands on a certain winner. An apparently new light was cast on Fallon's inexplicable error of judgement. *News of the World* claimed that Fallon had told the paper's undercover 'fake sheikh' reporters that Ballinger Ridge would lose to Rye. The report claimed that the champion had given them ten tips during the course of eight days at Lingfield, seven of which won. Other Sunday newspapers picked up the story for their later editions, but, in fact, as John Maxse pointed out the following day, the evidence for the claim of race-fixing against Fallon fell well short of the certainty demanded by the headline. That barely mattered. Through one of its most high-profile riders, racing stood condemned. Fallon had allegedly tipped Rye to beat Ballinger Ridge and, in the eyes of both his accusers and the wider public, had done his best to ensure that he was right. Two plus two seemed, on this occasion, to make a resounding four.

Fallon's innate ability to fan the flames was never more in evidence than in the days following the ride on Ballinger Ridge and the revelations in the *News of the World*. Understandably anxious to hide from the British press, Fallon went to Spain the following weekend to ride at Mijas, one of the country's few tracks. But his decision to arrive back at Stansted on the Monday morning after the *News of the World* 'exclusive', dressed in a leather jacket, eyes shaded by dark glasses, left arm firmly gripped by a burly minder was at best ill-judged, at worst downright tawdry. To add to the image, Fallon was involved in a pushing match with several photographers in full view of the Sky News cameras.

The racing authorities covered their eyes in shame and, in a desperate attempt to be seen to be doing something to stem the flow of bad publicity, charged Fallon with bringing racing into disrepute, a catch-all phrase borrowed from the Football Association. Almost lost in all the brouhaha was the twenty-one-day suspension duly handed out to Fallon for a breach of Rule 156 (i), a disciplinary charge that Fallon, through his legal representative, admitted. Calls for further punishment, such as the suspension of Fallon's licence, were rejected by the Jockey Club.

'On the evidence at the moment, there are no grounds on which we could withdraw his licence,' said Maxse. 'He's been suspended today purely for failing to ride out to the best possible placing.'

Fallon's twenty-one-day suspension included the Dubai World Cup, but he would be back in time for the Classic trials, the true start of the flat season. Betting on the jockeys' championship, for which Fallon was once again the odds-on favourite, was temporarily suspended. Fallon, some well-placed judges suggested, might retire there and then.

Fallon did indeed consider ending his riding career and retreating from the spotlight, an instinctive emotional response to the unwanted publicity. It was neither the first time nor the last that he would contemplate such a drastic solution. Fallon is an essentially quiet and private man, capable of changing mood from hour to hour, let alone day to day, but running through his core lies a streak of obstinacy stronger and more entrenched than any of his more mercurial emotions. David Walsh, one of the few journalists who have ever become close to Fallon, wrote a telling paragraph later in the summer, in the wake of North Light's brilliant victory in the Derby:

> Friends tell him to be polite to Jockey Club officials, to get the journalists on his side, to cut an inch or two off his hair. They might as well try to get horses to talk. He [Fallon] gives respect to those he feels deserve it, he remains suspicious of journalists and the hair stays at the length he likes it. For he cannot play the game.*

Compromise was not an option, not in the matter of riding winners and not in his reaction to adversity. Although surprised by the enormity of the storm breaking around his head, Fallon relished the battle to survive just as he had in his days in the boxing ring and in those early days when everyone else seemed to be moving up the ladder quicker than he was. The more people suggested that Fallon's career 'hung by a thread' – and the metaphor would be used extensively through the next three years – the more determined he became to prove them wrong. It made no difference whether it was a surgeon telling him his career was threatened by severed nerves in his left arm or, in a mind increasingly open to

* *Sunday Times*, 6 June 2004

conspiracy theories, whether it was the establishment press colluding with officialdom to drum him out of racing, Fallon perceived the challenge as a personal threat and responded with an animal-like intensity.

In an attempt to portray himself as an honest family man, guilty of stupidity but not illegality, Fallon made another elementary PR blunder. A day after his return from Spain, he agreed to be interviewed on ITV's early evening news alongside his wife, Julie, in a room at the Grosvenor House hotel in London. They both looked nervous and ill at ease. Fallon, dressed in black polo neck, the curl in his dark hair almost covering his left eye, strongly denied the allegations of race-fixing made in the *News of the World*.

'I've been very stupid,' he admitted. 'We've been warned about this [the set-up by reporters posing as Middle Eastern gamblers]. I was totally innocent myself about what was going on, but I've ended up being totally stupid.' Fallon also denied deliberately losing a race, calling it a 'ridiculous allegation'. 'For one thing, it would be impossible to fix a race because there are other horses that run and other people involved. It doesn't make any sense at all to lose a race. Most jockeys are hungry. It's a tough sport and the only way you're going to get anywhere is by winning, not losing.'

Typically, because attack was always his best form of defence, Fallon also said that he had ridden one of his best races on Ballinger Ridge, giving his horse a breather in the straight but just not getting home, and that he had not taken any money for the tips he had given the reporters.

'When the first couple of horses started winning for them, they did offer me money and I said, "What do you mean? Jockeys can't accept money." It got to the stage where they said, "If you are not going to accept any money, why don't we give you cars? Why don't you have a Mercedes?" I said, "It's against the rules of racing. I do very well out of racing. I make a good living – the cheque at the end of the month is very good. I'm happy, I don't need it." '

Yet it was actually Julie Fallon who made the most telling contribution to the interview. 'At the end of the day,' she said, 'all Kieren ever wanted to do was ride winners. It's all he's interested in doing.' If there was a hint of resignation in the voice, every wife of every jockey in the country would have understood the reason. The weighing-room houses more than its share of obsessive winners.

For the rest of March, the press made the most of racing's obvious vulnerability. Any incident on a racetrack deemed remotely dubious was hurled into the potent mix of speculation, claim and counter-claim. Alan Berry, son of Jack Berry, one of the north's most popular and powerful trainers, was arrested and charged over the running of Hillside Girl, who was pulled up early in a race at Carlisle after drifting markedly on the betting exchanges. In January 2008, the CPS dropped the case, saying he had no case to answer. The *Sun*, anxious not to be outdone by the *News of the World*, its sister paper, claimed that fourteen more jockeys were under investigation by the security department of the Jockey Club, a story strongly denied by the Jockey Club at the time.

Less than a week after Fallon's riding of Ballinger Ridge, another racetrack incident hit the national news. This time, jump jockey Sean Fox was accused of deliberately jumping off a horse called Ice Saint during a race at Fontwell. Again, the horse had drifted on the betting exchanges, from evens to 5–1, and on the course, and again it looked awful on camera, Fox being unseated so neatly he landed on his feet and walked away. Like Fallon, Fox was banned for twenty-one days, and protested against the ban, but coming so soon after the allegations against Fallon, the timing could not have been worse. Racing, no stranger to controversy, had hit its lowest point for more than a decade and Fallon, whether he liked it or not, was a central figure in the case for the prosecution.

The timing of the scandals could not have been worse for the advocates of the new betting exchange companies, either. They were fighting for their financial lives in the face of concerted opposition from the established bookmaking firms and some influential voices in government. At the heart of the debate was the right of the betting exchanges to function legally when, according to the bookmakers, they were encouraging their clients to act as unlicensed bookmakers. The tone of their opposition had changed markedly since Betfair, the oldest, largest and most powerful of the exchange firms, took its first tentative steps, in the summer of 2000, into a billion-pound market dominated by the 'big four' – Corals, Ladbrokes, William Hill and totesport. From patting Betfair on the head like a naughty schoolboy in the early days, the bookmaking industry had been forced to take the challenge to their supremacy in the betting market seriously. As Betfair's client base rose steadily, the big bookmakers realised they had misread the market and were scrabbling to retrieve lost ground.

The government had been equally slow to react and were belatedly drafting a new Gambling Act, in part to regulate the exchanges, which allowed markets to be formed between individuals via a computer terminal and not through a bookmaker. One of the key points in the case put forward by the bookmakers was that, on the exchanges, money could be made from losing, not just winning. So inside knowledge of any horse in any race could potentially be turned into profit. This, the bookmakers argued persuasively, was opening up whole new landscapes for corruption. John Brown, the chairman of William Hill, went on 'Morning Line', Channel 4's Saturday morning preview programme, to say that it was a dereliction of duty by the secretary of state not to close down these illegal businesses. The gloves were off.

Under pressure to defend themselves against the obvious charge of losing for profit, Betfair adopted a bold strategy. Evidence about 'drifters' and how punters could make more money backing them to win than to lose had failed to persuade doubters about the real benefits of this strange new form of betting in which sport, not just racing, seemed to be turned into an extension of the stockmarket.

'We needed to find a mechanism by which we could show people our data,' said a spokesman for Betfair. 'So we came up with the Memorandum of Understanding, MoU, which said that if you, the client, sign up with Betfair, we have the right to give your information to a named sporting body for the purpose of that sporting body being able to deal with any questions of corruption in their sport. If you don't want to sign up to that, then you have to close your account. We had to mail our entire user base, a hundred thousand registered customers maybe, and say we're making this change and this is why.'

The MoU, which was first signed between Betfair and the Jockey Club in June 2003, not only covered the leading betting exchange against the charge of corrupting racing, but gave the security department of the Jockey Club unprecedented access to individual records and betting patterns. Almost overnight, they had a new and powerful weapon in the fight against corruption and they used it to the full. Often, in those early days, Betfair resisted the call to release client information until a pattern had been established and a real case for further investigation outlined. This was entirely uncharted territory for both parties and the bookmakers, who had always prided themselves on their policy of privacy in relation to their clients, now found the ground swept from beneath their feet.

'One of the big reliefs about the Ballinger Ridge case was that we had the Memorandum of Understanding in place,' said Mark Davies of Betfair. 'If it had not been there, our lives would have been made virtually impossible. The MoU saved our skins because we were able to say that if something untoward had happened, it would show up in our betting records.'

Not for the first time, Fallon had put himself in the glare of a spotlight much more powerful than the mere winning and losing of a race. Although the charge of bringing the sport into disrepute initially brought against him by the Jockey Club was later dropped, the bad smell hung over racing and over Fallon's head in particular. In June, Fallon won the Oaks on the brilliant Ouija Board and followed up with his second successive Derby victory on North Light, but the seeds of suspicion had been sown on that ordinary afternoon at Lingfield when Fallon lost on a horse that had never won. When Fallon was arrested by the City of London police nearly six months later, the trail could be traced all the way back to Ballinger Ridge. Racing was no longer policing itself; the law of the land had taken an undue interest in its integrity as well.

The one happy postscript to the saga was provided by Ballinger Ridge himself, who returned to Lingfield a week later to win his first race by a handsome three and a half lengths at odds of 4–5 under a forceful ride by Martin Dwyer. He was then sold to a buyer in Ireland, blissfully unaware of his real place in the history books.

11

FRANKIE AND THE CHAMPIONSHIP

'When I first saw Kieren, I didn't realise how good he was.'

Frankie Dettori

Frankie Dettori tells a good story about the climax to the 2004 race for the jockeys' championship. He and Fallon had been going at it hammer and tongs through the closing months of the season, sometimes making pacts about where they would or wouldn't ride and mostly breaking them. Normally, on Champions Day, one of the highlights of the autumn calendar at Newmarket, both would leave it there. But as neither trusted the other not to sneak a few rides elsewhere, they flew to Wolverhampton together to continue the duel at the evening meeting on the all-weather.

'It was midnight by the time I got back, stressed and tired,' Dettori recalled later. 'We, Kieren and I, are speaking to each other, but it's not fun any more, it's become a chore. Because Kieren had said he'd be going to Musselburgh on the Sunday, I'd got some rides booked, too. So, bright and early, I'm up, absolutely knackered, but going to Stansted to catch the flight to Edinburgh. No Kieren, and he's not answering his mobile, either. So I get to Edinburgh and ring again. This time he answers. "I'm still in bed. You've won the championship," he says and puts the phone down. The bastard had stitched me up. He'd never intended to ride at Musselburgh, but it was my championship.'

Dave Pollington, Fallon's faithful agent, was left to explain to the newspapers and to some disgruntled trainers that Fallon had missed his flight north and wouldn't be coming. Dettori pulled out of the last race, citing illness. It had been an exhausting year for both of them.

That Dettori was involved in the title race at all was a surprise, but the real shock was that Fallon should fail to win it. That morning, he had been quoted in the paper as saying, 'The title's gone, I know that, but we'll keep going. Put it this way, I think I've got more championships left in me than Frankie has. Frankie knows he's got a gift this year.' Fallon's bravado was misplaced. This was the end of an era, the moment that two champions passed on their inheritance to the next generation. Two future champion jockeys had been stalking them all season. One, Seb Sanders, was to share the title with Jamie Spencer in a thrilling duel three years on. The other was Ryan Moore, son of the Sussex dual-purpose trainer, Gary Moore, and a newcomer to the professional ranks. Moore, his schoolboy face etched in a permanent scowl, had ridden 125 winners in his first full season and finished fifth in the championship. Spencer, Moore and Sanders shared the next three titles, quietly consigning the challenges of Dettori and Fallon to the past. Racing round the country, racking up the miles, riding obscure winners for pitiful reward – that was a game for younger men. For the older generation, there were just too many meetings, too many horses, too many bad races and way too many suspensions.

Although neither guessed it at the time, the race for the title in 2004 was the climax of a rivalry that stretched back twenty years to their days in the north when Fallon was a five-pound claimer with Jimmy Fitzgerald, and Dettori, the stable apprentice with Luca Cumani, was dispatched to the remoter tracks to learn his trade. Of the two, only Dettori, Newmarket-based and with a recognisable racing name, was likely to make it to the big time. He had the right pedigree and a natural confidence. But the extrovert Italian and the shy Irishman, five years his senior, struck up an unlikely friendship that survived a decade of fierce competition on the racetracks of the world. When Dettori finally won his Derby, on Authorized in 2007, Fallon sent him a huge bunch of flowers and a note of congratulations. 'We're good friends and we've been great rivals almost throughout our careers,' Dettori once said. 'I've never had any trouble from him on the track. We've had a very clean rivalry because we respect each other so much. Having Kieren there has made me ride better.'

In the autumn of 2004, having Kieren there made Dettori fight that much harder, too. It is doubtful if he would have kept up the relentless pursuit of downmarket winners at low-level tracks had Fallon not been hounding him at every turn. By rights, Fallon should have had the championship sewn up by the end of the debilitating schedule of evening turf meetings in late August. However, despite his second successive Derby win, he had not been firing with his usual consistency at the lesser meetings, which gave encouragement to all the chasing pack, including Dettori. The challenge to Fallon had been initially laid down by Darryll Holland, the self-styled 'Dazzler', who had always harboured pretensions towards Fallon's title. Holland had enjoyed huge success on Falbrav, a brilliant bull of a horse, for Luca Cumani in 2003, but had yet to break into the élite. At the start of 2004, he was in the twilight zone between top-class rider and true champion. Perhaps to motivate himself, perhaps to wind up Fallon – a forlorn hope – Holland had laid claim to the championship, Fallon's championship. He would, he said, go to the ends of the island to win it. He sounded serious. Fallon, though, was not worried about losing his title to Darryll Holland. But Seb Sanders, a Midlander with a serious work ethic? That was just possible. Unlikely, but possible. In part as a snub to Holland, Fallon named Sanders as his major rival for the coming season.

Being champion jockey, as A.P. McCoy (thirteen times and count-ing) will tell you, is not just a matter of winning races. A.P. is better than anyone else at doing that, but he and his agent, Dave Roberts, are equally brilliant at persuading others that only McCoy can win on their horse. When asked about young pretenders coming through to push him off the top, his response was telling. 'To do that, they need to have the opportunities,' he said, eyes narrowing. 'The trick is to stop them getting those opportunities.' How? By taking as many of their rides as he can, by dominating the psychological landscape like a tower block on a plain. Up until now, Fallon had exerted a similar influence on the track, but 2004 was different. The weighing-room, previously bullied into Fallon's way of thinking, sensed that their champion, distracted by the aftermath of the Ballinger Ridge affair, was unusually vulnerable.

When the stalls opened on the new season, Frankie Dettori was not an obvious challenger for the title. The presumption was that Frankie's days as champion had ended with his consecutive double centuries in 1994 and 1995 and his calculated decision to put quality above quantity. With a plum job riding some of the best Thoroughbreds in the world for the mighty Godolphin, why would Dettori want to fight for the title again, particularly against Fallon, who thrived on hand-to-hand combat? A snapshot of his way of thinking at the time was set down in the pages of his excellent autobiography, published in 2004.

> I thrive on the challenge of riding abroad, particularly in the key period when there are so many major races around the world between September and mid-November. Normally, I am bored by the demands of the domestic routine by then. Given the choice, I'd always prefer a long haul to Hong Kong or America to a dreary drive up the A1. I think it brings out the best in me.
>
> At home, we are slaves to the numbers game. That's crazy. If you don't do it every day, people start having a go, saying you're not interested any more, you're lazy and all that crap. I blame that stupid list of winning riders in the back of the *Racing Post*. It doesn't mean anything, it's just numbers.

For three seasons after the plane crash that nearly claimed his life, Dettori had failed to ride a hundred winners, let alone challenge for Fallon's title. His mind, understandably, seemed to be on other things, on business and a budding television career. Only in the middle of the 2003 season, when criticism of his riding had risen from a whisper to a clamour, did Dettori take himself away to Sardinia, as he always did at critical moments in his life, to seek the forthright and forbidding opinion of his father, Gianfranco, a former champion. He returned with renewed vigour, sure again of what he wanted from himself and his sport, and in the closing two months of the season almost doubled his tally of winners. For the first time in four seasons, he reached a century of winners. But no one expected the streak to continue into the early months of the following season.

By high summer of 2004, Dettori had 120 winners under his belt and smelt an unlikely third title. Fallon had set the pace, and Sanders, as Fallon had predicted, was keeping up a relentless pursuit, but Dettori was close enough to the action to be drawn into a succession of dreary drives up the A1, and hungry enough to provoke a head-on duel with his old friend. The sport had been anticipating such a battle for years, a thundering clash of character and style between the two supreme jockeys of their generation. No less than Borg and McEnroe, Dettori and Fallon had become defined by each other.

The parallels were closer than seemed obvious from the outside, but the styles, background and approach to life could not have been more different. If Fallon always envied Dettori's sleek outline on the back of a horse, the Italian envied Fallon's prodigious lower body strength. Dettori crouched low, American-style, more tight-reined, his knees high, his body moulded into the horse's neck. Fallon was more upright, sitting deeper into the horse, exerting control with his thighs and communicating urgency with his muscular torso.

Off the track, the contrast was just as stark. While Dettori's background as the son of a Classic-winning jockey and perennial champion of Italy provided him with a clear career path to the top, Fallon came from a non-racing family and could not have started from a lower rung of the ladder without digging a trench. Dettori was noisy, very Italian, and celebrated his victories with extravagant flying dismounts and kisses all round. Fallon's response to winning was a humble smile and a brief touch of his cap. When Dettori was in the weighing-room, everyone knew what mood he was in and where he was every moment of the day. Fallon sat in the corner and said very little. Fallon was the favourite of the regular betting-shop punters, who knew they would get a run for their money with the champion. Dettori was the darling of the five-bob irregulars, the people's champion.

'When I first saw Kieren, I didn't realise for a while how good he was,' Dettori said. 'That was in the north. I think I met him at Catterick one day and then went back to stay at his house in Malton.

We've been friends ever since. At the time, Kieren's way of ridings was very much of the Irish old school, not particularly stylish or impressive, but then when you began to start looking at his results, you began to understand his talent.'

Dettori has been watching Fallon from close quarters pretty well ever since and is still regularly baffled by his ability to keep something in reserve while seeming to be pushing for his life.

'He's ice cool and he's fearless,' said Dettori. 'He also has a knack of making his horses run. A lot of the time you think he's beat and then he'll come back and beat you. He's very difficult to read in a race. Kieren uses his body, so he's able to keep his horse revved up without asking him for a full effort. I'm more of an on and off style of rider. I can stop and start horses more quickly, he gets them revved up from much farther out than I do, which is partly due to his strength and partly to his ability to ride with a loose rein and still keep his horse straight and balanced. Not many can do it. You watch some young jockeys now and they're trying to copy Kieren with his long rein and they can't do it. It was like Lester. Everyone wanted to ride shorter than anyone else, but only Lester could do it. Kieren has another knack, too. He can see something happening before it happens. He can find his way out of trouble. I just try to keep it as simple as possible.'

Dettori's riding style was influenced hugely by his four years in the States in the company of such greats as Angel Cordero, his hero, Laffit Pincay, Willie Shoemaker and Gary Stevens. It was there that he developed the low, crouching style, mocked as a 'monkey on a stick' by the more classically trained home riders, who liked to see a bit of length in the stirrup and a bit of grip with the thigh muscles. Fallon spent a winter in California, while suspended for his assault on Stuart Webster, but whatever he learnt about switching a horse's leading leg and judging pace, no amount of tuition on the back stretch could teach him how to crouch low like an American.

'For me, aerodynamics plays a big part in it,' explained Dettori. 'In America, races tend to be shorter and they go hard from the start. If you crouch down, it gives the horse the message to run fast, but you can't do that over a mile and a half. You have to adapt. In America,

I didn't want to stand out – "Oh, there's that idiot kid from England" – so I learnt to ride like they did. But you try things throughout your career. I rode "acy-deucy" for a time, with one stirrup shorter than the other. I started with my whole foot in the irons and changed to ride with only my toes in the irons. Angel Cordero taught me to ride with my knees off the saddle so I'd create a better balance. You learn all the time and take what works for you.'

For a time, notably when he first arrived in Newmarket, Fallon seemed almost self-conscious about his upright and idiosyncratic posture, but he soon realised that no one has the patent on the right or wrong way to race-ride. Brough Scott, a good enough National Hunt jockey to ride a hundred winners, but a far better journalist, recalls a conversation with Fallon in his early days with Henry Cecil. Very much the new boy in town, Fallon's talent and character were the subjects of the closest scrutiny by the most critical audience in racing, and he wanted to explain his technique of riding to someone who would not only understand but translate it to a wider public. He was particularly stung by a comment made by John Francome on Channel 4. Francome, one of the most respected figures when it comes to judging jockeyship, had thought Fallon's style untidy and, typically, had said so on air. The implication was that Fallon was nowhere near the complete stylist expected of the heir to Cauthen, Piggott and Eddery at Warren Place. Scott went to see him and learnt a little about Fallon's psyche and a lot about his unorthodox approach to race-riding.

'He was aware that he was absolutely in the spotlight and conscious that people who didn't know him and hadn't seen him ride much were judging him. I can remember specifically him saying two things. One was that he was trying to be tidier in the saddle, but that he was never going to be as neat or stylish as Dettori, and the other was, "But, Brough, I can ride, you know." He told me how he used his body to propel the horse, which was difficult for people to see.

'Later, maybe a month on at York, when it had all died down a bit, he rode a big winner and he saw me and said, "You see, Brough, that's what I'm talking about." You can goad a horse into running faster by hitting it or shouting at it, but the only mechanical way you can make a horse go faster as a jockey is by thrusting your weight down the hind legs of the horse where the traction is. If you can actually get that extra eight stone of purchase through the back legs, it's the only way a jockey can physically make a horse go faster, particularly on soft ground. In my view, on pure mechanics, that's Kieren's secret.'

No less than Dettori, Fallon's style was a result of his upbringing, his physique and his intuition. No one had taught Fallon how to ride, so he had learnt the basics himself and then adapted them to the racetrack, influenced more by feel than fashion. Very early in his career, Fallon knew what worked for him. The trick was to persuade others that it could work.

Dettori also had to counter detractors, but he had help because others were riding in the American style. Alan Munro had adopted the crouch in a more exaggerated form than had Dettori, and was beginning to break through into the top rank of northern riders. He moved south to ride for Paul Cole, and partnered the brilliant Generous to victory in the 1991 Derby. Steve Cauthen, known simply in America as 'The Kid', had seamlessly adapted his way of riding to the more varied demands of the English racetrack without losing his rhythm or sacrificing his roots.

The old barriers to style were breaking down anyway as horses and top jockeys travelled more regularly in pursuit of the glittering amounts of prize money on offer in the Far East and America. Hong Kong, in particular, was a melting pot for jockeys from Japan, Australia and the UK. Racing, a slave to fashion but suspicious of change, began to accept that – with the exception of French jockeys, who were universally derided – race-riding, like a golf swing, could work in different ways for different riders. But they were still not quite ready for Fallon.

John Lowe, who was a regular work rider for Cecil and one of the best lightweight jockeys of his era, recalls a particular conversation with Cecil early in Fallon's career at Warren Place. 'Henry said to me very early on, "John, you know Fallon, can't you tell him to get hold of those horses' heads?" I said, "No, that's his style, Henry." Kieren played a lot of hurling when he was young and he boxed, so he's very strong in the legs. It's very unusual. Most jockeys ride too short to be able to do what

Kieren does. Kieren rides with a nice length of leg, he sits into a horse, not perched up like Lester or Jamie Spencer. Kieren is more like Joe Mercer [champion jockey in 1979] or Jimmy Lindley, and you don't see many of them now.

'You see kids now trying to ride like Fallon, with the reins being pulled through the hands, flapping all over the place, but they're riding two or three holes shorter [in the stirrups] than they should do. The strength comes from the calf muscles and the thigh muscles. You're holding a horse together, getting it balanced with your legs, squeezing away. If you're riding a yearling or a young horse and it starts to get edgy, you don't want to be yanking away on its mouth. You just squeeze with your legs, the horse feels it, comes back to you and relaxes. I think that's what Kieren does in a race. He uses his strength in his legs to get horses to pick up for him, and that's how he keeps them together. A lot of jockeys will pick up the stick first. Kieren throws the reins at the horse, but I can't believe that makes a horse go faster, so I think he's squeezing the horse to get it to lengthen its stride, which is what you do at home. It's a style he's developed and it seems very effective.'

Momentum, says Andrew Balding, one of Fallon's most eloquent advocates, is the key. 'He pushes forward through the horse rather than sitting on top and pushing down, so the horse builds up its momentum steadily. You can hear him coming, and then, if you're the jockey in front, you start to panic.'

By late August 2004, Fallon was 17 ahead of Dettori and 19 ahead of Sanders, and a seventh title – perhaps the most rewarding of his career – seemed assured. After August, the rhythm of the season slows perceptibly. Jockeys are no longer hurtling around the country, riding at two meetings a day, and the cards at a number of meetings are dominated by two-year-old maidens, which tends to favour the bigger stables. Closing such a wide gap appeared to be almost impossible for Dettori, and Ladbrokes closed its betting market.

However, events outside racing worked in Dettori's favour. On 1 September, Fallon was one of eighteen people arrested by City of London police investigating alleged race-fixing, the first move in a saga that, for Fallon, ended at the door of the Old Bailey three years and two months later. Distracted by the investigation, Fallon's stream of winners dried up just as Godolphin and Dettori enjoyed a glorious Indian summer. By the end of September, Fallon's lead had been overhauled and he trailed his great rival by six. When the *Racing Post* sensed a proper duel for the championship, and a good storyline to liven up the tail end of the flat season, Dettori stood on 163 winners and Fallon 157. Moreover, Fallon had gone 20 rides without a win in the last full week of September and had ridden a mere three winners in his last 48 rides. Something, not just the horses, was amiss.

Ladbrokes had Dettori odds-on favourite to win his third title and Fallon at an unsteady 6–4. In early October, the death of his old boss, Jimmy Fitzgerald, dealt another blow to Fallon's morale. Fallon's tribute to his long-time mentor at the funeral showed the strength of their friendship, but, at a time of turbulence in his own life, the loss of one of his greatest supporters was cruelly timed. At York that Saturday, Fallon rode Inchnadamph for Jimmy's son, Tim Fitzgerald. Out of sentiment more than logic, Inchnadamph was sent off 5–2 favourite in the last. The whole course sensed a poignant farewell to one of northern racing's true characters, but not even Fallon could coax a fairytale out of the two-year-old, and the pair finished a well-beaten and dejected eighth. (Three years later, the same horse carried Jamie Spencer to a share of the jockeys' title at Doncaster on the final day of the season.)

On Monday, 12 October, Fallon and Dettori journeyed to Leicester, with Dettori still ten ahead and within sight of the line. It was the decisive day of the championship. Already two more winners adrift by the second division of the fillies maiden, Fallon was hard at work on Sir Michael Stoute's Maritima when a horse stumbled alongside him and his horse was pitched into the rail, almost falling. Fallon was hurled to the ground and barely had time to curl instinctively into a protective ball before Bowled Out, the only horse behind him, trampled all over the prostrate figure. Fallon was stretchered away to Leicester Royal Infirmary, conscious but heavily bruised. To make matters worse, Dettori won the race on Saywaan to complete a treble.

Fallon was released from hospital overnight with bruising to his back and shoulders. He drove to the course the following day to take up his six rides, but failed to convince the course doctor that he was fit enough to do so. On the way out of the course, he had an altercation with a photographer, which was captured by another photographer and published on the front page of the *Racing Post* the following morning. The image cemented the consensus within racing that the right man was winning the title. These things are never spoken, not in racing, but during those final weeks of the season there was no question that the wind had turned in Dettori's favour. Fallon was still picking up his usual number of rides, but Dettori was getting the more fancied mounts. One of his winners was provided by Julian Richmond-Watson, senior steward of the Jockey Club, so he enjoyed Establishment support.

A few weeks later, Dettori duly usurped Fallon's title to become champion for the third time. Fallon put a brave face on the loss of a title he regarded as his personal property, but the title defined his status inside and outside the weighing-room and buttressed his often fragile self-esteem. While he was the champion, he felt inviolate, invincible. Stripped of it, by the establishment, he felt privately, as much as by Dettori, he felt diminished and vulnerable, no longer a champion, no longer the main man in a weighing-room he used to dominate. He had envisaged winning ten championships at least, possibly equalling Eddery's record of eleven, but although he talked with bravado of coming back stronger the following season, his days as a force of nature on the track, any track, were gone forever.

There was a postscript to the season. In the unlikely surroundings of Lone Star Park, Texas, Fallon rode a near-perfect race on Lord Derby's filly, the brilliant Ouija Board, to win the Breeders' Cup Filly and Mare Turf, following up his win on Islington the year before. Frankie had a winner that night, too, Wilko springing a huge surprise for Jeremy Noseda in the Breeders' Cup Juvenile. Dettori and Fallon had spent much of the week in Texas together and had shared notes on the idiosyncratic Lone Star Park. On the same night, Jamie Spencer, in his first season as Coolmore's stable jockey, brought Antonius Pius along with a smooth-looking run in the Breeders' Cup Mile, only for the notoriously fickle colt to duck away from the whip suddenly and allow Singletary to take the spoils. The young Irishman publicly blamed himself for giving Antonius Pius a third crack of the whip instead of riding out with his hands and heels, but for Spencer it was one mistake too many. His days at Coolmore were already numbered and Fallon's cool artistry under the same pressures needed no advertising down Tipperary way.

The following month, Fallon returned to the United States in controversial circumstances to take up a ride on River Belle in a Grade Two Stakes race at Churchill Downs. Fallon rarely needed an excuse to ride in the States, but his unexpected appearance on the card at Churchill owed as much to a boycott by local jockeys over insurance payments as his two victories on the same filly in England. His victory, by a fast-diminishing neck, earned widespread acclaim from one of the more hard-bitten audiences in world racing, even if the majority of the American jockeys were less than pleased at the lack of support from one of their own. Fallon claimed innocence of the whole affair. 'When I saw Pat Day [one of America's most respected jockeys] was riding, I thought it must be OK,' said Fallon, who completed a profitable double later on the same card. 'A vintage ride from a great jockey,' proclaimed the *Blood-Horse*, America's foremost racing publication.

That winter, Fallon flirted with the idea of staying in America to ride full-time. It was a place, he said, where he could be left alone and be himself, where they respected people. Sensing a good story, Greg Wood, the racing correspondent of the *Guardian*, flew to Florida to find out the seriousness of Fallon's intentions.

'The interview,' Wood later recalled, 'was to take place at Gulfstream Park, but a torrential downpour forced the cancellation of the afternoon's racing. Fallon was due to ride at Louisiana Downs the following day, so I got a ticket and headed to the airport the following morning, but the flight was delayed in Miami. I was just at the coffee bar at the airport when a familiar figure came and sat next to me. It was Kieren. We sat and chatted for two hours and he was in great form, talking about how much he enjoyed riding in America and how much he would learn about the American way of riding.'

Neither of them ever did get to Louisiana, but Wood got an excellent interview, which was published in the *Guardian* the following week. The tone was upbeat and positive, so Wood was surprised to get a phone call from Christopher Stewart-Moore, Fallon's solicitor, to say that Fallon had been unhappy with the piece. It turned out he'd not read it.

'My sense of the whole episode was that Kieren doesn't like his own company and therefore will do anything, talk to anyone, even a journalist, in order to avoid it,' said Wood.

Within a few weeks of stating his intention to stay in Florida to ride the winter season, Fallon had flown home. He didn't even tell his American agent he was going, but he had reason to leave America. Ireland was calling.

12

COOLMORE CALLING

'I'm pretty good at assessing how expert experts are.'

Michael Tabor

The statement when it came was as terse and unrevealing as anyone would have expected from the quiet men of County Tipperary. Michael Tabor, the former bookmaker from East London, John Magnier, son of a wealthy Cork farmer, and their newest partner, Derrick Smith, had not turned Coolmore into the mightiest breeding operation in the world by telling people their business. So, on the evening of 25 February 2005, several weeks of intense speculation in the racing and national press were ended by this simple announcement: 'Owners John Magnier, Michael Tabor and Derrick Smith are delighted to announce that Kieren Fallon will be the retained jockey for the horses at Ballydoyle and elsewhere for the 2005 season.'

Two things were interesting about the statement, which rightly sent a shiver down the spine of every trainer and owner in the global village of racing. One was that Fallon's jurisdiction would not end at the handsome gates to Ballydoyle, but take in opportunities afforded by Coolmore's operations 'elsewhere'. The other was that the deal, at least in the public eye, was for one season only. No football manager would consider signing a one-year contract, but if there were options for future years – and there were – no one at Coolmore was prepared to discuss them. The future could take care of itself; it was the present that required urgent attention. Perhaps, too, the preference for taking one season at a time reflected initial uncertainty at the long-term prospects of a rider who continued to be under police investigation, for all his protestations of innocence, and who had been the subject of too many lurid headlines in recent years to prompt an unequivocal investment. Fallon, the most prolific and the best jockey in the land, was a 40-year-old probationer.

Coolmore's multi-millionaire owners were businessmen first and racing men second, and, like all good businessmen, they knew the value of image. It would be extremely unlikely that, during the mating process, the new stable jockey had not been gently reminded of his obligations to his new employees, both in and out of the saddle. This was altogether a new venture for Fallon, one for which, in a sense, he had been preparing for his whole life. Stoute's loyalty, much tested through the previous few years, had been based on mutual understanding and downright pragmatism. Both men knew that. 'It was an interdependent relationship,' said Stoute later. 'Kieren was always good on the horses.' Winning was the key to their success. As long as Fallon helped to maintain Stoute's extraordinary record of consistency at the highest level, all was right with the world. That is not to say that the relationship was pure business. At times, Stoute treated his Irishman like a wayward son, just as he had the equally mercurial Walter Swinburn, and they developed an unlikely, but strong, friendship. Nevertheless, the deal was clear – on big days, Fallon had to produce.

The pressure would certainly be no less at Coolmore. Jamie Spencer, whose resignation as stable jockey ushered Fallon through the door, would confirm that. Back in Ireland under the Coolmore banner, Fallon was about to become a corporate employee, subject to one of the most successful cultures in racing. For once, he had entered a world with horizons bigger than his own.

This was not, though, a vintage time for Coolmore. As football managers will readily tell you, jobs don't tend to come up when clubs are winning. Still one of the biggest players in equine bloodstock, and in the world's most prestigious races, Coolmore was still winning, but it was just not winning enough, not winning as much as it did, say, in

2001 when a record 23 Group One winners emerged from the land they call the Golden Vale beneath the mountain of Slievenamon ('hill of the women' in Gaelic). At the time, the tally was deemed a freak, but every season has been judged by that high-water mark and the tide had been ebbing faster than the masters of Ballydoyle liked or anticipated. Mick Kinane paid the penalty at the end of an unexceptional 2003 season, and his replacement, the young and supremely gifted Jamie Spencer, lasted just a year. In both cases, Coolmore was shooting the messenger.

To his credit, the earnest young man at the heart of the whole operation, Aidan O'Brien, never once tried to deflect the blame for the lack of success. He admitted several times to having made mistakes, first in overtraining the horses, then in changing their feed and their routine. The change of jockey didn't help much. If Kinane was deemed over the hill, Spencer, at the age of 23, had barely crested the foothills of his profession, despite the fact that winning his first Classic at 17 had marked him out as a prodigy. By August, Coolmore had won just one Group One and Spencer's confidence was at an all-time low.

At the Arlington Million in Chicago, he rode the versatile but temperamental Powerscourt like a novice, bringing the four-year-old to challenge on the outside of the field but keeping his whip in his right hand as the horse veered across the track to the inside rail, severely impeding Kicken Kris and Epalo in the process. Spencer knew his fate as soon as he had crossed the finishing line, gesturing to the stands with a thumbs down. Powerscourt was quite clearly the best horse in the race, but was demoted to fourth, and Spencer's ears were ringing with the scorn of the US racing press, never short of a word or two when a European jockey messes up. The following weekend Spencer picked up his seventh suspension inside five months, a sure sign that he was trying that little bit too hard. There were rumours, wide of the mark as it happened, that Spencer and O'Brien did not see eye to eye. More specifically, as he stood down voluntarily from the job, Spencer blamed the intense and obsessive nature of life at Ballydoyle. It was, he intimated, a job for a more experienced hand. Against this background, Magnier, Tabor and Smith had little choice but to make a phone call to the coolest hand in racing.

Quite able to add two plus two, Fallon was ready for the call. He knew Michael Tabor from a few years back and had ridden for Coolmore on several occasions already. He remembered riding Louisville for them in the 2002 Derby when High Chaparral beat Hawk Wing to record a spectacular one-two for Aidan O'Brien. Fallon viewed the action from the safe distance of ninth, the forgotten man in the tableau. Magnier had still bothered to seek him out and thank him for taking the ride, an attention to human detail that appealed to Fallon. Magnier knew well enough that Fallon was a man to have on your side and now he was ready to listen to Tabor's advice and make the deal permanent.

The difficulty for Fallon as he flew to Barbados for a planned holiday that was now turning into a job interview, was the strength of his relationship with Stoute. Deep down, he knew he needed a change of scene, a chance to get off the treadmill of motorway driving and evening meetings he both loved and loathed. His beloved championship had gone, spirited away, he believed, by a combination of Frankie Dettori's brilliance and a concerted campaign by the establishment, his marriage was not in the best of shape and he was still under investigation by the City of London police, which affected his own self-esteem and enhanced his suspicion of the press. What better time to go back home and ride for, arguably, the most powerful stable in world racing, to take stock of life and settle down. By coincidence, the day initially set for the first negotiations at the Sandy Lane Hotel, Tuesday, 22 February, was the day of his 40th birthday. If that was not a thumping reminder of time passing, Fallon was beyond redemption.

All these thoughts crowded in on Fallon that February, but anyone who was ready to condemn him for what happened next has clearly never been given an unrefusable offer. Fallon's initial reaction on hearing the news that Coolmore wanted to speak to him was curiosity. What might they offer that he didn't already have? The answer was financial security beyond his dreams. He had already come a long way from Crusheen in County Clare to a fine house in Newmarket and the rewards that naturally follow being the best at your profession, but this deal promised to lift Fallon into the ranks of Premiership footballers, while taking him back to the land of his birth and a more favourable tax regime. And how many years did he have left at the very top? Five maybe. After all, Kinane had been deemed too old for the job at 44. This was not an offer that would come round again.

Delightfully, because this is his way, Fallon did not have an entourage of agents and lawyers ready to argue for every extra euro or comb every line of the small print on the contract. Fallon is quite capable of looking after himself in financial negotiations and, besides, for once in their business dealings, Magnier, Tabor and Smith were at a disadvantage. They needed Fallon more than Fallon needed them. That did not make the decision any easier for the wanted man. There were considerable drawbacks to returning to Ireland. One was his conscience and the call he knew he would have to make to Stoute, a call he was dreading. Another was the prospect of losing the ride on Motivator, the firm favourite for the Derby, and – if he knew it – a place in the history books alongside Steve Donoghue, who was the only jockey to win three successive Derbies (1921–23). Not even Lester had managed that. Then there was the weighing-room and the prospect of regaining his jockeys' title one last time, just to show them, and the seductive and exhausting rhythms of English racing in high summer, the sheer thrill of riding winners and going for the championship. Coolmore, as young Spencer had found, would be a different way of working, a commitment to a single flag that might not appeal to a restless soul such as himself.

According to an inside source, Fallon was offered a three-year deal worth 'four times' more than he was earning in England. Back in Newmarket, Stoute knew the partnership was ended, and Fallon, even before he left England to return to his winter base in America, knew he knew. But the mind plays tricks and when Fallon blithely announced to the *Racing Post* on 14 February that he was 'very much committed to Sir Michael', he was not wilfully leading the press up the garden path, one of his favourite pastimes. He was saying what he wanted to believe. That he drifted on the exchanges to 49–1 for the job, as Johnny Murtagh was installed as the favourite for the post, was not Fallon's fault any more than the accompanying headlines, which highlighted his disloyalty to his old boss. Fallon sensed the charge more keenly than anyone, knew how it would look and vowed to make sure he told Stoute exactly how he felt when he returned to Newmarket.

Stoute was finally told of his jockey's defection by David Walsh, the *Sunday Times* journalist, and his reaction was typically hard-headed. Not an ounce of sentiment clouded his assessment, nor would he be drawn into any accusations that he might later regret. What angered Stoute was the timing of the departure, just a few weeks before the start of another critical season.

'I expected to be retaining him in 2005 and we were only weeks away from the start of the season, so it was late,' he said later. 'But the decision has been made, and we have since been able to make alternative arrangements.'

He made the split seem no more significant than a minor hitch in some holiday plans, but, privately, Stoute had been hit hard by the loss of a man whose judgement in matters of the Thoroughbred he trusted implicitly and whose spirit he much admired. Names mentioned in connection with the vacancy were Robert Winston, a close friend of Fallon's and from a similar background, Johnny Murtagh, Mick Kinane and young Ryan Moore, the riding revelation of the 2004 season. Stoute pointed out that in 1997 and 2000, both years in which he had been deprived of his stable jockey through illness or injury, he had been champion trainer. Just to prove the point once more, the championship was duly won in 2005 with a variety of riders, including Fallon.

Who, then, were the men with whom the six-times champion had now thrown in his lot? Michael Tabor, John Magnier and Derrick Smith were neither especially colourful – the adjective often used to describe them – nor particularly colourless. They went about their business on the racetrack with the detached and determined air of city brokers in search of a deal. They rarely spoke to the press, almost never smiled and never quite banished the special suspicion reserved by racing's true patrons for those who regard the Thoroughbred in all its majesty as no more than a means of making money. More money. Yet no one can possibly doubt that in bringing the principles of a multi-national corporation to the imprecise art of breeding and racing Thoroughbreds, in refining the system first established by Robert Sangster in harness with Vincent O'Brien at Ballydoyle, Coolmore has revolutionised the racing industry and established an unprecedented dominance over it. The exploits of Sadler's Wells, one of the greatest sires in history, set the organisation on its way, and now the stud has his son, Montjeu. Coolmore's roster of stallions in Ireland, America and Australia reads like a who's who of great champions – Galileo, Rock of Gibraltar, High Chaparral, Hawk Wing, Giant's Causeway. Those they don't breed themselves, Coolmore buys in, notably, Choisir, the great Australian sprinter, and Hurricane Run, bred by Dietrich von Boetticher at the Ammerland Stud near Munich.

Of the trio, Michael Tabor has the most exotic past, and marginally the most amiable presence, although conversation about anything other than the state of the weather is rarely encouraged by any of the men dubbed the 'Coolmore mafia'. Tabor has every right to be proud of what he has helped to build because he has travelled the farthest. He was born and brought up in Forest Gate in the east end of London. His father was a glassmaker, whose own father had brought the family to England from Vilna – now Vilnius, the capital city of Lithuania – to escape the rising tide of anti-Semitism in eastern Europe. In transit, they lost two syllables of their original surname, Taborosky becoming Tabor, a decision that suggests both a strong sense of pragmatism and a yearning for anonymity in their brave new world. Tabor was educated at East Ham Grammar, left school at 15 and rejected jobs at the Co-op and a potential career in hairdressing before succumbing to the lure of the track, in this case the humble surroundings of the dog track at Hendon. 'My grandfather was the real gambler,' Tabor once said. 'So I suppose there was a natural affinity between us.'

Having bought two rundown betting shops, Tabor quickly turned his analytical mind and gift for mathematics to profitable use, building up the Arthur Prince – not Prince Arthur as one American newspaper recently had it – chain of bookmakers, and establishing a reputation for shrewdness and hard-nosed business dealing. He was helped on the way to the top – and being a successful bookmaker in the East End through the seventies and eighties could not be classed as a sweeping highway – by a chance association with a punter in the Midlands, whose phenomenal eye for finding winners stemmed from the principles of rigid discipline and sound temperament that Tabor himself followed in a spectacular career in the betting ring. Tabor hired him as a paid adviser, but to this day will not reveal the man's name.

'If you have done your homework conscientiously, you must trust your principles and stick to them consistently,' he once told an interviewer. 'The right temperament is essential. When some people back a couple of losers, their principles go out the window. You must have real confidence. There are days when you are wrong and that's the end of the story.' Tabor's ability to be right more often than not and, in his own words, to be good at 'assessing how expert experts are' has been the key to his success.

Other methods of finding an edge were less well tolerated by the people who ran the sport. In 1970, Tabor was banned from the racecourse for life by the Jockey Club for paying two jump jockeys – Duncan Hughes and Tom Jennings – for information. On his second appeal, the ban was commuted to three years. Tabor still believes he was merely doing what all good bookmakers did in trying to gain an advantage over the punter and over his rivals. The authorities saw it differently. Yet, by the early eighties, Tabor had taken his first tentative step in racehorse ownership, paying £3,000 for a horse called Tornado Prince, trained by Neville Callaghan, which, much to the delight of its owner, won a selling race. Another connection catches the eye here. On 8 August 1988, in the high summer of his first season in England, a young five-pound claimer called Kieren Fallon made his first foray south from his base in Malton to an evening meeting at Newmarket, where he rode Notion, a two-year-old maiden, into third for trainer, Neville Callaghan. Callaghan, one of the great survivors of the turf, became a long-time friend of Michael Tabor's, and so Fallon's connection with the former East End bookmaker extended further back than was at first presumed when the pair were reunited at Coolmore.

Tabor's own fortunes as a poacher-turned-gamekeeper owed very little to Tornado Prince and pretty well everything to Thunder Gulch, one of the legends of the American turf, who was bought for $475,000 and won two legs of the US Triple Crown, including the 1995

Kentucky Derby. Tabor had just sold his 114 betting shops to Corals for £28 million, but Thunder Gulch provided the real ticket to the jackpot. Most owners wait a lifetime to own a horse as brilliant as Thunder Gulch. Tabor, with the help of Demi O'Byrne, one of Coolmore's key horsemen, managed it in one spectacular leap.

Tabor sold a half-share in the colt to John Magnier, and the horse stands at the Ashford Stud in Kentucky, still one of the mainstays of the Coolmore empire. That year, Tabor also bought in to Coolmore, forming an alliance of skills with Magnier, which, no less than Thunder Gulch, took them straight to the heart of a national obsession.

In Ireland, the horse is a working animal, not a plaything or a domestic pet, treated with due reverence, for sure, but with the lack of sentimentality accorded any other potential investment. In rural Ireland, having an eye for a horse is essential to survival both in business and in society. Horsemanship is learnt from the cradle. As the son of a farmer in Fermoy, County Cork, Magnier had all the natural advantages of the Irish gentry, but was pitched into the world of the adult more quickly than he might have liked. When his father died, Magnier left school at the age of 15 to help his mother run the family's stud and cattle farm. The family had bred horses since the 1850s, including Cottage, sire of Cottage Rake, the triple Cheltenham Gold Cup winner trained by Vincent O'Brien, the greatest trainer of them all. In 1975, John Magnier married Vincent O'Brien's daughter, Susan, and, along with five children, a racing empire was born. In Magnier, whose teeth, it was once said, are the softest part of his head, Tabor quickly sensed a fellow traveller, in ambition and attitude if not in background. Above all, Tabor was smart enough to realise his own strengths and weaknesses in the partnership. He is not the keenest judge of a horse, but his business instincts are unerring. Coolmore needed a cool head on the big day and no one was cooler than Fallon. The hiring of the six-time champion was a gamble, he knew, but it was worth the risk.

Once the dust had settled, there was precious little time for Fallon to acquaint himself with the very particular rhythms of Ballydoyle, or with Aidan O'Brien, the quietly spoken genius at the heart of a great racing empire. Fallon had done his homework well enough and the thought of riding some of the better bred two-year-olds in the land would undoubtedly have helped to sway his thinking about the job. Although Ballydoyle has a Kremlin-like attitude to outsiders, the word on the wind was that Coolmore had a special crop of juveniles coming through, among them, as it turned out, Horatio Nelson, Dylan Thomas and George Washington. Again, Fallon had timed his move to perfection.

Yet as he moved to his homeland to take up his new job, Fallon had concerns, both personal and professional. It was one thing to move himself close to Ballydoyle, which the job, if not his contract, truly demanded, but quite another to uproot Julie and the three children from Newmarket. Fallon went on his own, initially, expecting the family to follow. There was also the nagging concern over why Spencer had left Coolmore so abruptly. Had the secretive, corporate culture of the place scared Spencer away, or did he know something about the crop of Thoroughbreds that were due to carry the famous colours through the coming season, the key to Fallon's well being back in Ireland? Spencer was reticent on the matter, saying only that if he was not happy, it didn't matter how good the horses were or how profitable the job. The question of why he wasn't happy was left largely in the air, but there was a sense that the rhythms of Coolmore, the unwavering intensity of O'Brien himself and the total commitment demanded of the stable jockey were at the root of Spencer's departure.

Yet the parting had been amicable enough. Spencer rode for Coolmore during the 2005 season, but went away to tracks north, south, east and west to perfect his art. By the end of the season, he was champion jockey, an achievement greeted no less enthusiastically by Tabor, Magnier and Smith than by anyone else. Many people genuinely warmed to the boyish charm of the new champion. The job, quite simply, had come too soon for Spencer and he knew it, but there will be a few willing to bet that he will be back in full Coolmore livery before the end of his career.

Fallon's first duty as stable jockey was to get to know the new crop of Classic hopefuls, among them Footstepsinthesand, Virginia Waters, Grand Central, Gypsy King, Ad Valorem and Oratorio – and the older horses were an untried generation. Yeats, ante-post favourite for the Derby, was ruled out of Epsom three days before the big race and did not run again, while Wolfe Tone was considered big-race material until torn back muscles ruled him out for the season. With that eye for assessing a horse's ability and temperament that so benefited Stoute during their association, Fallon quickly latched on to the talents of Footstepsinthesand and Virginia Waters, aware, too, that Oratorio had more to him than he was prepared to show each morning on the Coolmore gallops.

However – and it may become a decent quiz question for anoraks in the coming years – Fallon's first official racecourse duty in his new colours came in the unlikely surroundings of the Cheltenham Festival when he rode Refinement into fourth place in a bumper for Jonjo O'Neill. It would have been typical of Fallon to mark his new role by entering the winner's enclosure at Cheltenham accompanied by the full-throated roar of his countrymen, but, in the event, he had to wait a few weeks for his real baptism, at the Curragh at the start of the Irish flat season.

The partnership began promisingly enough, yet the first real test came back on the familiar ground of the Rowley Mile at Newmarket, scene of so many of Fallon's triumphs, and not a few of his disasters. In the weeks before the Guineas, Coolmore, as ever, kept their counsel. Footstepsinthesand, winner of his two races as a two-year-old and the subject of an unusually hefty gamble in the second of them, was set to carry the first colours in the season's first Classic, with Oratorio regarded, in the bookmakers' eyes at least, as the second string. Neither came over from Ireland accompanied by a clarion call.

'We're expecting both of them to improve a good bit,' said the taciturn O'Brien. 'It has been a very wet spring and most of the horses we have run so far have needed the race.' Footstepsinthesand, he added, 'could be anything', but Fallon, it seemed, had no hesitation in choosing the 170,000-guinea son of Giant's Causeway as his first Classic mount for his new employees. Oratorio, Fallon believed, would come into his own later in the year. He was spectacularly right, in both his assessments.

In all honesty, neither O'Brien nor Fallon were brimming with confidence, despite Motivator having been controversially rerouted to the Dante at York two weeks later in preparation for a tilt at the Derby, his number-one target for the season. Dubawi had enjoyed such an impressive two-year-old campaign, culminating in a thoroughly professional victory in the Group One National Stakes at the Curragh in mid-September, that he was not only touted to be Frankie Dettori's first Derby winner, but rated pretty much a certainty for the Guineas by Michael Stoute, whose own unproven colt Rob Roy was an uneasy second favourite. According to the Newmarket grapevine, a private trial at Godolphin's winter training camp in Dubai had more than proved the son of Dubai Millennium's well being through the off season, and by 3.15 p.m., Dubawi had maintained his hold over the betting offices and on the course. Little attention was given to either of the two Coolmore runners, Fallon wearing the distinctive blue and orange colours of Michael Tabor, Murtagh wearing Mrs John Magnier's dark blue livery.

Leaving nothing to chance, although the colt had shown little sign of a wayward temperament so far in his career, Fallon took Footstepsinthesand down to the post early, a trick he had used to good effect for both Cecil and Stoute on big days. For Fallon, this is vital educational time, a chance to relax a highly strung Thoroughbred and to ensure that every ounce of energy is conserved for the more serious work on the way back.

Keeping Footstepsinthesand handily paced throughout the straight mile, Fallon was always going conspicuously well in the centre of the track as Kandidate, Tony James and Party Boss streaked clear of the field, almost giving a heart attack to the evergreen, ever optimistic, Clive Brittain, who trained all of them. In contrast, Dubawi was visibly struggling on the firm ground and had no answer when Fallon asked his mount to quicken and put the race beyond doubt. The response was immediate and decisive, the one and a half length gap at the winning post barely a measure of Footstepsinthesand's control. Behind him, significantly perhaps for those judging the quality of the race, came Rebel Rebel, trained by Neville Callaghan and ridden by the Spaniard, Oscar Urbina, and Kandidate, ridden by Eddie Ahern, both 100–1 shots. The race was quickly labelled substandard by the experts, but

The Master of Epsom: Michael Stoute described Fallon's victory on Kris Kin in the 2003 Vodafone Derby as one of the 'great Derby rides'. The apparent ease of Kris Kin's win on the line belies the ground he made up in the final two furlongs. On the rails, Pat Eddery's dreams of winning one last Derby on The Great Gatsby are snatched away. *(PA Photos)*

A smile of satisfaction lights up Fallon's face in victory. Once again, he has answered his critics, including the owner, Saeed Suhail, who is leading Kris Kin back to the winner's enclosure. The Fallon Factor was deemed by bookmakers to be the cause of one of the biggest and most costly gambles in Derby history. *(Getty Images)*

The defeat which launched a thousand conspiracy theories: Ballinger Ridge, under Kieren Fallon (seen here leading into the straight), was caught on the line at Lingfield by Rye, March 2004. Fallon was banned for 21 days for dropping his hands and allowing Rye to overhaul him. *(RaceTECH)*

Fallon's 2004 season ended with his arrest by the City of London police on charges of race-fixing and the loss of his jockeys' title to Frankie Dettori, but for two days at Epsom Fallon was once again peerless. *(Above)* The brilliant Ouija Board, trained by Ed Dunlop, spreadeagles the field in the Oaks in the historic colours of Lord Derby, while *(left)* Fallon acknowledges his third Derby victory on North Light for Michael Stoute. *(PA Photos/Getty Images)*

The happy postscript to a dispiriting 2004 came in the Breeders' Cup at Lone Star Park when Ouija Board, ridden with calculated verve by Fallon, pounced off the final turn to win the Filly and Mare Turf to establish Ouija Board's reputation as a globe-trotting star. Fallon had won the race the previous year on Islington. *(Getty Images)*

Julie Fallon, daughters Natalie and Brittany and son Cieran join their father in the winner's enclosure after Footstepsinthesand's victory in the 2000 Guineas in May 2005, Fallon's first Classic ride for Coolmore, his new employers. *(Racingfotos.com)*

Virginia Waters goes to the post for the 1000 Guineas at Newmarket under a tight rein as Fallon tries to relax the filly in the critical moments before the race. Fallon's ability to educate highly strung thoroughbreds was a priceless asset. Moments later, Virginia Waters completed the Guineas double for Aidan O'Brien, Coolmore and Fallon. *(PA Photos)*

Harry Can Win. Fallon betrays relief as much as joy after Hurricane Run's extraordinary triumph in the Prix de l'Arc de Triomphe at Longchamp, October 2005. Fallon's nerve and confidence were never more evident than on that rainy Sunday afternoon in Paris. Shuffled almost to the back of the field, Fallon negotiated a perilous path along the rail to snatch an improbable victory. *(Racingfotos.com)*

The birth of a legend. Despite the coaxing of both O'Brien and Fallon, George Washington refuses to walk into the winner's enclosure at Newmarket after his electrifying victory in the 2000 Guineas. *(Racingfotos.com)*

The long eye of the law: Fallon emerges from Bishopsgate police station in July 2006 after being charged with race-fixing. Suspended by the UK racing authorities pending the trial, Fallon has not ridden in England since that summer. *(Getty Images)*

Fallon and Aidan O'Brien in earnest conversation after Dylan Thomas won the Irish Champion Stakes in 2006. O'Brien was an eloquent defender of Fallon's talent and a robust supporter of his stable jockey through the troubled prelude to the trial at the Old Bailey. *(Racingfotos.com)*

The unwanted headlines from Fallon's arrest hit racing and the jockey equally hard. *(George Selwyn)*

Left Fallon discusses future plans with Coolmore connections after Myboycharlie wins the Prix Morny at Deauville, 19 August 2007. Results of a drugs test taken that day later proved positive for the second time, and Fallon was banned for eighteen months. *(AFP/Getty Images)*

Right The look that Fallon reserves for *Panorama* investigators and intrusive photographers. Fallon returns home from Spain after the *News of the World*'s allegations of race-fixing to find the world's press on his doorstep. He was not amused. *(Racingfotos.com)*

Fallon's last ride? Dylan Thomas wins a second Arc for Fallon on the eve of his trial at the Old Bailey, prompting emotional scenes at Longchamp. The Irish flag later draped around Fallon's shoulders could have been a curtain call for his career. *(George Selwyn)*

The following morning, 8 October 2007, Fallon appears at the Old Bailey on the first day of his eleven-week trial, which ended in an embarrassing and expensive defeat for the City of London Police and the Crown Prosecution Service. *(AFP/Getty Images)*

Free at last, but not from himself. A weary Fallon faces the cameras after his acquittal at the Old Bailey, 7 December 2007. But Fallon did not look like a free man. The following morning news broke of a second positive drugs test, which seemed certain to signal the end of his career. *(Getty Images)*

neither Fallon nor O'Brien cared to debate the historical merit of their victory right then. Like Cecil and Stoute before him, Fallon had crowned a new partnership with a Classic victory – Sleepytime for Cecil in 1997, King's Best for Stoute three years later, now Footsteps-inthesand. Had he stayed in Newmarket to ride for Stoute, Fallon would have finished plum last on Rob Roy, a cruel irony that did not need spelling out in the triumphant aftermath of Coolmore's success.

'Kieren had great faith in him all along,' said O'Brien later. 'When he started riding work, he was the only horse he wanted to ride all the time.' Yet it was Fallon, ever suspicious of what might come round the corner next, who sounded a note of caution.

'It's going to be hard to recapture a day like today,' he said. 'It's a crucial point in my career because it was a big decision to go and ride in Ireland. There were a lot of changes to make, but now I've got my career in order, hopefully I can continue.'

If Footstepsinthesand's success was not entirely unexpected, 13–2 reflecting a realistic assessment of his chances, Virginia Waters was utterly unfancied to complete a double for Coolmore and the full set of English Classics for O'Brien. The defection of the brilliant French filly, Divine Proportions, and John Gosden's highly rated Playful Act had certainly opened up the field for the fillies Classic. Admittedly, Virginia Waters' two-year-old form did not warrant too much attention, but Fallon had been deeply impressed by the three-year-old's impressive victory in the 1,000 Guineas trial at Leopardstown the previous month.

Once again, fortune smiled on Fallon, who might have been tempted to ride Damson for David Wachman had not the Michael Tabor-owned filly been withdrawn a few days before the race. Who's to say Damson wouldn't have won anyway, but she would have needed wings to catch Virginia Waters. Once Fallon had set her alight, the twenty-strong field was reduced to slow motion. This was vintage Fallon. With three furlongs left to run, Virginia Waters was last, but if there was once a panic button at the tip of Fallon's fingers, he has long since mislaid it. 'You have to lose the fear of being beaten,' the great American jockey, Angel Cordero, once told Jamie Spencer. Fallon has long since lost that, too. Instead, behind Fallon's intimidating gaze lies a mind like

Calculus and the nerve of Houdini. With the whole field in front of him, Fallon barely moved until the time was just right. Hitting the front inside the final furlong, Virginia Waters quickened clear to win by two and a half lengths at 12–1 from the favourite, Maids Causeway. It could easily have been more. 'She's a better filly than I thought she was,' said Fallon, his face wreathed in smiles.

From failing to win a single Classic at home or abroad in 2004, O'Brien had claimed two in two days. Not since Noel Murless and George Moore with Royal Palace and Fleet in 1967 had the same trainer–jockey combination completed the Guineas double. O'Brien, ever a creature of habit, returned swiftly to Ballydoyle by helicopter to supervise the return of his heroine and, quite probably, oversee the homework of his four children. Humility has ever been one of O'Brien's qualities, painful humility at times as he struggles to feed the press the exact emotion they want while staring at his shoelaces and rubbing his hands like a priest after Mass. Those close to the young master of Ballydoyle are concerned that he will worry himself to an early breakdown, but his wife, Anne-Marie, and his family – frequent visitors to the racetrack – act as buttresses against the overwhelming forces that, at times, have threatened to engulf the boy wonder. Besides, as Fallon found out swiftly enough, O'Brien's meek and mild manner hides a ferociously competitive spirit.

If there was any doubt about Fallon's impact on the new partnership, it was dispelled by the time Gypsy King, rapidly emerging as Coolmore's principal Derby hope, had been coaxed, kidded and cajoled into winning the Dee Stakes at Chester a few days later. That O'Brien had scheduled runners for the tightest track in the country was a surprise to many. He had never done so before and Fallon's hand was clearly at work in persuading the trainer of the merits of the quirky old Roodee.

First came Almighty, a touch disappointing in his opening run of the season and out to make amends in the Chester Vase. Although installed as the 100–30 favourite, the O'Brien colt was beaten cosily by Clive Brittain's Hattan. Even with the improvement promised by the trainer for next time, the half brother to Arc winner Sagamix did not look to have the class to win a Derby. So attention turned to Gypsy King, a handsome son of Sadler's Wells, seeing a racecourse in earnest for only the second time in his young life. Against him were ranged the Queen's Forward Move and the Michael Stoute-trained duo of Mordor and Zalongo.

Mostly, as jockeys will generally tell you, horses win races and jockeys lose them. Were he blessed with the ability to talk, Gypsy King would say different. From the moment he fell out of the stalls to the moment he thrust his head across the line to snatch victory from the 33–1 shot, I'm Spartacus, Gypsy King tried his hardest to lose the Dee Stakes. He loitered through the first few furlongs, jumped an imaginary fence on the bend and then stumbled over to the stands into, rather than away from, Fallon's right-hand whip. Had Fallon donned a mortar board and stood at a lectern, he could not have administered a finer lesson in the art of race-riding. Even as he gathered to deliver the decisive challenge, Fallon held an inch or so of rein more than any of the other jockeys driving to the finish.

'It would have taken two months at home to learn what he did here today,' said O'Brien.

The question was whether Gypsy King could afford to show such a quirky attitude over the more testing terrain of Epsom. It was a ringing endorsement of his jockey's skill that the lightly raced colt should be promoted above the mighty Motivator and the Guineas winner Footstepsinthesand to the head of the betting for the Derby. Halfway through the Dee Stakes, punters on the betting exchanges were offering 50–1 about a Fallon–O'Brien victory. Deep down, though, Fallon knew the true odds of winning his third successive Derby.

One other horse in the O'Brien arsenal had made a favourable impression on the new stable jockey. As early as April, O'Brien had taken the measure of the bay son of Danehill and deemed him a talented idler, the sort of schoolboy you summon to the front row to keep an eye on.

'All he does is eat and sleep,' said the trainer. 'He would be happy doing nothing else.' Fallon recorded roughly the same sentiments at season's end – 'Bone idle,' he laughed.

It was Oratorio who carried on the campaign for Ballydoyle through the major middle-distance races of a long season and who, with some dual feelings for his jockey, handsomely downed the colours of Motivator, the pride of England and the one horse Fallon would have brought with him across the Irish Sea.

No one could argue with Oratorio's work rate – he ran seven times as a two-year-old and a remarkable eight times as a three-year-old – but he tended to run his own race when it suited him, at least until Fallon found the key halfway through his Classic season. Oratorio had rounded off his two-year-old campaign with an enigmatic, slightly fortunate, victory in the Prix Jean-Luc Lagardere at Longchamp and by finishing second to Shamardal in the Dewhurst Stakes at Newmarket. If that was the best Coolmore had to offer, the experts thought, then the next season was going to be as tough as the last for O'Brien. For the first half of the season, Oratorio was not even Spencer's preferred mount, and even Fallon ignored the claims of the horse for the first two colt Classics of the season, rightly preferring Footstepsinthesand for the 2,000 Guineas and Gypsy King for the Derby. Gypsy King finished fifth, Oratorio a desultory tenth, but that was the last time Fallon bequeathed anyone else the ride because he had already deduced that Oratorio firstly had more ability than he was letting on, and, secondly, would take longer to get fit than some others at Ballydoyle.

Brought back to a mile for the St James's Palace Stakes at York (Royal Ascot), Oratorio was again well beaten by Shamardal. However, aimed for the first time at one mile and two furlongs in the Coral-Eclipse at Sandown the following month, Oratorio finally justified the faith placed in him by both trainer and jockey. It's possible that Oratorio needed his third Group One run in just under a month to bring him to full race fitness. It's equally possible that both O'Brien and Fallon had been fooled into thinking a mile was his ideal range after a lacklustre showing in the Derby, and only split the difference at ten furlongs as a desperate last resort. Not all campaigns are meticulously planned, whatever trainers might tell you. Whatever the cause, when Oratorio suddenly decided to go racing again, he proved a formidable opponent, twice defeating Motivator, the runaway Derby winner widely regarded as invincible.

As his rider the previous year, no one had a better understanding of

Motivator's mentality and potential weakness than Fallon, and it was clear from the way both the Eclipse and the Irish Champion Stakes unfolded that his inside knowledge had been put to good use. In varying the pace of the Eclipse at Sandown, Fallon deliberately prevented the free-moving Motivator from exerting the effortless dominance he had shown on Derby day. Under pressure throughout the race, Johnny Murtagh brought the odds-on favourite through to win his race, only for Oratorio, under the fiercest persuasion by Fallon, to battle back close to home. The winning distance was half a length and the odds of 12–1 reflected the suspicions with which Oratorio was viewed. The Sandown crowd, who had come to acclaim their champion, were stunned into silence. This was not the Motivator they knew. More significantly, it was not the same Oratorio either.

To prove that was no fluke, Oratorio repeated the performance two months later in the Irish Champion Stakes at Leopardstown. This time, the odds were closer, Motivator starting at 3–1 second favourite behind the well-backed Azamour and Oratorio 7–1. Once again, Motivator set sail for home first and, once again, under the strongest possible driving from Fallon, Oratorio wore him down to win, also by half a length. Returning to Newmarket where his season had begun in the spring, on an afternoon his jockey would rather forget, Oratorio was narrowly beaten in the Champion Stakes by David Junior, and by the time of the Breeders' Cup Classic, at a freezing Belmont Park in New York in late October, the talented but temperamental colt had decided enough was enough.

'This horse needs understanding,' O'Brien had said halfway through the season. 'He's been given a masterclass.'

If Fallon was having difficulty adjusting to the obsessive demands of the Coolmore corporation – and there were suggestions that his time-keeping of a morning was not always to O'Brien's liking – Fallon's horsemanship on the big day more than compensated for his personal failings. More worryingly for his own well being, Fallon's family had decided to stay in Newmarket, depriving him of stability and routine away from the track. Idleness is not an ideal companion for a man as restless as Fallon and, as the season wore on, his appearances back on

English tracks became more frequent. Fallon was missing the very thing that had driven him back to his homeland, the frenetic rhythms of high summer in English racing, the daily grind of riding winners the length and breadth of the country. Above all, he was missing his title.

'I don't know Kieren particularly well, but I reckon he's a bit like me,' Tony McCoy, the obsessive harvester of winners, once said. 'He loves the Monday to Thursday stuff, the Windsors and the Pontefracts and so on. He loves riding winners.'

Yet compensation came in the form of some of the best and most expensive horseflesh in the world and, on one autumn afternoon in the suburbs of Paris, a victory that defied superlatives and defined a career.

13

HARRY CAN RUN

'You have to have nerves for that ride, I think.'

Diettrich von Boetticher, breeder and
former owner of Hurricane Run

In Paris on 2 October 2005, the day dawned grey and damp. It was the day of the Prix de l'Arc de Triomphe, when Longchamp, the preserve of the smart and chic Parisian, is traditionally invaded by uncouth hordes from across the Channel. On any other day of the year, Longchamp moves to its own gently élitist rhythms. Racing in France is not a sport of the people, at least not in Paris, and so some of the most expensive Thoroughbreds in the world go about their business on one of the most picturesque racetracks in the world in front of crowds sparser than can be found on a midweek afternoon at Lingfield Park. The Arc, though, is different. On Arc day, Longchamp comes alive, galvanised by the need to protect French pride from the infidel and to ensure that a race with a uniquely French ambience remains in safe keeping for another year. The air crackles with the intensity of a prize fight, for although no championship is at stake, the winner can lay strong claim to the season's middle-distance crown. Sea-Bird, Mill Reef, Vaguely Noble, Dancing Brave, Peintre Célèbre, Montjeu, the history of the Arc is recited like a creed, but late-developing, lightly raced three-year-olds, or older horses trained specifically for the autumn – All Along, Carroll House, Marienbard – have also graced the honours board, which makes the race a true test of a champion's quality. There

191

is no such thing as a bad Arc, but there is a lot of bad luck in the Arc.

Longchamp is a difficult track, not as topographically extreme as Epsom, but undulating and with a long sweeping bend from the end of the back straight down into the home straight that tests the nerve and balance of both horse and rider. Jockeys not familiar with the idiosyncrasies of Longchamp can be seduced into pushing for home too soon, or find themselves pinned against the rail, and hampered by the early leaders retreating through the field and the gathering posse of challengers on the outside. Jonathan Pease, the English-born, French-based trainer of Bago, the defending champion in 2005, warns his jockeys not to follow overseas riders. It is a course where experience is paramount, patience is rewarded and panic punished. The timing of the race is critical. October is late in the season for Classic contenders, who might have been racing since May, and the ground is often softer than ideal. Winners of the Arc need to have a high cruising speed, at least two changes of pace and bottomless reserves of stamina and courage to last out the punishing mile and a half.

'On some courses you can get away with mistakes, but not at Longchamp,' commented Gary Stevens, the great American rider who learnt to ride the track as well as any European jockey during his spell in France with Andre Fabre. 'It's a very, very tactical course, very fair if you know where you're at. The best horse wins if the jockey does his homework. It's my favourite racetrack in the world.'

Cash Asmussen, another American rider who enjoyed huge success over many years in France, came to observe a few cast-iron rules over the treacherous contours of the Arc course, and put at least a few of them into practice in guiding Suave Dancer, a horse initially bought and conditioned by his father Keith, to victory in 1991.

'I remember that day on Suave Dancer. I was three to five lengths farther back from the lead than I really wanted to be down the back. But Generous [the 1991 Derby winner ridden by Alan Munro] was going a helluva pace up the front. I had to make a big decision. I could have moved closer by going wide or I could sit and wait and suffer. I chose to stay where I was and it paid off. The problem is that once the bend starts, it turns right away from you almost all the way so you can be three horses wide at the top of it and end up at the bottom what seems like six wide. It's a racetrack where you gotta be patient.'

Fallon knew the required virtues both from watching previous races, which he does avidly, and from riding in the race himself, but he did not know the character of his horse as well as he did Motivator's, winner of the English Derby and, ironically, one of his chief rivals that afternoon. Fallon had ridden Motivator throughout his two-year-old career, but today he was allied to another imposing bay son of Montjeu, the mercurial and talented Hurricane Run, trained by Andre Fabre. Fallon had become acquainted with the Hurricane only in mid-summer, when his new employers had reportedly invested £7 million into luring the French Derby second to Coolmore. For a horseman who specialised in educating and understanding his mounts, this was a steep learning curve and although Fallon's confidence in Hurricane Run's ability would have been shaped by their victories in the Irish Derby and the Prix Niel, a preparation race for the Arc, he had no idea how the horse would react under the sort of pressure exerted by a large field of top-class Thoroughbreds in the Arc.

At the Curragh in June, Fallon had done the sensible thing, not always his forte, and simplified his tactics. The Irish Derby was a race Fallon had never won and his desperation to set the record straight emerged in the genuine depth of his emotions in the winner's enclosure afterwards. In a conveniently small field, Fallon knew the qualities of at least two of his main market rivals, Scorpion and Gypsy King, from riding them on spring mornings at Ballydoyle. He knew, too, that he had the best horse and that human error would be the most likely cause of defeat. So Fallon pulled Hurricane Run wide off the turn, gave him plenty of daylight and asked him to quicken down the vast expanse of the Curragh straight. The response was, to most eyes, workmanlike rather than electric, but the result was never in doubt once Hurricane Run had headed Scorpion inside the final furlong. The sad postscript to the race was the injury to Gypsy King, who broke a shoulder and had to be put down.

The victory was particularly sweet for two reasons. One was that Fallon's career had come in a neat circle, back to the days of his apprenticeship with Kevin Prendergast on the Curragh, when he had dreamed of winning his own Derby, and the second was that he was wearing the colours of the owners who had given him his first international Group One winner, on the filly Borgia at Baden-Baden in September 1997. 'They've been lucky for me,' he said. Although Coolmore had paid handsomely for the privilege of owning Hurricane Run, part of the deal was that Fallon should carry the green and red livery of Dietrich von Boetticher, the owner and breeder, one last time in the Irish Derby. Fallon was only too happy to pay his respects to the tall, urbane, Munich lawyer, who had for so long championed the cause of the German breeding industry from his Ammerland Stud in Bavaria.

For von Boetticher, too, this was an extraordinarily emotional moment, the culmination of a dream hatched fifteen years earlier when he bought a rundown farm on the edge of a lake about an hour's drive south of Munich and started his own stud.

'Everyone told me to forget it,' he recalled in the spring of 2006. 'They told me I would never produce a decent horse in Bavaria. But the soil here is created out of the glaciers that once stretched all the way to Munich from the Alps, and it's beautiful limestone soil, high in calcium, like Ireland. We began with one building and now we have ninety hectares of land and thirty mares. The horses like it here. They like the views.'

From the moment he was born, the Montjeu colt had something about him that was different. Unlike many Montjeus, he had a cool and controlled temperament, but he was good and he knew it well enough. He was nicknamed Harry, as in Harry Can Run, by Daniela Nowara, the manager of the Ammerland Stud.

'Some horses give you a feeling, if you see them and handle them every day,' she said. 'Harry gave me that feeling.'

So instead of being kept in Germany, Hurricane Run was sent across the border to the master, to Andre Fabre at Chantilly, and when a fax arrived a few days later from the Frenchman, saying simply, 'I'm impressed by your Montjeu colt,' the sense of expectation stretched all the way from Paris to Munich. Soon afterwards came another missive from Fabre: 'Your Montjeu colt is a good mover.'

Neither Fallon nor von Boetticher could know the full circle that would unite them on the Curragh. In a way, they shared an unlikely background, the one a son of landed gentry in Latvia, who had been brought up hunting and fishing before the outbreak of war pushed his family out of their home and into permanent exile, to the west. Fallon's exodus to the east, from the tiny village of Crusheen and an upbringing typical of the rural working-class in Ireland, took him on an equally winding path to fame and fortune. Von Boetticher was born in Poland, but found his home in Germany, and he tells a touching story of his parents, who always believed that one day they would return to Latvia to resume their lives. Dietrich bought them the tickets to Riga after the collapse of the Soviet Union. 'They went and came back, understanding that Germany not Latvia was now their home,' he said.

But if von Boetticher had inherited his father's eye for a horse, another gift he shared with the Irishman, and had developed it through competing in dressage to national level, he also had strong opinions about how to bring the best out of a racehorse. Walter Swinburn had ridden Luigi, Ammerland's first stallion, to victory in the German Derby and now, with Borgia emerging as a filly of international class, von Boetticher had noticed the peculiar bobbing action of another Irish jockey just making a name for himself in England.

In the autumn of 1997, Fallon was still two months away from landing his first championship, but he had shown enough panache and power to bring Sleepytime home in the 1,000 Guineas for his first Classic win and to render all the criticism of his appointment as stable jockey to Henry Cecil not just wrong, but vacuous.

'I had always studied English racing and I liked his way of riding,' said von Boetticher. 'It's hard to find a rider as involved as Kieren is. He makes use of his whole body, it's a very active style of riding. He doesn't just sit on a horse and ride, he educates it and gives it all he's got. He told me that he owed a lot to his time in the States where he learnt about timing and balancing a horse. He doesn't look too beautiful, but it's very effective.'

Von Boetticher recalled Boreal's victory at Epsom in the Coronation Cup some years later, the second success by a German horse in a Group One in Britain.

'Even though he won by four or five lengths, Kieren was still out of breath when he was being interviewed afterwards. It wasn't lack of fitness. He'd just put so much effort into the ride. It was a big move for him, as well as for me, when he came to Baden-Baden back in 1997, because Borgia was still an outsider on the international scene.'

No less so than Fallon, but together they flourished, finishing third behind Peintre Célèbre and Pilsudski in the Arc, second to Chief Bearheart in the Breeders' Cup Turf at Hollywood Park the same year, and fifth in the Filly and Mare Turf at the 1999 Breeders' Cup, beaten less than a length and a half by Soaring Softly, the American four-year-old. By the time the brilliant filly retired, she had won two Grade Ones, more than £1 million in prize money and Ammerland was no longer just an unknown fishing community in the lee of the southern Alps. When Borgia was succeeded by Boreal as Ammerland's star, Fallon's star, too, was on the rise and he was not always available to take the ride. Victory in the Coronation Cup was particularly sweet, but neither von Boetticher nor Fallon could have anticipated the resumption of their old partnership on the imposing Montjeu colt in the summer of 2005, although it might just have helped the negotiations between von Boetticher and Coolmore over the sale of Hurricane Run that Fabre would be retained as the trainer and Fallon would be contracted to ride. Von Boetticher was impressed, anyway, by Coolmore's calm and stylish conduct.

No longer involved in the preliminaries, von Boetticher watched the Arc from behind a phalanx of umbrellas. At Ammerland, little excuse is needed to rerun the tape of Borgia's greatest moments and each time they laugh at the bobbing cap that shows Fallon and Borgia at full tilt. Obscured by the rain, the umbrellas and a wall of horses, von Boetticher had all but given up on Harry when the field swung into the straight.

'I thought that was it,' he said. 'I couldn't imagine them getting through all those horses. You have to have nerves for that ride, I think. What if the gap doesn't open up?'

Daniela Nowara watched the race from a private box alongside Andre Fabre. It is the only time she can recall the instinctively aloof French trainer shouting at the television like a punter in the betting shop.

'When Borgia was running, I was always nervous,' recalled Nowara.

'With Hurricane Run, I always had confidence, in the horse and in Kieren. How did Fallon manage to keep the horse straight when, with (Christophe) Soumillon, he tended to go left and right? Fabre said he never saw Borgia run as well as she did for Fallon and it was the same with Hurricane Run.'

From the start, when Hurricane Run had been knocked and pushed to the back of the field, to the bottom of the hill, the Arc could not have gone worse for Fallon. But, having won the previous two Group One races of the afternoon, he was full of confidence and as the gaps opened up in front of him down the rail, he rode his luck with all the bravado of a Las Vegas gambler on a roll. The Arc can be won down the inside and Martin Dwyer proved that the Epsom Derby can be won by the same route when Sir Percy squeezed through the latest and tightest of gaps to seal victory in 2006, but to come from near last to first at Longchamp within the space of no more than a furlong, to hold position and nerve in the face of such imminent disaster, took a horse of rare courage and class and a jockey utterly oblivious to the consequences of defeat. His best piece of luck, as he modestly admitted later, was to be on a horse at the height of his powers.

'In that Arc, for the first time, Hurricane Run had to come from behind, from a long way behind,' said Fabre later. 'He had never done that and, you know, that day I saw an acceleration I had never seen before and that I did not know he had. Kieren found something in the horse no one else did. But this is a talent possessed by all great jockeys. Hurricane Run was a very powerful horse with a very generous nature. He wanted to be respected and, if he was, he gave that respect back. I think that was why he got on so well with Kieren. They had the same attitude.'

The closing stages worked out perfectly for Fallon as Hurricane Run cut down the gallant Westerner to win by the margin of four lengths. Motivator, the main hope of the English, who had seemed the likely winner a furlong from home under Johnny Murtagh, faded into fifth, while Bago finished a creditable third in his attempt to become the first horse to defend the title since Alleged in 1978.

'I don't think I've ever ridden a horse with a turn of foot like that,' said Fallon in the winner's enclosure. 'I got shuffled back at the start, farther back than I wanted to be, but I was lucky to have the horse and I wasn't worried because the pace was so strong, and I always thought they'd come back to me. Things got pretty tough on the home turn, but luckily all the problems happened to my left and I just skipped through it all.' It was Fallon's first Arc, Fabre's sixth. His seventh would come twelve months later with Rail Link.

Winning three Group Ones in succession on Arc day was, Fallon admitted, as good as it gets – but it was more than that. Fallon's win on Hurricane Run was his signature ride, just as the essence of Lester Piggott's brilliance over five decades was distilled into his victory on Royal Academy in the 1990 Breeders' Cup. Luck, judgement, defiance, cockiness, contrariness, coolness, concentration, fatalism, addiction to danger, strength, an absolute mastery of time and space, every one of the forces shaping Fallon's individuality was present in the two minutes 27.4 seconds it took for Hurricane Run to win the Arc. Later, Walter Swinburn spoke about the ride.

'I went that route along the rail on All Along to win in 1983,' he said. 'The difference is that I was on a sixteen to one shot, Kieren was on one of the favourites. He would have known that every set of binoculars was watching him about to mess up. That takes some nerve.'

Even Fallon's normally taciturn post-race demeanour deserted him. He seemed almost overwhelmed by the accolades, as if he was only keeping them safe for someone else. 'It's definitely the best day I've ever had riding,' he said. Those proved to be poignant words. The 50,000 crowd at Longchamp that rainy afternoon included Fallon's solicitor, Christopher Stewart-Moore, who, a few days later, had to accompany Fallon to a London police station to answer bail following his arrest in connection with allegations of race-fixing. At Ammerland, they drank a toast to the jockey, *their* jockey, that night and to a horse called Harry that had carried their flag, if not their colours, into the winner's enclosure of one of the most prestigious races of them all, while the words of another Arc winner echoed all the way from the living room of a ranch in Texas – 'They only pay out at the post,' Cash Asmussen had said. 'I believe that's still the same as it was in my day.'

14

A SEASON ON THE BRINK

'When one burns one's bridges, what a very nice fire it makes.'

Dylan Thomas

Not even Fallon's most rabid critics or most devoted followers could have charted the highs and lows of a season that began with an almost unbroken run of success in Britain and Ireland and ended in banishment and ignominy. It was as if the twin forces of Fallon's life, all the brushes with authority, all the bans and the controversies, all the brilliance, the bravado and the bravery had fused into one single, electrically charged year.

It was the year of George Washington, Alexandrova and Dylan Thomas, all Classic winners, but it was also the year that left Fallon with no hiding place. Far from being absolved from any connection with the race-fixing enquiries being carried out by the City of London police, as he had fondly and naïvely believed, on the morning of 3 July 2006, at Bishopsgate police station, Fallon, the six-time champion and the foremost rider of his generation, was charged with conspiracy to defraud the customers of Betfair, the leading betting exchange.

This was no longer some minor misdemeanour open to absolution in the stewards' room or by the disciplinary committee at Shaftesbury Avenue. This was out of Fallon's jurisdiction, way beyond the boundary where his reputation and his charm might be influential. This was the law of the land and conviction would mean not another suspension, but a prison sentence. Fallon had only to pick up the phone and dial the number of Timmy Murphy, another supremely talented but wayward Irish rider, to appreciate what that might mean. Murphy, a reformed alcoholic, spent three months in Wormwood Scrubs for assault on an airline stewardess and, although Murphy is back doing what he does best each afternoon at the racetrack, the scars from the experience will never fully heal. As well as Fallon, ten others were charged with a variety of offences. They included trainer Alan Berry and Miles Rodgers, a former director of the Platinum racing syndicate, which owned several of the horses at the centre of the investigations, and jockeys Darren Williams and Fergal Lynch, as well as Lynch's brother Shaun and Philip Sherkle. Racing stood in the dock alongside them.

Fallon knew his fate before he arrived at the police station that July Monday, which only makes his ice-cool performance on Dylan Thomas at the Curragh the previous afternoon all the more miraculous. No emotion can ever be straightforward with Fallon and the cheers for the winner as he returned to the paddock after a blistering victory in the Irish Derby had barely died down, as many of them raised in honour of their champion rider as for an indisputably brilliant three-year-old, before British racing was reduced to stunned silence by the implications of the routine police statement delivered less than twenty-four hours later. What sort of man could keep a clear head, compute all the complex calculations required of a Classic and reject so easily the demons that must have been crowding in on him that afternoon at the Curragh? Dylan Thomas certainly made the job easier than it might have been by producing the best display of his young life, but the very fact that Fallon could face the demands of his profession with such utter assurance while deep down fearing for his future – as he had done for much of the season – merely endorsed what friends and enemies had known all along about the hard man from Crusheen.

With the toughness comes an acceptance of what life brings, an understanding that if you give it out, you have to take it back. That's the way of life. But there's more to it than that. In common with Paul Gascoigne and Wayne Rooney, Fallon finds release in the activity he does best. On a horse, he is in control, at one with himself and his surroundings; off it, he is subject to the considerable faultlines of his own character, and to the complexities of everyday existence. He is, by his own admission, a bad judge of character, which is a dangerous failing in a world as enticing to rogues as racing. McCoy has sacrificed everything in his life to the cause of riding winners. Family apart, he has no life outside that relentless pursuit, which even he finds hard to quantify or explain. Fallon gets bored more easily. For his most memorable seasons, when he was pursuing his title from meeting to meeting, day in, day out, Fallon was cocooned in his own obsession, but even then the compulsion to break free was never far below the surface. He has to see how far he can push his luck, just for the fun of it.

In the summer of 2006, there was no way out, not any more. The net was closing. In the police station's incident room, an inner sanctum rarely visited by anyone except the suspicious and the suspected, the walls were covered with images of one, instantly recognisable, face. Wherever you looked, there was Fallon, and yet the file handed over by the Horseracing Regulatory Authority in 2004 included no mention of him. Only when the City of London police began to follow up leads on a series of races between 1 December 2002 and 2 September 2004 did a pattern emerge, with Fallon as a linking motif.

By the time he was charged, Fallon had been on bail for twenty-two months, since his initial arrest on 1 September 2004. It was a long time to be a very public figure under suspicion. He kept riding with the same resolution and confidence, of course, notably in winning both 1,000 and 2,000 Guineas at Newmarket in his first season for Coolmore and, at the end of the same 2005 season, three Group Ones at Longchamp, including the Arc on the peerless Hurricane Run. But in private, Fallon was struggling to cope with the attention.

'I just want this nightmare to end,' he said in *The Times* early in the 2006 season. 'I want to clear my name. I've done nothing wrong, that's the sad part. It cost me the jockeys' championship two seasons ago with all that was going on. I suffered from a lack of concentration, and though things improved last year when I went to Ireland, I was just getting by. I can switch off and forget everything when the gates open, but at other times, like at night when I'm trying to get some sleep, it can get on top of you.'

This was a rare admission of weakness from Fallon, a glimpse of the desperate vulnerability that lay beneath the rock-hard exterior. An interesting divide had opened up across the Irish Sea. In England, Fallon had become a hugely popular figure on the racetracks, where punters spoke with their wallets about his prowess, coolness and, above all, consistency in the saddle. Not the least of the ironies associated with the whole case was that for seven seasons, punctuated only by injury, Fallon was the most prolific race-winning jockey since Sir Gordon Richards. To the betting-shop brigade, the people who really keep the whole crazy carousel turning, Fallon was a hero, like Lester Piggott before him, a jockey who would give your last tenner a decent run. Punters demand no more than effort, or at least the perception of effort, from the jockeys chosen for their investment, and with his rhythmic, relentless, driving style, Fallon not only rode winners from nowhere, he quite demonstrably gave every one of his rides a chance. And that was good enough for them. If there were rides that did not match up to the stringent criteria of the pen-and-paper faithful, then they either forgave their man for his error or pretended not to notice. In that sense, at least, being a convicted winner was a decent cover for losing.

On the track, though, the image of Fallon was not quite so healthy. A chequered past, a natural antipathy to authority and an intimidating presence did not prompt the sort of warmth unequivocally accorded the arch showman, Frankie Dettori. The flying dismount was just not the appropriate trademark for Fallon, who greeted his big winners with a handsome smile but no flamboyance, and although Fallon had learnt to handle authority and was a persuasive speaker in front of the stewards when a winner was at stake, there was a sense, compounded and finally proved in the latter stages of the 2004 season when he and Dettori were fighting for the title, that Fallon, in the corridors of racing's ultimate power, was not a popular champion. In the summer of 2006, the difference of opinion assumed an altogether more familiar dimension.

'The Irish view is that he's one of our own, a young Irish lad who has come from nothing, has done good over in England and now he's come back and good on him,' Donn McClean, the Irish racing correspondent of the *Sunday Times*, said at the time. 'I don't think there would be much debate that he's the best rider around at the moment, and the people over here are behind him now, for sure. The punters love him because he gives everything a ride, and people are willing to overlook his other side because they regard him as a genius and all geniuses have their flaws.'

Fallon, wearing jeans and a striped black T-shirt, arrived at Bishopsgate police station just after 9 a.m. on that summer morning, the first of the twenty-eight people summoned to answer bail. Confirmation of the charges took a mere twenty minutes, but racing was feeling the aftershock many months later. Jason Weaver, an old weighing-room friend, now a pundit for At The Races, one of two dedicated racing channels, rang Fallon late that morning to say how shocked he was to hear the news. 'Not half as shocked as I am,' replied Fallon, deadpan. Racing's reaction was much the same. All along, while Fallon was technically under arrest yet still riding, the suggestion was that, not for the first time, the law had over-reached itself. The scepticism stemmed in part from the arrests of Jamie Osborne, Dean Gallagher and Leighton Aspell eight years earlier in a case that had all the makings of a Whitehall farce. No charges were ever brought against any of those jockeys, yet all of them were kept under suspicion for four months. Years later, Osborne was able to laugh about the dawn raid on his cottage in Lambourn and his subsequent questioning in a Reading police station. As he was released on bail after a morning's interrogation, the police still had one more question to ask. 'Got a winner for this afternoon, Jamie?'

Racing still believed that somehow it was above the law of the land, unpoliceable, a no-go area, subject only to its own rules, which were enshrined in a hefty handbook compiled by the former Jockey Club and indecipherable by anyone raised outside the confines of this bizarre little kingdom. How could the police understand the complexities of the handicapping system, or know the difference between a brilliantly constructed betting coup and a criminal offence? The police had largely stayed clear of the sport of kings until it became entangled in a wider criminal net. The case of Brian Wright, a drug dealer and sponsor of a widespread doping ring, revealed the extent of potential corruption inside racing, and the 'nudge-nudge, wink-wink' culture that inadvertently encouraged it. At the heart of the controversial 'Panorama' programme broadcast by the BBC in October 2002 was the Jockey Club's inability to regulate its own sport effectively, to distinguish the difference between outright corruption and institutionalised collusion. It made its point well enough to prompt a significant re-examination of racing's relationship with the courts. Given unexpected help from the increasingly powerful betting exchanges, the new Horseracing Regulatory Authority, which had taken over the role as racing's official rulemaker from the old and outdated Jockey Club,* professionalised its security department, broadened its range of intelligence sources and started to view the practices deemed acceptable for three centuries through a more powerful set of binoculars. The more regular beat of the officers of the City of London Police was business fraud. Now racing was being judged by the same standards as the stock exchange. Insider trading – the passing on of information for profit, information unknown to the general public, which was standard practice for years in the Square Mile and no less on the racetrack and in the betting shop – was now deemed a criminal offence.

With the case costing £3 million already, and sceptical judgement being passed on their competence – notably by Christopher Stewart-Moore, Fallon's lawyer – Steve Wilmott, head of the City Economic Crime Division, was at pains to stress the extent of the investigation.

'The amount of work undertaken by the investigation team has been immense,' he said. 'During the course of the investigation, we have arrested thirty-four people, conducted over five hundred interviews, taken more than thirteen hundred statements and provided over five thousand exhibits and nearly forty thousand pages of evidence to the Crown Prosecution Service and counsel.'

The City of London Police were under almost as much pressure as the champion jockey. Now that they had charged one of the most high-profile figures in the sport, their work was guaranteed national headlines on television and in every newspaper. Operation Krypton, the codename

---

* On 3 April 2006, the Horseracing Regulatory Authority (HRA) replaced the Jockey Club as the governing body of UK racing. On 31 July 2007, the HRA merged with the British Horseracing Authority (BHA).

for the investigation, had to produce a result. Even the *Financial Times*, not noted for its dedication to racing, carried the story of Fallon's criminal charges on its front page. But few, even at the HRA, knew the extent of the evidence or the breadth of the investigation. Racing took a deep breath and braced itself for the inevitable backlash. Corruption in racing, race-fixing, was once again headline news and whether anyone liked it or not, innocent or guilty, Fallon was the symbolic bad penny.

The charges were not the only piece of bad news for the former champion, not by a long shot. As soon as he was charged, Fallon's licence to ride in the UK was automatically suspended. Fallon's riding licence was issued by the racing authorities in Ireland, who made it clear that their man was innocent until proved guilty and would be allowed to continue riding. However, to ride in the UK again, Fallon had to apply to a hastily convened three-man panel for the return of his licence. With a trial probably more than a year away, by conservative estimates, and the Coolmore operation reliant for much of its business on winning the big races in England, it was not just Fallon's reputation at stake, but his livelihood and his career. If the panel denied Fallon's appeal, he was effectively banned from UK racetracks until further notice. The panel heard the case on Friday, 7 July, the day before Fallon was due to ride Aussie Rules for Aidan O'Brien in the Coral Eclipse Stakes at Sandown Park, one of the major set-piece races of the season.

There might have been an omen in the fact that Fallon's first ride of the season, back in April, had been in the Crimestoppers Handicap at Windsor. Even Fallon appreciated the black humour of it. He had taken the winter off, but his face reflected the strain of the past year. Jockeys' faces can pinpoint the time of the season as clearly as the trees or the sky. Bright and clear in spring, their eyes are dark and ringed by high summer as a relentless round of evening meetings and endless hours on motorways takes its toll. It's rarely a good idea to interview a jockey in July or August, unless you want to do it on the run, or write in monosyllables. Fallon's face at Windsor, tight and drawn, was a weary, mid-August face. For once, he looked every one of his 41 years, as if the cares of the world had fallen squarely on his slender figure, a symbol of a troubled season ahead.

His private life did not offer much support or respite from the outside world. In February, Sam Wallin, a former assistant trainer with Mark Wallace in Newmarket, had again claimed that Fallon was the father of her young son, James Kieren Wallin, having previously claimed he was the father of her unborn child, then subsequently retracted the claim. Fallon himself has always denied paternity, and his name is not on the birth certificate. Julie Fallon had already had to endure a succession of tabloid stories about her husband's alleged affairs, the most recent of them had linked him with Kerri Radcliffe, a bloodstock agent fifteen years Fallon's junior, and it was no surprise that she returned to Newmarket from Ireland with the three children in the summer of 2005, effectively ending the couple's eleven-year marriage.

Yet, of all the jockeys setting out in pursuit of their hopes and dreams in the spring of 2006, Fallon had the most to savour. Four or five potential Classic winners could be ready and waiting for the Guineas, any one of which would be the star in other stables. This would also be the first season that would fully reflect Fallon's influence at Coolmore, on the way that horses had been taught their business on the gallops and on the racetrack. A successful season for Coolmore would bring further proof of Fallon's unparalleled horsemanship and intuitive understanding, the qualities that had once led Aidan O'Brien to describe his stable jockey as more like an assistant trainer. Privately, Fallon harboured thoughts of a record-breaking season, for him and his employees.

'I wanted to ride more Group One winners this season than I had ever ridden before,' Fallon told Donn McClean later in the year. 'I thought we had the horses to do it.'

Among them, one stood out, for ability and personality. The mere mention of George Washington would lighten Fallon's face in those early spring months. You didn't need any further explanation, the quiet smile said it all. This one could be something special. In his five starts as a two-year-old, the bay son of Danehill had recorded four victories, his only defeat coming in his first start, in May 2005, when he ran a little too freely down the Newmarket Heath. Three weeks later, he broke his maiden impressively, Fallon giving him a copybook ride over six furlongs at the Curragh, and he followed up in the Group Two Railway Stakes when the first signs of real temperament began to show.

After preening himself in the winner's enclosure for a while, George Washington refused to relinquish his place and return to the shadows of the stables until coaxed away by handfuls of grass and the enticement of a stablemate. It was not the last display of exhibitionism by a horse who was quickly dubbed Gorgeous George by the racing press. George was always looking for the red carpet.

Only in August, on the day of the Phoenix Stakes, did the full extent of George Washington's star quality become evident. In a race that Aidan O'Brien had dominated, but had not initially considered as ideal for a horse bred to stay farther, George Washington produced what James Willoughby, chief racing correspondent of the *Racing Post*, described as 'the two-year-old performance of the season'. The standard of the opposition was open to question, but not the distance of eight lengths that separated him from stablemate Amadeus Mozart, or the time, which Willoughby, a student of these things, thought 'sensational'. Using the phrase 'natural speed' comes as second nature to Aidan O'Brien, partly because it is a quality cherished by breeders – and from the moment they walk on to a racetrack, all Coolmore horses are walking billboards – and partly because Ballydoyle horses are bred to possess it. So the animation with which the usually taciturn and quietly spoken O'Brien talked about George Washington suggested that this one was different.

Just how different, we found out on the day of the 2,000 Guineas at Newmarket, the opening Classic of the 2006 English flat season. In the calm and logical way in which they do things at Coolmore, Fallon was left to sort out the tactics of the race for himself. It's on days like these that the instinctive trust between jockey and trainer is tested to its absolute limit. Getting the fractions right in a seller at Wolverhampton is one thing; keeping cool under the pressure of a Classic, where the difference between a right and a wrong decision can be measured in seven figures, is quite another. Although a master of detail, and very far from the gentle soul seen so often in the winner's enclosure, O'Brien resisted the temptation to overburden his jockey with any tactical masterplan. Top jockeys, the ones you want on your side on the big day, are marked out by their flexibility of thought, by their ability to compute the percentages and switch plan in a matter of strides. A gap appears sooner than you want, do you take it and risk reaching the front too soon? Do you leave it and risk being boxed in? The best jockeys have all done their homework, but they also have an intuitive sense of where the gaps might come and how horses might run in front of them and around them. They also get the big decisions right. Jockeys will say that good horses make good jockeys, just as Michael Schumacher was only as good as his car. It is an immutable law of sport that the best drivers tend to find the wheel of the best cars and the best jockeys tend to ride the best horses. Still, with the hype surrounding George Washington building by the hour and the money pouring on to his white blaze – and a 1.15 million guinea price tag to justify (he was the most expensive yearling in Europe in 2004) – there was no margin for error.

Fourteen runners went to post for the 198th running of the Classic, and all morning and through much of the early afternoon only one name rustled the spring leaves in the Newmarket paddock. Plenty of Coolmore horses had floundered here in previous years but there was a persistence to the whispers this time that brooked no argument. Coolmore had a serious horse on its hands and the rest of us were about to find out just how serious. The sense of anticipation was suffocating, the same tightening of the grip that prefaces the starting gun at an Olympic 100m, the knowledge that in a twinkling of an eye a reputation will be made or broken. Brough Scott, a brilliant chronicler of racing's moods, wrote of the next one minute 36.86 seconds of pulsating action:

> The best horses I have seen up the Rowley Mile have been Nijinsky, Brigadier Gerard, El Gran Senor and Dancing Brave. After each one, there was a moment of buzzing wonderment…as Kieren Fallon loosed his bright bay partner past the pacemaking Olympian Odyssey and Sir Percy, that moment came again. This horse, and here comes another dangerous word, was different class.

At face value, the two-and-a-half-length victory over Sir Percy did not warrant such classification, but so positive had been the vibes for the runner-up from Martin Dwyer, the jockey, and the trainer, Marcus

Tregoning, that they seemed mildly shell-shocked by the ease with which their flying colt had been dismantled by the winner. It was in the berth for second place that George Washington's performance was truly defined. The amiable Tregoning, still searching for his first Classic winner – he did not have to wait long – and Dwyer, the ebullient Liverpudlian, consoled themselves with the thought that Sir Percy had run a top-class trial for the Derby. Yet in the preliminaries they would not hear of defeat. As it turned out, Sir Percy could have occupied the spot for the winner anyway.

At Newmarket, the winner's enclosure is situated at the end of a curved walkway down into the paddock. After a big race, the public gather on the steps to welcome home the winner, while the press and photographers hover around the connections, waiting for the best quotes and the best photos. Gorgeous George had other ideas. In defiance of 197 years of tradition, he had decided that enough was enough, that he could take or leave the plaudits for the victor. Despite the coaxing of Fallon, O'Brien and Pat Keating, Coolmore's travelling head lad, George Washington had seen the pre-parade ring where he had been saddled and decided, quite logically, that he would only be unsaddled in the same spot. The crowds gathered on the terracing around the paddock waited in vain to acknowledge the new champion while a rather embarrassed O'Brien was left to explain himself and his horse beneath the tree in the antechamber.

'Sure, he has this way with him,' said Fallon, as if talking about an errant schoolboy. 'He hung back behind the stalls before the start but in the race he just blew them away.' Both Fallon and O'Brien were winning their fourth 2,000 Guineas.

'He doesn't believe any horse or human being should tell him what to do,' O'Brien explained. 'We never had a colt that had such a domineering instinct. In the barn, he can intimidate other horses just by looking at them. Other horses get out of his way. If he was in the wild, he would run to the front and then pull up. We've never had anything like this.'

For the usually taciturn O'Brien, this was the Gettysburg Address, delivered with all the animation of a soapbox orator. Now we knew we had seen something special. Now we knew exactly why Fallon had smiled like the Mona Lisa at the very mention of the name and why, having suffered a deep cut in his right foot just days before the Guineas, he had not even considered the prospect of bequeathing the ride on George Washington to anyone else.

Fallon made a particular point of thanking the doctors at Limerick Hospital for patching him up in time. In truth, they had no option. Fallon's unshakeable confidence in George Washington had carried Coolmore through the week and he was not going to miss the moment of vindication. There might not be many more left. Coolmore were widely tipped to repeat their double of the previous year with victory in the 1,000 Guineas, but Rumplestiltskin failed to emulate the feat of her grandmother Miesque in 1987 and could finish only seventh behind Speciosa, trained by Pam Sly, a farmer from the Fens with a small stable and a character almost as quirky as her wonder horse. Aidan O'Brien and Pam Sly? Racing had never seen glory shared by such an odd couple.

Just a week later, Fallon proved his mastery of Longchamp once more by conjuring a run up the rails on Aussie Rules in the Poule d'Essai des Poulains, the French 2,000 Guineas, every bit as audacious and calculated as his astonishing victory on Hurricane Run the previous autumn.

'I was a little bit frightened in the straight,' commented O'Brien on Aussie Rules' victory, 'but Kieren had told me beforehand what he was going to do.' And, Fallon claimed, he had been told what to do by Michael Tabor before the race. If so, it was an unlikely conversation.

To confirm the well being of the Coolmore horses, stablemate Marcus Andronicus finished second, while O'Brien also landed a double at Leopardstown on the same afternoon, Dylan Thomas winning the Derrinstown Stud Derby Trial in fine style under Seamus Heffernan, Fallon's understudy at Ballydoyle, and Queen Cleopatra taking the 1,000 Guineas Trial. As Sinndar, Galileo and High Chaparral had completed the Derrinstown–Derby double in successive years, Fallon now found himself with a lively chance of winning his third Derby in four years. The bookmakers were certainly taking no chances, cutting the odds on Dylan Thomas from 14–1 to 8–1. His problem was which horse to choose. Just days before, Fallon had guided Papal Bull to victory in the Chester Vase for his old boss, Sir Michael Stoute, in the familiar dark colours of Susan Magnier. Horatio Nelson, another of Coolmore's brightest prospects, had also caught Fallon's well-trained eye and when Septimus bolted up in the Dante, the race that had produced the last two Derby winners in North Light and Motivator, the extent of Fallon's dominance was equalled only by the breadth of his dilemma.

'It's going to be a tricky one to get right this year,' he said. No one was betting too heavily on defeat for Coolmore this time.

The season rolled on, not always according to the plans laid down in County Tipperary. On unseasonally heavy ground at the Curragh, George Washington was beaten by Araafa, fourth in the 2,000 Guineas three weeks earlier. Araafa proved himself a top-class horse in the St James's Palace Stakes at Royal Ascot a month later, but two days after his inexplicable defeat, George Washington was found to be lame. Some sceptics, those who had pronounced that George Washington might never be seen on a racecourse again after the Guineas, presumed that this was the ready excuse Coolmore needed to protect their future investment. Bow out while the lasting memory was of a horse at his peak on Newmarket Heath, cash in on the stud fees for a horse compared, if only for ninety-six seconds, to Nijinsky, Mill Reef and Dancing Brave. But O'Brien was not finished with Gorgeous George, not by a long way. Fallon, though, would never ride him again on the track.

On the Tuesday before the Derby, Fallon rode all four of the prospective Coolmore entries in their final piece of serious work – Horatio Nelson, Septimus, Dylan Thomas and Mountain. Privately, he still favoured Dylan Thomas, but so strong and powerful did Horatio Nelson feel that morning he was forced to change his mind. It proved a fateful decision. Bookmakers talked of the 'Fallon Factor' in the wake of Alexandrova's impressive victory in the Oaks the day before the Derby in a bid to whip up a challenge to Visindar, the long-time favourite from Andre Fabre's Chantilly stable, at the head of the market. It didn't work. On the day, Horatio Nelson went off at 11–2 while Visindar strengthened to 2–1.

In extricating Alexandrova from an unpromising position at the bottom of Tattenham Hill in the Oaks, Fallon had showed an unusual streak of caution in his decision-making. In the past, he might well have persevered with his challenge through the centre of the field or up the rail, but riding for Coolmore had instilled in him a new sense of confidence and trust. It was the same philosophy adopted by Aidan O'Brien: 'I've been given some of the best horses in the world to train. All I have to do is not mess them up.' Fallon was learning, as Jamie Spencer did not, that the same principle applied to the stable jockey. In the decisive move of the race, Fallon switched his filly to the outside and simply pressed the button. Alexandrova swept past the field, her turn of foot drawing comparisons with Reams of Verse and Ouija Board, two of Fallon's other three Oaks winners, to win by six lengths. 'I didn't think she would improve that much,' he said. The following morning, the *Racing Post* featured a full-page photo of Fallon on its front cover, taken, inevitably by Edward Whitaker, the supreme photo-chronicler of racing's many moods. Fallon's gloved hand is acknowledging the reception for Alexandrova. There is no hint of flamboyance or arrogance in the gesture, but the smile shows the champion, for the split second of a camera shutter, at peace with the world and with himself. The strapline asks readers a serious question: 'He won the Oaks yesterday – can you afford to ignore the king of Epsom on Derby day?'

The answer this time was a categoric 'yes'. Fallon had chosen Horatio Nelson as his Derby mount, but as Martin Dwyer found the narrowest of gaps on the rails to bring a fairytale win for Sir Percy and his owners, Anthony and Victoria Pakenham, eyes were inexorably drawn to another, contrasting, tableau back down the course. Fallon had been concerned enough about Horatio Nelson's action to summon the vet to the start. In consultation with O'Brien, Jenny Hall, the course vet, passed the second favourite fit to race, but just as Fallon was asking his mount for a final challenge at the two-furlong mark, he heard the agonising crack of a broken bone. Fallon was commendably swift in realising the problem and dismounting. Part-owner John Magnier praised the rapid response of the ambulance services and the vets and, although callers rang and e-mailed the BBC to ask why the horse had been allowed to take part if his fitness was in doubt, no blame could be attached to the connections. None of that lessens the sickening sense of doubt that lingers in the mind of the jockey, who can do nothing but calm his stricken horse and pray for the best. With a cannon-bone badly fractured, a fetlock joint dislocated and potential infection to the open wounds around the injury, the vets had no alternative but to put Horatio Nelson down. Fallon gave up his ride on Indian Trail in the last and headed for home, unrecognisable from the smiling champion of the previous afternoon.

A story told to me later by Andrew Balding is pertinent to Fallon's response at Epsom. Ironically, it features that old rogue, Top Cees, who had brought the Ramsdens and Fallon to court to defend their integrity all those years ago. Since the Ramsdens' retirement, Top Cees had been transferred to Kingsclere, where he was nominally trained by Ian Balding, but actually in the care of young Andrew, who had known the horse from his days in the north.

'He came down to us and we missed a whole season with him because of injury,' Andrew recalled. 'Then he won up at Ayr with Kieren and it was like they had won the Derby, Kieren was so pleased. The following season, we took him back to the Chester Cup. He was ten, but he was still joint third favourite. I went to collect the saddle from the weighing-room and Kieren told me not to run him. "The ground's dried out," he said. Dad was holding the licence, but Top Cees was always my horse, so it was my decision. I thought, "Christ, he's on the front of the *Racing Post* or whatever, he's one of the favourites for the race and the owner's come over from Monaco to see him run." I told Kieren, "We'll have to run him, but just look after him." "How the fuck can I look after him in the Chester Cup?" he said. Sure enough, the horse breaks down after six furlongs. Kieren was absolutely foul and he was quite right. He only calmed down when I rang him later to say the horse was all right. It was a bad decision by me, but his reaction was just because he genuinely cared about the horse.'

Fallon's reaction to the loss of Horatio Nelson would have been no less emotional just because, in contrast to Top Cees, this was a young horse. If Fallon had doubts about the wisdom of the decision, he was wise enough not to express them in public. Few people could have resisted the pressure, within minutes of the start, to take a chance and run the second favourite in the Derby. It just so happens that Kieren Fallon, Aidan O'Brien and John Magnier are three of the people who could.

'He was just one of the best little horses I've ever been around,' Fallon said at Chantilly the following day. 'He wanted to do everything for you and those are the horses you want to be associated with, but if I wasn't happy with him, I wouldn't have gone around there on him, especially down that hill.'

The emotional index over those twenty-four hours at Epsom mimicked and mocked the course of the following two months. At Royal Ascot, Fallon was fortunate to survive a stewards' enquiry to win the Queen Anne Stakes on Ad Valorem, who veered violently towards the rails in the closing 300 yards, impeding both Peeress and the eventual runner-up, Court Masterpiece, ridden by Jamie Spencer. Fallon was found guilty of careless riding and banned for four days, but to the surprise of everyone bar the bookmakers, who had interpreted the rules more astutely, Ad Valorem was allowed to keep the race after a fifteen-minute deliberation by the stewards. Two days later, Yeats brought Fallon and Coolmore their second winner of the meeting in the Ascot Gold Cup. Victory by a cool four lengths at odds of 7–1 suggested two things. One was that, at last, at the age of five, Yeats had found his optimum distance over the Gold Cup trip of two and a half miles, and the other was that the public had long given up on this enigmatic under-achiever. How else do you explain those insultingly long odds? Fallon was just delighted to bring O'Brien his first Ascot Gold Cup winner and to be contemplating a trip to Australia in the autumn for the race that 'stops the nation', the Melbourne Cup.

As significant for Fallon was the announcement by the Horseracing Regulatory Authority in the week before Royal Ascot that two jockeys, Dean Williams and Brian Reilly, had been charged in a new corruption case involving ten races over a fifty-two-day period between December 2004 and February 2005. They were subsequently banned by the HRA for eighteen months. Owen Churchill, a bookmaker and former owner, was also charged with the laying of horses in those races and banned for eight years by the HRA. A familiar pattern to the investigations was starting to emerge after the five-year ban imposed on Gary Carter by the disciplinary panel of the HRA the previous autumn. Central to all the cases was the ability of the security department, headed by Paul Scotney, a former policeman, to monitor client accounts through their Memorandum of Understanding with Betfair, and to persuade the High Court to allow investigation of individual phone records, often without the knowledge of the individuals concerned. Carter's links to the accomplices, who laid eight horses to lose in a systematic and corrupt betting operation, could be traced through his phone records. Carter did not defend himself, because, he said, of the costs involved, and was already out of the country by the time his ban was announced. Scotney's point, made forcefully in an article in *Owner and Breeder* magazine in May 2006, was that many of the people involved in the HRA's investigations had been corrupting the sport long before the introduction of betting exchanges. What had changed was not just the technology of betting but the technology of policing.

The charges laid against Fallon on the morning after his victory in the Irish Derby on Dylan Thomas brought into question the whole credibility of the sport. 'Royal jockey is charged with throwing races' ran one headline in the *Daily Mail*. 'Fallon charged in £10m race-fixing scandal' roared the *Sun*. Less obviously anticipated were the immediate implications for Fallon's career. The difference in the attitudes of the two racing authorities in Ireland and the UK became apparent within hours of the news from the City of London police.

'We have noted what has happened with the Kieren Fallon situation,' said Denis Egan, chief executive of the Irish Turf Club. 'We may or may not be asked by the British authorities to reciprocate the ban on him riding. However, if we are asked, it is highly unlikely that we would ban him. He has been charged and we will await developments. Our attitude is one of a person being innocent until proved guilty and for that reason we would be most unlikely to ban him from riding in Ireland.'

The Irish authorities could not have fired a louder warning shot across the bows of the HRA and its disciplinary panel had they summoned the Irish Artillery. But this was a steelier governing body than before, better able to look in on itself from the normal world and to look itself in the eye. By the evening of 7 July, Fallon knew it, too. He had hoped to be free to partner Aussie Rules in the Coral Eclipse the following afternoon. Instead, he was locked in a fight for his future. If Fallon was surprised by the extent of the charges laid against him by the City of London Police, he was devastated by the decision of the three-man panel, which effectively banned him from riding in the UK until the end of his trial. Fallon, who appeared at the hearing in dark suit and tie, left through an underground car park just after midday, shielded from photographers, before the decision was announced but issued a statement through his solicitors, Burton Copeland.

'I am obviously devastated by the decision,' he said. 'I cannot under-stand it as I am confident I have done nothing wrong. My lawyers are confident that the case against me has no validity. Unless my suspension is lifted, my career is in ruins. I cannot ask owners and trainers to support me elsewhere when I am prevented from riding in the UK.'

The nub of the panel's decision, said Michael Connell, the chairman and former High Court judge, lay in balancing the rights of the individuals to pursue their livelihoods and the potential damage that might be done to racing, both in reality and perception, if 'persons the subject of a serious criminal charge are permitted to ride pending trial'. The panel concluded that the 'damage done would be very hard to repair and, as the regulator, we are anxious to avoid the damage'. Fallon's lawyers argued that the original case against him had no substance and that, at the very least, their client should be allowed to continue riding pending a hearing to prove it. But it was not, added Connell, the job of the panel to 'assess the strength or otherwise of the prosecution case', nor was it their task 'to decide on guilt or innocence' nor 'to second guess the Crown Prosecution Service or the Director of Public Prosecutions'. It was a very public statement of intent by the HRA, who invited proper scrutiny of the logic by releasing the panel's ruling in full to the press. The panel recognised the hardship that would be caused to Fallon, Lynch and Williams by a ban, even acknowledging that Fallon might lose his contract with Coolmore, which was due to expire at the end of the season. But the ban still stood.

Fallon swiftly announced his intention to appeal against the decision, but, in reality, he knew that his chances of overturning the ruling either through the HRA or in the High Court, which had always shown a reluctance to intervene in the disciplinary procedures of sporting authorities, were negligible. Fallon returned to Ireland and the familiar routines of his life. In Ireland, he was innocent until proved guilty; in England, he felt persecuted and, in his darkest moments, which were many, hunted. The establishment, he told those close to him, had always been against him and now they had got their man. It was left to Aidan O'Brien to articulate the feelings not just of Ballydoyle and Coolmore, Fallon's outwardly supportive employers, but of a broad section of the racing community, who similarly felt that one of their own was being hounded from the sport.

Unless the subject is George Washington, O'Brien is not the most forthcoming of trainers in victory or defeat. He is courteous and attentive to the press, but acutely wary of how costly a misplaced word might be to Coolmore and the future earning power of its expensively bred inmates. But, on the Friday of the July meeting at Newmarket, the flow of O'Brien's rhetoric reached all the way to the steps of the HRA's new headquarters in Shaftesbury Avenue, and because it was O'Brien speaking, there was a widespread feeling that this was Magnier, Tabor and Smith talking, too. Initially reluctant to speak, when cornered, as he knew he would be, by the daily racing reporters, O'Brien became so caught up by his own passion that he spoke almost without punctuation for almost fifteen minutes. Fallon's ears must have been burning.

'Kieren is the most unbelievable jockey that we have ever dealt with,' O'Brien began. 'He is an absolute master of his craft. We go back and look over the records – we keep records – and he senses things other people don't. So instead of condemning him, we should be celebrating him, not, like a lot of geniuses are, when they are dead and gone for twenty years.'

More pertinently for the potential battles ahead, O'Brien also highlighted two specific attributes of his stable jockey. One was his incredible will to win, the other, his sparing use of the whip, which stemmed, said O'Brien, from his absolute respect for the horse. Privately, O'Brien spoke of his surprise that the evidence of an Australian expert on race interpretation might be regarded as critical to the case, pointing out the very different styles of whip use in the two hemispheres.

'Nobody gets as much out of a horse without hitting him,' O'Brien continued. 'Kieren very rarely uses his stick. He won a handicap at Naas the other day, you should look at the tape. Though he was still two lengths down, he put his stick down and won by a head. He knew the horse was giving as much as he could. He has such respect for the horses. Speak to the other trainers, any of the trainers he rides for, and they will all say the same. Kieren wants to win every race he rides in, but not at the cost of the horse. If he does have a fault, it's that he is too open with people, but I just hope everyone can get out of this mess without anyone looking stupid.'

In the most telling analogy of all, O'Brien said that losing Fallon's services in the UK was 'like taking a wheel off a car', but he also outlined a continuing role for the beleaguered jockey in the hierarchy at Bally-doyle, which was aimed as much at Fallon as the journalists surrounding him in the parade ring. 'Kieren would still be totally involved in those horses he can't ride,' he added. 'He will be able to say how to ride them and will want every horse to win, even though he is not riding. That's the way he is. Kieren would die for horses. He wouldn't come back from the injury like he has unless he loved it like nothing else. Kieren is going to get better, if racing allows him. I just hope that the most unbelievable talent we have had doesn't get destroyed.'

Spoken in the very heart of the English racing establishment on the very day that the HRA released its reasons for rejecting Fallon's appeal, O'Brien's pleas reverberated like thunder through the corridors of power and deep into the offices of the City of London police. This was not just a brilliant young trainer speaking – 'the Kid' as Magnier refers to O'Brien – but the voice of a great racing empire. It was also a touching personal reference for a colleague down on his luck. When the stream of words had dried up and O'Brien had walked away, the press were too stunned to speak. The racing would not be getting much coverage that day.

O'Brien was not the only spokesman for the beleaguered former

champion. Surprisingly perhaps, given the paper's topsy-turvy relationship with Fallon down the years, the *Racing Post* came out in favour
of allowing him to ride in a strongly worded editorial on Friday, 7 July.
The majority of Fallon's trainers also voiced their public support, but
the HRA were determined to stick to their position. On the evening of
his appeal hearing at HRA headquarters, Fallon returned to Naas,
recording a treble on Flamingo Guitar for David Wachman, Hitchcock
and Savannah for O'Brien. Clearly, Fallon's judgement on the racetrack
was immune to the debate swirling around his head, and when Alexandrova won the Irish Oaks for Fallon and Coolmore two days after
O'Brien's passionate outburst, there was a growing sense that, not for
the first time, an innocent Irish lad had been subject to some rough
British justice. There was no other way to interpret the thunderous roars
that greeted Fallon's return to the winner's enclosure at the Curragh on
that blisteringly hot afternoon. 'For the racing public, the moment was
all about solidarity,' wrote Alastair Down in the *Racing Post*.

In truth, this was not one of Fallon's most taxing tactical rides. It did
not need to be, so confident was he in the quality of his filly, and so
effortlessly did Alexandrova answer her jockey's call to cut down the
six-runner field two and a half furlongs from home. Once Fallon had
manoeuvred the odds-on favourite to the rail, the race was effectively
decided. Alexandrova accelerated smoothly along the rail, took up the
running a furlong out and had a comfortable four lengths to spare over
Sir Michael Stoute's improving filly, Scottish Stage, at the finish.

'We were here for the Derby a couple of weeks ago and that was a
really good feeling,' said the winning jockey. 'The reception I got was
the best in the world and it was no different today. It does help, it's
a little pick-me-up, but I'm quite relaxed about it all because I know
I have done nothing wrong.'

The majority of the Curragh seemed to know it, too, but the confidence was stripped bare the following day when Fallon lined up with
ten others behind a glass panel at the City of London magistrates court
number 1 to hear the charges and to apply for bail. In less than fifteen
minutes, the formalities were over. All eleven were granted unconditional bail, with Fallon due to stand in the first of three separate trials

alongside Miles Rodgers, Fergal and Shaun Lynch, Darren Williams and Philip Sherkle at a date and venue to be announced. Shorn of the lustre of the racetrack, Fallon's face was pale and pinched, his expression barely changing as he left the court and contemplated his appeal to the High Court, his last possible hope of overturning his ban in the UK.

Fallon returned to Ireland to a routine that was both comforting and depressing. Jockeys ride out in the mornings only on the tacit under-standing that they might have a chance of riding the same horses in the afternoon at the racetrack. Fallon's role at Coolmore was different in that it involved educating young Thoroughbreds each and every day, then educating them some more under the pressure of a race. Coolmore loved the continuity of thought that Fallon brought to the process and the swift understanding he had struck up with O'Brien. They seemed to talk the same language and share the same sense of respect, which augured well for a prosperous future. Now Fallon's part in a complex operation had been diminished. He could still work with the horses on the gallops, prepare them and educate them as Coolmore promised that he could do, but on big days at Newmarket, Ascot and York, Fallon would have to give up his most significant role to an understudy, someone who might not be able to communicate so effectively either with the horses or the humans at Coolmore. He could still ride in France and Ireland – possibly America and Hong Kong – but the geographic parameters only heightened the strange sense of isolation Fallon felt back in his new home inside the grounds of Ballydoyle. He was doing half his job and that, from his days back in Crusheen, had never been his way.

If Fallon did not fully comprehend the severity of his sentence, he surely did so during two days at the end of July when the renewal of the King George VI and Queen Elizabeth Diamond Stakes, back at Ascot once more, marked the apex of the English flat-racing season. Fallon's desperate hope was that, on Friday, the High Court would overturn the HRA's ban and allow him to take up his King George appointment with Hurricane Run, on whom he had won the Arc so spectacularly the previous autumn. But, in a seventy-minute hearing, Mr Justice Davis dismissed Fallon's appeal with a faintly damning assessment of his case. The interim case summary provided by the Crown Prosecution Service indicated seven different areas of evidence against Fallon. 'It does not,' said Justice Davis, 'rest solely on video evidence of races that Fallon rode in. It would have been inappropriate, unfair and potentially misleading to have considered partial evidence leading to a mini trial.'

Worse was to come on the following afternoon, not in the sense that Fallon would begrudge the connections of Hurricane Run their victory, but that he was not there on the day his battle-hardened partner joined the illustrious company of Ribot, Ballymoss, Mill Reef, Dancing Brave, Lammtarra and Montjeu in winning both an Arc and a King George. Whether by design or accident, Christophe Soumillon, the nerveless young Belgian standing in for Fallon, conjured up a run down the rails almost as audacious and every bit as successful as Fallon's at Longchamp. The one consolation for Fallon was the news that John Magnier had at last voiced his support with the withering suggestion that he would be reading *Alice in Wonderland* because he gathered there was more fact in it than the case against his stable jockey, and that the battle being waged in the English courts was 'far from over'. It sounded remarkably like a threat. Fallon was equally gratified to be asked to ride a horse owned by Vincent O'Brien – and trained by his son, Charles – at Leopardstown on Saturday evening, an ostentatious show of support from Ireland's greatest horseman. On Sunday, Fallon journeyed east to ride in the Turkish Derby, happy perhaps to find another country where he could readily ply his trade. His mount, though, finished well down the field. More ominously, Fallon reportedly put up eight pounds overweight.

In England the season rolled on through the dog days of August when the shadows lengthen under the eyes of jockeys travelling too many miles to ride in too many races. Depending on who you listened to, the weighing-room collectively breathed a sigh of relief that they could get on with the job of race-riding without the taint of suspicion prompted by Fallon's presence, or fell into a heap of depression at the loss of their spokesman and considerable champion. Both opinions were expressed in private. The prevailing mood was of uncertainty and fear. If Fallon, the most successful jockey in the game, was wanted in a court of law on what seemed the flimsiest of evidence, who would be next? Like the patron of the peloton in the Tour de France, Fallon shaped opinion in the weighing-room and events on the racetrack through sheer force of personality. He knew it and others knew it, too. Few were prepared to oppose him too openly.

Fallon's popularity was genuine, though. He was generous with advice, quick to help the younger generation and utterly loyal to the intimacy of the tightest knit community in sport. Hayley Turner still recalls a quiet exchange from early in her career. 'Hayley,' said a familiar voice as the horses were pulling up, 'hitting the shit out of tired horses won't make them go faster.' It was Fallon, so she listened, and because Turner is smart and industrious, she remembered, subsequently becoming not just the first female champion apprentice but comfortably the most accomplished woman rider of her generation. If an apprentice had forgotten his goggles, Kieren always had a spare pair and he never asked for them back. Whichever view you took, the weighing-room was an eerie place without one of its most recognisable inmates.

In early August, Robert Winston, a close friend of Fallon's, whose career had followed a distinctly similar path, was charged by the HRA with corruption along with three other jockeys, Fran Ferris, Robbie Fitzpatrick and Luke Fletcher. Winston received a one-year ban from the HRA, with Ferris getting two years and Fitzpatrick and Ferris banned for three years. Three months later, Shane Kelly joined the list of jockeys under investigation and was eventually banned for a year by the HRA. At the same time, Fallon was finding out the extent of the HRA's international jurisdiction, having been denied a licence to ride in the Arlington Million in Chicago by the US authorities, a decision that effectively ended his hopes of partnering Coolmore's challengers in the Breeders' Cup in New York in late October. The potential significance of Fallon's absence became clear in the Celebration Mile at Goodwood.

The race marked the much-heralded return of George Washington. Mick Kinane, once the stable jockey at Coolmore, replaced Fallon and, according to O'Brien, would face a 'big learning curve' in trying to understand the quixotic ways of the brilliant 2,000 Guineas winner. Although impeccably behaved in the preliminaries, George Washington ran too freely in the early stages of the race over the rolling downs of Sussex, and Kinane could only watch in mild horror as David McCabe on board River Tiber, the nominal Coolmore pacemaker, disappeared at a cracking gallop, ignored by the rest of the field. By the time Kinane had gathered the odds-on favourite together for a challenge, Frankie Dettori and Michael Hills, two old pros who knew exactly what was happening, had stolen the finish for themselves, Godolphin's Caradak prevailing by a short head from the 50–1 shot Killybegs. Had Fallon been riding for Coolmore, the outcome might well have been the same, but the race did nothing to lessen O'Brien's belief in the importance of continuity in the whole Coolmore operation. Fallon, as Kinane had before him, provided that extra vital layer of understanding.

Fallon settled into the life of a part-time jockey, riding out every morning and racing in the afternoon. But the rhythm of racing in Ireland is very different from in England, as competitive, but gentler and less frenetic. Fallon, although a proud Irishman, was not particularly enamoured with the facilities at many of the tracks and had voiced his criticism sharply since his return home. He was used to better and he felt his fellow jockeys should be treated better. For a man returning home, Fallon felt a stranger, forced to fight every inch of the way in 25-runner fields against jockeys who all wanted his scalp. It wasn't quite as he had imagined. He had a lot of time on his hands.

George Washington came to Ascot for the Queen Elizabeth II Stakes and showed himself every inch a champion by dominating a high-class field in a race marred by controversy. Pushed wide on the bend by Seamus Heffernan on Ivan Denisovich, George Washington's stable-mate, a furious Frankie Dettori dismounted Librettist and immediately accused Coolmore of employing blocking tactics. The stewards agreed and Heffernan was banned for fourteen days. That infuriated O'Brien and the angry exchange between Dettori and O'Brien, two of the sport's most respected figures, in the weighing-room afterwards – and in the press – merely highlighted the state of war that now existed between Coolmore and Godolphin, the world's two most powerful breeding empires. Heffernan took his case to the HRA and was absolved of deliberate blocking tactics but still suspended for seven days.

Everyone felt good for Mick Kinane, the winning rider, and for George, who had justified much of the hype hanging over his handsome head. But it was late September, tempers were getting shorter with the days and Fallon, for one, could not wait for a tortuous season to end.

Consolation came in the form of Holy Roman Emperor, the most promising of Coolmore's two-year-olds. He won the Phoenix Stakes in a canter under Fallon but was subsequently well beaten by Teofilo, trained by Jim Bolger, when odds-on in the National Stakes at the Curragh. Teofilo, the powerfully built son of Galileo, confirmed the form in the Dewhurst Stakes at Newmarket in mid-October, the most significant pointer to the early Classics the following year. The commanding nature of Teofilo's victory, his second over the best of Ballydoyle's crop of juveniles, brooked no argument and Bolger, not a man generally given to hyperbole, even talked of attempting the old-fashioned Triple Crown – 2,000 Guineas, Derby and St Leger – last won by Nijinsky in 1970. But although Holy Roman Emperor, under Mick Kinane, did not have the best of it, an air of quiet satisfaction still settled over Ballydoyle as O'Brien and his team reviewed the tape of the race and looked forward to an unusual winter, shorn of the pressure of housing the favourite for either the 2,000 Guineas or the Derby. They looked forward even more to the re-emergence of Holy Roman Emperor in the spring and to reversing the form with the unbeaten hotshot over the same turf in May.

Fallon's state of mind was a cause of more concern at Ballydoyle. In mid-October, the *Sunday Times'* Irish racing correspondent, Donn McClean, an excellent correspondent but no particular friend of Fallon's, was surprised to find his request for an interview granted. When Fallon seeks out a journalist to talk to, he has something he wants to say, and that proved to be the case. McClean met Fallon in the weighing-room at the Curragh on Beresford Stakes day. Fallon seemed surprisingly relaxed, much like his old self, still beating himself up for his dilatory ride in the Arc aboard Hurricane Run, the very same horse and at the very same venue that had proved a passport to glory just twelve months earlier.

'All week I was going to make the running and I never change my mind,' Fallon told McClean. Then he changed his mind. Some of the other jockeys in the stalls were saying that Dominique Boeuf was going to make the running on Irish Wells. Fallon didn't want to get into a duel at the front with a virtual no-hoper, so he listened for once and changed his mind. 'It may have cost us an Arc.' Fallon, John Lowe once noted, hates to let people down. Yet, by the end of the following month, there were plenty at Coolmore and beyond, those friends who had supported Fallon through some dark patches in his life, who felt deeply let down.

But that afternoon at the Curragh, Fallon had something else to say and he wanted to say it by megaphone so that the people in London, those responsible for spin-drying his life, would know he was serious.

'If we don't convince them that there is no case to answer,' Fallon told McClean, 'the top and bottom of it is that I'm gone. These boys [at Coolmore] can't hang on any longer. They haven't said anything to me, but that's what I think. If we had to wait for a court case in September or so, that would just be too long. They've got the best horses in the world and it's frustrating having to sort out jockeys. We thought it would be all over by now.' There was more. 'I'm going to train,' Fallon added when asked about his future. 'I've just decided over the last couple of weeks. A friend of mine in the UK has asked me and I have been thinking about it for a while.'* It seemed as if he was talking about sooner rather than later, but by the Sunday morning, when he was en route to Milan for the Group One Gran Criterium, the timescale had changed subtly. 'Eventually I will do it,' he told a *Racing Post* reporter. 'Ideally, it will be in a few years' time because I want to keep on riding. But I could be out of a job and as I want a career in racing, training appeals to me a lot.'

To occupy his mind and stop his stable jockey from brooding over his latest setback– a ban from riding at the Breeders' Cup in New York – O'Brien sent Fallon to Australia for the Melbourne Cup, extending his duties from riding Yeats, the Coolmore representative, to looking after every facet of the horse's well being in the lead-up to the race. In effect, Fallon was assistant trainer-cum-jockey. Off the track, Fallon was

* *Sunday Times*, 15 October 2006

meticulous in his duties, but, in a reversal of usual form, on it he came within a whisper of disaster. On his first ride in Australia, Fallon was deemed to have cut across the entire field at the start and was handed a ban that expired on the eve of the Melbourne Cup itself, nearly three weeks later. In an interview with Alan Lee of *The Times*,* Fallon sounded another sombre note about his impending retirement.

'If I sound disillusioned,' he told Lee, 'it's because this thing [the court case] has hung over me too long and time is running out. If I don't get it resolved before the start of the next Flat season, that's me finished. I'll have to retire.'

From the other side of the world, this sounded remarkably like another threat, but the chances are slim that the City of London Police read the racing pages, so it doubtless fell on deaf ears. Fallon would have to wait like any other for the wheels of justice to turn. But Lee perceptively noted one other aspect of Fallon's nature that afternoon as they watched the racing at Flemington. 'He [Fallon] was constantly anxious not to be offending anyone by sitting where he should not,' Lee wrote. In a strange environment, Fallon remained suspicious and insecure. The problem was that the environment he knew and loved had now shunned him. The hurt was beginning to show.

Yeats ran creditably enough to finish seventh in a race dominated by Japanese horses. Europe has yet to crack the Melbourne Cup, a slog around a tight oval track on treacherously hard ground against local hard nuts, but Fallon was philosophical enough in defeat. Three weeks later, with the flat season over, came the final indignity of an ignominious year. This time Fallon could blame no one but himself. On 29 November came news from France that Fallon had tested positive for cocaine after a routine drugs test taken at Chantilly in early July. There had been rumours of a positive test for a high-profile jockey for a few weeks, and the name of Fallon had increasingly been linked to the case, but when it was confirmed, the news prompted a collective shake of the head. The automatic six-month ban ruled Fallon out of race-riding anywhere until early June 2007, but many believed that the latest line

* *The Times*, Monday, 6 November 2006

in a chapter of controversies would prove to be the last. He had a right to appeal, but as both A and B samples were positive, no lawyer in the kingdom could recommend further legal action. Coolmore issued a terse statement acknowledging the suspension of their stable jockey by France Galop, the French racing authority, and saying only that, during the period of the suspension, they would use the best jockeys available.

Just before Christmas, Fallon returned to London for a case management hearing at the Old Bailey and used the opportunity to set a few things straight with the media. In another remarkable and contrary interview, with James Willoughby, chief racing correspondent at the *Racing Post*, Fallon denied that he had hinted at retirement and reported himself to be physically and mentally better than ever. Why, he asked rhetorically, would he ride out three lots every morning come rain or shine if he was going to quit? He talked animatedly of the young horses he was learning about every morning on the gallops and the potential physical improvement of both Dylan Thomas and Holy Roman Emperor.

'I am,' he announced blithely, oblivious to his downbeat mood just a few weeks before, 'in the best shape of my life. I could be like this for at least five more years.'

For a moment, he was just another jockey thinking big in winter. Only when Aidan O'Brien referred obliquely to the necessary discipline of riding out every day did an air of realism penetrate the fog of subversion. After the most turbulent year of his life, it became increasingly clear that Fallon's mental state was as changeable as ever. One moment he was quitting the saddle and turning to training, the next riding out every morning and loving every minute of it – optimistic, depressed, always on the brink of reform. He no longer knew what to say or what to think.

15

ON TRIAL AGAIN

'The land that Kieren lives in a lot of us don't understand.'

Aidan O'Brien

For much of the summer of 2007, Fallon had to watch from his home in Tipperary as other jockeys took his rides. Worse still, it was a decent, if not a vintage, year for Coolmore. So Coolmore horses did a lot of winning without Fallon. To make matters even worse, the jockey who benefited most from Fallon's inability to ride in the UK and America because of the criminal charges pending against him was Johnny Murtagh, not one of Fallon's best friends in the game and a rider who had largely been frozen out of the Coolmore reckoning the year before.

Peeping Fawn, for example, was unraced as a two-year-old and took four races to win her maiden, then won four straight Group Ones. At least Fallon was available to ride her in the Pretty Polly at the Curragh on her debut success in Group One, but Murtagh was on board – with Fallon elsewhere – for the Irish Oaks, the Nassau Stakes at Goodwood and the Yorkshire Oaks at York. If there were some comforting moments for Coolmore's stable jockey, they were provided by Dylan Thomas, who carried the flag for the Coolmore team in a relentless programme of top-class racing from April through to December. In that time, the extraordinary four-year-old had ten races, nine of them in Group One company, emerging with four Group One victories, including the King George at Ascot and the Arc at Longchamp. Of those ten races, Fallon was available to ride just two, winning both times in the Irish Champion (for the second year) and the Arc. The frustration seemed to spread through Fallon's normally irrepressible personality and even to fray the edges of his habitually nerveless race-riding.

Confined to the mundane midweek evening meetings at some of Ireland's more downhome tracks, Fallon was expected to return to his roots and make a strong bid for the Irish jockeys' title, despite his late start. He didn't. By the end of the season, Fallon had ridden just 24 winners in his native land, a tally that mocked the statistics of his heyday. But it was not just the total of winners that was a concern for everyone who knew how dangerous Fallon could be with time on his hands – it was the number of rides, a mere 198. Pat Smullen rode 94 winners from 672 rides to become champion ahead of the rising star of Irish racing, Declan McDonogh, son of Dessie, who trained Monksfield to win two Champion Hurdles in the seventies. Young McDonogh rode a career-high 82 winners from 602 rides and put himself on the list of potential long-range recruits for the job at Coolmore. Even Seamus Heffernan, Fallon's understudy at Ballydoyle, managed a pretty handsome 76 winners from 625 rides. No wonder O'Brien, Michael Tabor and John Magnier spent much of the season worrying about the health and the state of mind of their stable jockey.

At the Ballydoyle Open Day in April, Fallon was conspicuous by his presence, wearing a different coloured jacket from the neatly regimented ranks of work riders. O'Brien likes team players and he likes his stable jockeys to ride work every morning. And that means every morning. As Jamie Spencer, Fallon's predecessor in the job, found, Coolmore can be a claustrophobic place, for all the acres of prime horse country enveloping it. This is the racing equivalent of playing for Manchester United and nothing other than 100 per cent commitment to the colours is tolerated. For all his angelic appearance, O'Brien can be a tartar, a man of obsessive and wearing attention to detail. Although being gently punished by his employers for getting into trouble, Fallon was still determined not to conform entirely to the dress code, his blue jeans and a silk-like blue top contrasting with the black and burgundy livery of the other riders.

There wasn't much communication between O'Brien and Fallon that morning, nor was there much of a chance to learn the thoughts of the stable jockey about the firepower being unveiled before the assembled media on a dank morning in County Tipperary. O'Brien was in surprisingly relaxed mood, given that his leading Classic contender for the season, Holy Roman Emperor, had been whisked away to perform the stud duties of the infertile superstar, George Washington. The early retirement of Holy Roman Emperor had left a big hole in O'Brien's ammunition for the coming spring and, like a football manager who has just lost his centre-forward to injury for the season, O'Brien was casting around for a suitable substitute in the ranks of immaculately bred horseflesh circulating the indoor school at Ballydoyle. O'Brien would have known more than he was prepared to tell the press that morning, but he did seem entirely genuine in wondering out loud which ones might emerge as his Classic prospects. Fallon's uncanny ability to sense the potential of an undeveloped horse was invaluable in the process of selection. The only problem was that Fallon would not be available to continue the education on the racetrack, at least not for any of the English Classics, which was a source of untold frustration for trainer, owners and jockey. How can you be part of the team and not play in half the matches?

When he had finished his last lot riding out, Fallon emerged to give an interview about the potential in the stable and about his renewed love of squash, a sport that, he said, was now keeping him fit while the English courts stopped him from doing his proper job.

'I play squash with a cousin of Mick Kinane's, Brendan,' he told James Willoughby of the *Racing Post*. 'He's a very good player and he kills me every time, but it's competitive and that's what I love. I'm just passing time. By the time I've ridden four lots here, it's one o'clock. I have a shower, something to eat and then nearly every day I'll have a round of golf and play badminton or squash in the evening. A lot of the lads go home to bed for a couple of hours, but I could never do that. I'm so used to going racing every afternoon. It's a routine thing that Aidan started and it has worked out for me.'

He sounded bright and positive, happily reformed again, certain that the whole terrible misunderstanding with the City of London police and the UK authorities would be cleared up in a trice and that he would be back doing what he does best before the summer was out. Tacitly understood in his analysis was the need for him to keep busy, a fact equally understood by O'Brien.

The previous December, in response to the six-month ban imposed on him by the French authorities, Fallon had vowed to clean up his act and come back stronger and fitter.

'I will be better than ever next year,' he said at the time. 'I've been riding well, but mentally I've been making a few mistakes. I was worried at the start of my absence. For one thing, I didn't think I would have a job. But now I feel I have so much to look forward to. If I can get this thing in England out of the way, I could start to live my life again. Next year, I will be sharper than ever because I will appreciate being able to ride these good horses all the more. I have really good people around me and I can't wait to get back.'

It sounded brave at the time, and because people wanted him to be telling the truth, they believed him. In another interview, he embellished the point.

'It's a little bit like rehab, when you take the time to look back on your life, how you've been abusing yourself, it's been similar. I think I'll be better because I'll be hungrier now. It's kind of like starting over again.'

Fallon has a talent for making people believe him and believe in him. It's part of his charm. By the end of the year, the words seemed hollow and sad, the shibboleths of an unreformed, addictive personality.

There were high spots for Fallon in an understandably low-key season. On 7 June, he returned to race-riding just down the road from Coolmore at Tipperary Junction. His first ride at the evening meeting was on The Bogberry and everyone in the land, including the crowd of 3,000, much greater than the usual numbers on a midweek meeting in these parts, knew what would happen next. Typically, it was not a straightforward race. Knocked back on the bend to second from last in the seven-runner field, The Bogberry had to be properly balanced again before mounting a serious challenge to the leaders. With a furlong to run, the two-year-old was still only fourth, but Fallon had the measure of the pace by then and urged The Bogberry forward, using the stick just once to introduce him to the task but not giving him a hard race. An impressive burst of acceleration settled the issue within sight of the line. Donn McClean, who has an eye for the moments that really matter, watched Fallon in the race and watched him return through the crowds.

> If Fallon was expecting 'Welcome Back Kieren' cards or 'After You Kieren' gaps from his five weighing-room colleagues, he is disappointed. A seven-and-a-half-furlong breeze this is not. Kevin Manning makes sure that Fallon won't get off the rails easily as they round the home turn. Fallon takes a tug in order to get around his rival but, as soon as he does, Pat Smullen arrives on his outside. That's race-riding. Fallon has to drop back in order to go forward. A furlong and a half to go and at least four lengths to make up, the perfect result looks unlikely. Even Chris Hayes, nineteen-year-old Chris Hayes, with scant regard for seniority or six-time champions, kicks for home for all he is worth on Rainbow Crossing, but Fallon and The Bogberry catch them. Just … Before they [Fallon and The Bogberry] are engulfed by the inevitable heart-felt applause, a lady sitting by the entrance to the parade ring shouts, 'Nice to have you back, Kieren.' Fallon turns his head, seeks out the lady, meets her gaze and responds, 'Thank you.' '

The Bogberry won 'with something to spare', according to the official race-reader, who also rated the son of Hawk Wing a 'smart prospect' for the future. The reception for Fallon as he made his way back to the winner's enclosure was warm and genuine, the evening was made for reminiscence. It was Fallon's first ride since Yeats in the Melbourne Cup in November 2006 and in one short burst he had reminded his employers just how much he had to offer on horseback. More importantly, he had rediscovered the biggest high of all, the feeling of winning.

'I thought that this day would never come,' Fallon told McClean in an interview later that evening. 'I've been riding four lots a day and riding out at Newmarket, and I was over in Canada for a couple of weeks. I enjoyed what I was doing, but it's great to be back race-riding.' Mind you, he added, the 'boys were sharper than me tonight.'

The problem was that riding winners at Tipperary and Listowel was not high on Fallon's list of things to do before he retired, nor could they provide enough of a buzz to keep him interested while Dylan Thomas was winning a King George at Ascot and the brilliantly progressive Peeping Fawn was sweeping aside the best English and French fillies in high summer without him. His views on the facilities at most provincial Irish tracks had been well documented and were far from favourable. If Ireland is to be taken seriously as a racing nation, he said, there has to be some notable investment in the basic infrastructure of most Irish tracks. He knew no one would be listening, but the fact that Fallon had made the remarks at least made the headlines in the Irish newspapers. The attraction of riding out on a crisp spring morning has nothing to do with the stillness of the surrounding countryside or the beauty of the morning light. No, the attraction of riding out is that, on a racetrack somewhere soon, the horse cantering beneath you might win a big prize.

'Riding work, I'm in among them and thinking all the time,' Fallon said that spring. 'Our gallops are laid out like a racecourse and when we work in bunches of five or six, I'm doing everything I would in a race.' Except winning and losing, which is the point of the whole exercise. When the season starts, riding out becomes a chore. Everyone wants to be at the races.

At Saint-Cloud late in June, Fallon rode Mountain High, a significant step forward for two reasons. One was that the Grand Prix de Saint-Cloud was his first Group One success for eight months, and the other was that the winner was trained by Sir Michael Stoute, who had shown almost as much faith in his former stable jockey as had Coolmore. Eagle Mountain was not able to bring Fallon his third Irish Derby victory a week later, but when Dylan Thomas swept home in the Tattersalls Millions Irish Champion Stakes in September to become the first horse to win the Champion for a second time, Fallon was so emotionally bound up in the moment, he uttered the words jockeys always try to avoid. 'This is the best horse I have ever ridden,' said Fallon of the 8–15 favourite, a statement utterly justified both then and certainly a month later, but designed to irritate the owners and trainers of Ouija Board,

Hurricane Run, Golan and Bosra Sham, to name but a few. Ladbrokes, never a bad reflector of racing opinion, trimmed Dylan Thomas to 6–1 from 7–1 for the Arc. To crown another extraordinary day for Aidan O'Brien and Ballydoyle, Dylan Thomas was chased home by his stablemates, Duke of Marmalade and Red Rock Canyon.

'I'd say Dylan Thomas is the best I've ridden,' said Fallon. 'He's going from strength to strength. He's a very high-class horse whether it's a mile and a quarter or a mile and a half.'

Fallon, too, was making history at Leopardstown, winning the race for a third successive year after Oratorio's victory over Motivator in 2005. Students of Fallon's style of riding might care to look at the brilliant photograph of the closing stages of the race taken by Caroline Norris and published in the *Racing Post* on Sunday morning. While Seamus Heffernan has a taut rein and an arched back aboard runner-up Duke of Marmalade, Fallon's reins are hanging loosely down the neck of Dylan Thomas and his seat is low in the saddle. He pushes with his hands and you can sense the horse stretching for the line beneath him. The pair were to enjoy one last moment of sunshine in the twilight of a forgotten season.

Hanging like a thunder cloud over every step, intruding on every night's sleep, were the charges demanding defence in an English court. In the rare interviews he granted through the long summer months, Fallon never gave any indication that he understood the case, or even had a glimmer of guilt on his conscience. The whole thing, he said, was baffling, wasteful and downright degrading. His defence team, led by John Kelsey-Fry QC and Christopher Stewart-Moore, Fallon's solicitor, friend and advisor, were convinced that they would be able to persuade Mr Justice Forbes, the presiding judge, to dismiss the case well before the legal system cranked into action on 24 September, the date set for the trial. Fallon was led to believe it would soon be over, but Justice Forbes rejected the pleas from Fallon's counsel in a private hearing and ruled that, on the evidence laid out before him, there was indeed a case to answer. In the press room, no one knew quite what to make of the whole affair. Fallon's talent for race-riding was no cause for debate, but this was not the first time his integrity had been subject to the most intense scrutiny. When, in the age of betting exchanges, tightened security regulations and more intrusive surveillance, did an honest tip for a horse become a case of conspiracy? When did a good old-fashioned betting coup become a criminal offence?

To find Court 12 at the Old Bailey, you need to climb three broad flights of stairs or take one of the six lifts to the third floor. Court 12 is at the end, separated from the broad waiting areas outside by a little vestibule. Imagine a big classroom with three long rows of desks and the teacher's chair at the front and that is roughly the layout of the court. The defendants sit at the back of the court, behind a glass screen, the jury and the press sit on one side, facing inwards down the rows. Between the main body of the court and the raised dais for the judge are the stenographers and the clerks of the court. The judge, robed and bewigged, enters from a door to the side; the QCs wear dark robes and wigs. The public gallery is stepped steeply like the upper circle in a theatre and with almost as bad a view. The overall feeling is surprisingly intimate. Time seems to pass in a different warp from the outside world. It's like watching a game in which only a privileged few know the rules. When the judge enters and leaves, the whole court stands. There are more upheavals in a daily session in court than a Catholic Mass. The rhythms of court life were not new to Fallon, although the consequences of the Top Cees case were rather less severe than the potential two-year jail sentence available to the criminal court for conspiracists.

From the moment Jonathan Caplan rose to present the case for the prosecution, it was clear that Fallon would be the dominant figure in the trial and John Kelsey-Fry the highest profile defence QC. Fergal Lynch and Darren Williams were lesser jockeys and so the focus of the trial seemed to be off them. Fallon had first to present himself in front of the court on 24 September, but two weeks of legal argument concerning the admissibility of different witnesses and of evidence on both sides postponed the actual start of the trial for two weeks, time enough for one of the most extraordinary victories in Fallon's life.

Only rarely had Fallon confided in the press his true feelings about the effect of the court case. His background was a source of protection, up to a point. It had taught him not to worry too much about what others said, but his natural shyness, his social reticence and awkward-ness, worked against such a careless attitude. Fallon did care what people thought and said, not about his riding, but about him. In a revealing interview with Alan Lee after the court case, Fallon said how embar-rassed he was to see Sir Michael Stoute, Luca Cumani and John and Ed Dunlop voluntarily coming to court to testify for him (even though they were theoretically supposed to be witnesses for the prosecution). He had wanted, he said, to hide behind the rows of books in front of him so that Stoute, in particular, one of his most loyal supporters, couldn't see him. 'What they said made me feel so humble,' Fallon told Lee, who was the only journalist to speak to Fallon directly on the afternoon of his discharge from court.

In darker moments, in the winter of 2006, another side of Fallon emerged, not the chipper Irish boy who would always survive, but the weary champion who, on some days, had no more stomach for the fight. Fallon felt that he was being watched and criticised every time he left the weighing-room. In the past, he had always been able to separate his insecurity with people from his utter certainty on a horse. Now, one had begun to infiltrate the other and, by his own admission, at the start of the 2007 season, he had not been at his sharpest on the track. He highlighted some bad rides on Arc day in 2006, a day that just a year earlier he had dominated. His mood was very different from the day of his victory on Hurricane Run two years before. So much more than a mere horserace rested on the outcome.

It was touch and go whether Fallon would be fit to ride Dylan Thomas in the 2007 Arc. The top brass at Coolmore had debated the decision long and hard, but it was O'Brien's belief that Arc day would once again bring the best out of his stable jockey, and events at the Old Bailey, in the form of a leaking pipe that flooded Court 12 and caused a well-timed adjournment two days before the weekend, also worked in Fallon's favour. In a sense, the remarkable thing about Dylan Thomas's victory in the Arc was not that Fallon was able to conjure a pearl of a ride under such pressure, but that he was asked to do so in the first place. If there was ever a ringing endorsement of Fallon's temperament, it came on 7 October 2007.

In the bull-like Dylan Thomas, he had a willing accomplice. In Fallon's absence, Kinane, Murtagh, Seamie Heffernan and Christophe Soumillon had all experienced the relentless surge of power and the absolute concentration of energy that have marked the success of Dylan Thomas in five Group Ones. Despite the disruption in the saddle, Dylan Thomas's appetite for the fray had never been questioned. The only complication on Arc day was that Coolmore was fielding another, increasingly favoured, challenger. Soldier of Fortune, under Johnny Murtagh, had recently won the Prix Niel, historically the most significant preparation race for the Arc. The only blemish on Soldier of Fortune's three-year-old career had come at Epsom on Derby day when he finished fifth behind Authorized, the second of Coolmore's ludicrous posse of eight runners, but while Dylan Thomas had been taking on all-comers over a variety of distances in top-class company through the summer, Soldier of Fortune had been put away since his romping victory in the Irish Derby and looked ready to make further progress over the one mile and four furlongs of the undulating Arc course. The profile – lightly raced, trained for the moment – seemed to match so many of the French three-year-old Arc winners down the years, not least because he preferred the soft ground. Fallon said later that he was only dissuaded from switching to Soldier of Fortune by O'Brien, who assured him the ground would dry out just right for Dylan Thomas. The more likely truth was that Fallon wanted to stay with the trusty four-year-old all along and O'Brien was happy with Murtagh riding Soldier of Fortune.

Fallon travelled over to France on the day before the Arc to prepare himself. If he needed his confidence bolstered, the sight of the strapping Dylan Thomas would have been a far stronger boost than the memory of two years before and the impossible victory of Hurricane Run. This time, Fallon did not go into the Arc with a memory bank of winners to call on. He had not been riding with his usual force, and other riders had begun to take advantage of the lapses. Fallon needed a ride to restore his reputation, and he needed a winner to restore his confidence. Dylan Thomas went to post at 11–2, Soldier of Fortune was a 100–30 shot, but the hordes of English racing fans, who make their trip to Paris an autumnal party, would not hear of defeat for Authorized and Frankie Dettori. The Derby winner was 11–10 favourite.

The absence of the French superstar, Manduro, had depleted the international quality of the field, but, like most Arcs, it had the feel of a proper heavyweight contest, even without the champion of France. Two things began to go Dylan Thomas's way in the lead-up to the race – the field of twelve runners was one of the smallest for a decade, and, as Aidan O'Brien had promised, the ground was drying out. Yellowstone had been included in the field by Coolmore to ensure a good early pace under Pat Smullen, but there was no surprise when Fallon eased Dylan Thomas sweetly through the field at the two-furlong mark and dashed him into the lead more than a furlong from home. Strength and stamina were always Dylan Thomas's strong points. The rest now had to catch him. For a split second under pressure, Dylan Thomas drifted into the rail, squeezing up both Zambezi Sun and Soldier of Fortune, but Fallon had the line in his sights. What was it Stoute had said? Kieren knows where the finishing post is. A couple of strides beyond the finishing post, Mick Channon's Youmzain would have been declared the winner. Where it mattered, Dylan Thomas and Fallon still had a head to spare.

Coolmore do not go in for animated celebrations – this is business, after all – but Fallon looked as if the cares of the world had just been lifted off his shoulders, if only for a few, precious, minutes. He smiled, he waved the Irish tricolor above his head and then he waited. Jockeys will tell you that the moment after crossing the line first, and walking back to meet the connections of the winning horse, is the best feeling in sport, no matter the prestige of the race or the prize at stake. Multiply that feeling by a factor of ten and both Coolmore and Fallon had every reason to be smiling that late afternoon in Paris, except that the French stewards, notoriously strict in their interpretation of the rules on the track, were analysing the incident a furlong from home. 'Please wait,' said the Longchamp announcer. 'There's a real enquiry. We are not sure of the outcome.'

Fallon and all the backers of Dylan Thomas held their breath. The omens were not good. On board Zambezi Sun was Stephane Pasquier, one of the top riders in France, but not a man particularly welcome in the weighing-rooms across the water. In the Grand Prix de Paris in the summer, Fallon had been brought down on Eagle Mountain, suffering a bad enough injury to put him out for a week. Publicly and wisely, on the advice of John Magnier, Fallon said nothing. France was, after all, one of the few countries where he was welcome to ride. Privately, he was seething with Pasquier for causing the interference and potentially putting his life at risk. Back in England, Jamie Spencer, for one, expressed his disgust that the authorities had taken no action against the Frenchman. His criticism was spoken with feeling. Spencer himself had suffered a ten-day suspension for an offence he considered rather more minor than depositing a jockey over the rails. The general feeling was that if one rule applied to overseas jockeys in the French stewards' room, there was quite another for the locals. Here now, late on a blissful autumnal afternoon in the suburbs of Paris, Fallon's future and Dylan Thomas's Arc depended substantially on the testimony of Stephane Pasquier and on the unwritten etiquette of the weighing-room.

Jockeys understand that six times in an afternoon they bequeath their lives to the common cause not just of winning but of surviving. The rules are largely laid down by the jockeys themselves. Jockeys will shout, holler and, just occasionally, blaspheme in the name of getting a clear run and, nine times out of ten, those who know their chance of winning has gone will try to keep out of the way or even make room for a rival on the tacit understanding that, sometime down the line, the favour will be returned. The same system works in professional cycling, with favours asked and returned every afternoon on the road. In race-riding, there can be no other way. By leaning on Eagle Mountain in the Grand Prix de Paris so heavily that Fallon had been unshipped, Pasquier had infringed the unwritten rules. Fallon had kept his counsel and now the Frenchman, who had professed his innocence all along, duly returned the favour in the best possible way. Had Zambezi Sun come second, placing an Arc within reach, the outcome might have been different, but the French challenger had faded into eighth and so Pasquier had nothing to lose by telling the truth. The interference had not caused him to stop riding, nor did he think Fallon's move across to the rail was deliberate. After ten minutes, which seemed like a lifetime, the announcement came. The result remained unchanged.

'He [Pasquier] owed me one, but I think he has paid me back now,' said Fallon. 'I've always thought, ever since he won the Irish Derby [2006], that he was going to be a great horse,' he added, warming to one of his favourite themes. 'It's unlucky I haven't been able to ride him in England. I know the horse well and I get on well with him because he's not the easiest of rides. I could feel Youmzain coming at me but mine was doing nothing in front. If he'd gone round again they would not have got by him.'

Not for the first time, O'Brien was effusive and eloquent in support of the jockey who had just won him his first – and Ireland's sixth – Arc de Triomphe.

'With everything that's been going on with Kieren, we weren't even sure he would ride this weekend,' he said. 'But what a masterful ride. When Kieren gets up on a horse, he just goes off into a different land and the land that Kieren lives in a lot of us don't understand. He's a unique talent.'

For Fallon, the celebrations were short-lived. He had another appointment in London the next morning.

16

A CASE WON, A CAREER LOST

'Everyone knows that Kieren has an addiction problem, that he had one before he came to us and that he had it when he came to us. Obviously, anyone like that deserves help rather than anything else.'

Aidan O'Brien in the *Racing Post*, December 2007

Kieren Fallon emerged from the Old Bailey at just before 1 p.m. on Friday, 7 December 2007 and, strangely, he looked very far from being a free and vindicated man. For almost the first time in eleven weeks, which he later described as the worst of his life, Fallon's face betrayed weariness and desolation. He was ushered over to hear a statement read out by a spokesman for his lawyers, mumbled a few words of gratitude to his employers at Coolmore and his legal team, who had mounted such a brilliant defence of his reputation in Court 12, and was bundled into the back of a black car. It was as if, after months of putting on a suit and tie and a brave face, he had finally confronted the truth of his life and wondered, perhaps for the first time, where it had all gone so wrong. He should have been in Hong Kong preparing to ride Dylan Thomas in the Hong Kong Vase, but Hong Kong was another racing no-go area for him. He owed Dylan Thomas one, for the way the brilliant colt had battled all the way to the line for him in the Arc on the eve of his trial. Yet, on a grey, mid-winter afternoon, he was emerging from the Central Criminal Court in London, free at last from the charges laid against him, but not free from himself, not free from his own capacity for self-destruction. One of his first calls after the verdict was to Aidan O'Brien. Fallon wanted to tell him the good news. The bad news was yet to come.

Outside Court 12 that lunchtime, the mood seemed to match Fallon's own. A few punters – always his most faithful constituency – cheered their hero, and a few bemused office workers wondered at the commotion, but Fallon might have lost his case, for all you could tell. The long and tiring farce had ended moments before with the discharge of all six defendants by Justice Forbes, but no one seemed moved to celebrate their freedom. The co-defendants drifted back into obscurity, all except Fallon, who had been in the full glare of publicity for almost three months. By the time Justice Forbes entered his court just before 11 a.m. for the final day of the trial, everyone knew what he was about to say. The court was packed, the press seats full to overflowing and news reporters sat on the edge of solicitors' desks at the side of the court. For such a full house, the court was unusually still. It was an unlikely venue for another of the Irishman's astonishing comebacks.

Fallon sat at the back of the court flanked by his defence counsel, staring without expression towards Justice Forbes.

'Do you find the defendant, Kieren Fallon, not guilty?' the clerk asked the head of the jury.

'Yes,' came the reply.

'And is that the verdict of you all?'

'It is.'

Shortly afterwards, Justice Forbes dismissed racing's 'trial of the century' with four simple words: 'The defendants are discharged.'

There was no cheering from the gallery, no shouts of glee from within the court, just contented smiles from the defence counsels, and the anticipation of a decent celebration over lunch. Fallon shook hands with his lawyers and left the court. The strange irony was that Fallon was a far greater danger to himself out on the streets than he was safely cocooned inside the warm embrace of proceedings in Court 12. Travelling in each day from a friend's house in Hendon, having to be prompt for a 10.30 start most mornings, was akin to the familiar routine of the racetrack that Fallon knew so well and loved so much. If he was in court, Fallon could not get himself into trouble. No one had quite anticipated how swiftly trouble would tumble down on him once he returned to real life.

The case against all six of the defendants was brought by the Crown Prosecution Service on behalf of the City of London police. Alongside Fallon, jockeys Darren Williams and Fergal Lynch, together with Miles Rodgers, Philip Sherkle and Shaun Lynch were charged with conspiring to defraud the customers of Betfair, the betting exchange company, by laying horses to lose in a series of races between December 2002 and the end of August 2004. Miles Rodgers, formerly a director of the Platinum Racing Club and a big-time gambler, according to the prosecution, was alleged to be the mastermind behind the attempt to fix races and profit from them through a series of internet-based accounts with Betfair. Shaun Lynch, Fergal's brother, was a friend of Fallon's from their days growing up together in County Clare, and Philip Sherkle was a friend whom Fallon had met at The Cock pub in Kentford near Newmarket a few years before. (In a police interview he could not remember the exact date.) There was, Jonathan Caplan QC for the CPS claimed in his opening statement to the jury, an unlawful agreement or conspiracy between these defendants and other persons that these races should be fixed. The fixing was not to ensure that the horses in the twenty-seven races under investigation won, but that they lost. 'The object of the conspiracy,' the prosecution claimed, 'was to wager large amounts of money on a particular horse to lose in each of those races whilst knowing that the jockey was prepared, if necessary, to cheat by stopping the horse.'

The consensus of opinion in the run-up to the trial was that the City of London Police had compiled a strong case against the six-time champion and his five co-defendants. They must have done, surely? In the summer, a submission by Fallon's defence counsel for 'no case to answer' was heard by Justice Forbes, who had listened to the outline of the evidence and ruled in favour of the Crown Prosecution Service. There was indeed a case to answer, said Justice Forbes, and racing nodded its head in agreement.

The case, as both sides knew, was not really a trial of racing at all but of Kieren Fallon, who stood, whether racing liked it or not, as one of the sport's great champions and therefore one of its figureheads. Fallon was, as one senior member of the former Jockey Club said privately, the 'trophy'. Yet Fallon was not central to the evidence initially handed over to the City of London Police by the security department of the Jockey Club back in early 2004. Fallon had a disciplinary record that stretched out like the Dead Sea Scrolls, but none of it had ever involved criminal activity.

The non-combatants viewing the case from the press seats or the public gallery, those who remembered how the Top Cees case nearly a decade earlier had floundered on the inability of the *Sporting Life* to substantiate claims of 'cheating' in the running and riding of Top Cees, trained by Lynda Ramsden and ridden by Fallon, were wary that the law of the land would once again become entangled in the linguistic and technical complexities of the sport of kings. If Fallon – and his other five co-defendants – were to be convicted on the charge of a conspiracy to defraud the clients of Betfair, by knowingly and systematically fixing the outcome of races, it had to be proved beyond reasonable doubt to a jury. Trying to prove this to a jury who had no previous understanding of horse-racing, that a jockey, and no less a jockey than the six-time champion, should have gone right instead of left in the middle of a seven-furlong sprint at Goodwood was a pointless exercise. The prosecution needed to present incontrovertible evidence of criminality – that the conspirators had intended to fix races and that Fallon, the central figure in the drama, had benefited financially from the fixing. It emerged through eleven long weeks that it could fulfil neither duty. By the time Fallon had won races he should have lost, by the defence counsel's reckoning, he had lost his 'conspirators' more than £300,000. No wonder Fallon looked so confident.

By the time Fallon's court case had settled into its daily ritual, the attention of the country had moved on. Elsewhere in the Old Bailey, the Metropolitan Police were in the dock over the shooting of the innocent Brazilian, Jean Charles de Menezes, at Stockwell Tube station two and a half years earlier, and racing's 'trial of the century' had been reduced to a meaningless sideshow to all but the occupants of Court

12. Most mornings, a posse of photographers would lie in wait outside the Old Bailey, corralled into a pen on the pavement or, when the local police were in a bad mood, banished to the opposite side of the road, where their views of the comings and goings were likely to be obscured by the regular traffic of taxis passing up and down an unremarkable street with one of the most recognisable names in the capital.

Mostly, Fallon came and went unnoticed; sometimes his arrival prompted a stirring and whirring in the ranks of photographers. Fallon being Fallon – and therefore not given to making life easy for the press in general and photographers in particular – would make a dash for the door. He was always immaculately dressed, neat suit, smart tie, as if arriving for a full book of rides at Royal Ascot. Inside the court, he was always more attentive than either Fergal Lynch or Darren Williams, following the lengthy and often mind-numbingly tedious tiptoe to justice with the look of a man who already knew the outcome. Either Fallon was putting on a brave face or he was whistling in the dark to keep up his spirits, but half of him seemed to enjoy the regularity of the ritual and the increasingly cosy community in the court, like an off-season weighing-room. Then there was the mobile phone game, which Fallon particularly enjoyed. After proceedings had twice been interrupted by the ringing of a mobile phone in the press area, Fallon took to brandishing his phone in the air as a reminder to the fourth estate. The irony, not lost on Fallon, was that his possession of a bewildering number of phones, at least one unregistered, formed one of the minor strands of evidence against him in the trial.

It summed up the prosecution's hapless timing that when Fallon returned to court for the true start of the trial, he did so as the Arc-winning jockey, a result obliquely referred to by his QC, John Kelsey-Fry, in his opening speech to the court. Fallon, said Kelsey-Fry, was driven by a desire to win and was still a jockey at the height of his powers.

Rodgers, it was claimed, used numerous different accounts to lay the horses to lose on Betfair. The total amount laid on the twenty-seven races was £2.12 million. Fallon was one of three riders in question, having ridden in seventeen of the races. Twelve of his horses lost and five won, Caplan said, resulting in a net loss of about £338,000 for the alleged conspirators.

'The plan was not – and could not be – foolproof because you could not always stop the horse if in the particular circumstances it would look too obvious,' said Caplan. 'A horserace is a dynamic event and anything can happen. But the plan worked most of the time.' The contention was later ridiculed by Kelsey-Fry, who noted the 'absurd equation' of this 'extraordinary case'.

Two races were picked out for particular attention. One was Fallon's ride on Ballinger Ridge at Lingfield on 2 March 2004, a race on which Rodgers had staked £72,312 to win £26,599. The other was the Lockinge Stakes at Newbury in May 2004, when Fallon won on Russian Rhythm, which had cost Rodgers £160,256. The jury heard how Ballinger Ridge had built up a huge lead turning into the straight at Lingfield that afternoon. According to the prosecution, Ballinger Ridge 'should have won in a canter' but did not do so because Fallon stopped riding and the horse lost momentum. Ballinger Ridge was beaten a short-head by Rye. 'Was this just a terrible mistake or did he [Fallon] want Rye to beat him?' asked Caplan. The defence's interpretation of the race was that Fallon simply made a blunder, mostly in failing to see Rye, his nearest rival, when he looked over his shoulder to assess the danger before giving his mount a 'breather'. Fallon was subsequently banned for twenty-one days by the stewards for being in breach of Rule 156, i.e. the horse did not achieve the best possible placing because of a jockey's error. The period of the suspension, the defence noted, included the lucrative Dubai World Cup meeting at the end of the month at which Fallon could potentially have earned a lot more than in losing a minor race at Lingfield.

In contrast, Fallon's riding of Russian Rhythm in the Lockinge, a Group One race at Newbury, was particularly commended by the trainer, Sir Michael Stoute. Stoute, the defence said, thought his stable jockey at the time had given the filly a 'tremendous ride'. How was it then, asked Kelsey-Fry, that the communication between Fallon and Rodgers, through the intermediary, Shaun Lynch, had gone so wrong? After several texts and phone calls between Fallon and Shaun Lynch and between Rodgers and Lynch, Rodgers began to lay the horse roughly forty-five minutes before the off. After the race, which Russian Rhythm won by half a length, Rodgers telephoned Shaun Lynch five times between 3.19 p.m. and 7.47, presumably to find out what had gone wrong.

Russian Rhythm's victory, the jury was told, had three consequences for the alleged conspirators. One was a trip by Shaun Lynch and Rodgers to Leicester racecourse three days later, which resulted in Fallon receiving a lift in Rodgers' car to East Midlands airport. The second was a trip by Rodgers, Shaun Lynch, Philip Sherkle and Daniel Kinahan, not one of the defendants, to Newmarket in an attempt to confront Fallon in the early hours of 27 May 2004, and the third, the activation on 27 May of two mobile phones, which were to be used by Sherkle and Rodgers to provide a more secure method of communication with Fallon on racedays. The prosecution alleged that, unhappy at the loss on Russian Rhythm, the conspirators came to Newmarket to make a more reliable working arrangement for stopping horses in the future. The defence maintained that Fallon did not know who Miles Rodgers was and that if he had known him – and known he was banned from all racecourses by the authorities – it would have been 'suicidal' to be seen in his company in the car park of Leicester racecourse.

The jury was also asked to consider exactly what the little 'n' meant in the communications between the alleged conspirators on the morning of fixed races. On 14 August, Fallon rode Goodwood Spirit at Goodwood. The horse was 2–1 favourite. That morning at 11.43 and 12.04, Fallon called Philip Sherkle. At 12.08 he texted him. At 12.09, Sherkle texted Rodgers: '6.55 no 4 n'. Between 6.35 and 6.51 p.m., Rodgers laid Goodwood Spirit for £116,738 to win £29,822. Goodwood Spirit finished third. According to the prosecution, the 'n' denoted non-trier; according to the defence, it meant negative or 'not fancied', a contrast with another text message, which had 'p' in the text, for positive, said the defence. The probe evidence from telephone conversations, much of it inaudible, also suggested, according to the prosecution, regular contact between the conspirators or, with Fallon, through an intermediary. Rodgers is heard to tell Fergal Lynch one afternoon at Ripon:

'You cannot afford to make a mistake on this one', which was taken to be a reference to the third in a sequence of fixed races at Ripon. That morning Rodgers had been taped saying, 'little Fergal's coming out to play today'.

The most revealing set of texts concerning Fallon came the morning after he had ridden Daring Aim, the Queen's horse, to victory at Newmarket on 23 July. The texts were sent to Sherkle on an unregistered phone recovered by the police from the glove compartment of Fallon's car. One text read: 'They will take my licences off me if they drift like that last night. They are watching me.' Another read simply: 'No, I can't chance it.'

In reality, once John Kelsey-Fry had reported that Fallon's strike rate (percentage of winners/rides) was 29.4 per cent when he was supposedly trying to lose, and 19 per cent when he was trying to win, and that this was a six-time champion who had won more than anyone else over much of the past decade, the prosecution was already on the back foot. The court was shown a series of videos of the races under investigation, and no one had to be a racing expert to know that the victory of Russian Rhythm in the Lockinge and of Beauvrai at Goodwood were minor gems of race-riding, whatever the activity raging on the betting exchanges. They showed Fallon not at his worst, but close to his cool and calculating best, and Fallon must have enjoyed the spectacle as much from the back row of the court as he had at the time. Once again, racing was starting to make a fool of the law.

The mechanics of the trial were interesting in the way that they reflected on Fallon's attitude. One moment he was texting tips to a man he had met a few times in the local pub, without, it seems, giving a thought to any motive or what might be done with the information; the next, he was riding races of near perfection to ensure that everyone lost other than himself, the owner and trainer. Did anyone expect anything different from Fallon? Yes, in a word, they did. Racing did. The transcripts of five interviews carried out by officers from the City of London Police in September 2004 and June 2006 showed the state of Fallon's contacts with Sherkle, who was, claimed the prosecution, one of the intermediaries used by Rodgers before he placed a bet. Asked if he ever offered Sherkle tips, Fallon replied: 'He often asked me. I often tell him what I fancy or I didn't fancy. He'd often ring me, I'd often text him, but he'd more so.' Fallon said that he did not know that texting from the weighing-room during racing hours was illegal; nor could he tell police which of his many phones he had used. 'I don't know. I had so many phones. I always keep quite a few phones.' Fallon was also asked by Detective Constable Matthew Hussey of the City of London Police about the potential for race-fixing. 'It's impossible,' replied Fallon. 'Horses have minds of their own.'

Fallon could summon some staunch support to his cause. Racing's good and great filed out from Newmarket to sing their champion's praises. Sir Michael Stoute pronounced Fallon's ride on Daring Aim at Newmarket in July 2004, one of the races under investigation, as 'brilliant'. Daring Aim, he said, had been given one smack of the whip by Fallon and had not liked it. 'So he put the whip down quickly and that has won her the race.' Fallon's former boss was equally effusive about Fallon's ride on Krynica a month earlier at Pontefract. 'He is squeezing her and encouraging her. It's beautiful horsemanship – and she was not very good.' Michael Bell joined in the chorus of praise, referring to Fallon's pillar-to-post win on Barking Mad as 'a very good ride'. Ed Dunlop, for whom Fallon had won the Oaks on Ouija Board, excused Bubbling Fun's third at Lingfield on the grounds that the horse was 'very ordinary', while David Loder, who has subsequently retired from training, described Bonecrusher, who finished fifth at Epsom in July 2004, as 'thoroughly unreliable'. Fallon sat at the back and, in his own words, hid his face, embarrassed partly at the unconditional strength of their support but mostly by the fact that he should need it.

The case had wobbled along for a few weeks before it came to what, Justice Forbes noted later, was the real crux of the legal argument. The week that Ray Murrihy, a chief steward of New South Wales racing, spent in the witness box, painstakingly analysing videos of all the races, irrefutably turned the tide in favour of the defendants and, in particular, Kieren Fallon. Fallon was outraged that a man who had never ridden a race in his life, nor, by his own admission, knew much about the workings of racing in the UK, could be used in judgement on a six-time

249

champion. He had some sympathy, even from his fiercest critics.

The defence claimed, among other things, that Murrihy had been prompted in his analysis of the races by the officers of the City of London Police, a view Murrihy denied repeatedly, but he had been set up. Murrihy, as he said frequently in court, had merely been asked to give his expert opinion, as one of Australia's most respected stewards, on the twenty-seven races sent to him by the police. Crucially, though, he would go no further in court than expressing his concerns about the actions in some of the races. Even in the notorious case of Ballinger Ridge, Murrihy would venture only that the race cried out for investigation, not that it had, in his opinion, been deliberately fixed. Justice Forbes thought this a significant omission and made it central to his decision to dismiss the case a month later.

Murrihy was clearly out of his depth talking about British racing in an English court, and John Kelsey-Fry took great delight in proving it. Poor Murrihy was left naked, stripped bare by his inability to put the races he was judging into any context or to highlight the particular running patterns or quirks of the horses in question. But there was still one big looming danger for Fallon. It was Ballinger Ridge and the fact that, for a jury of non-racing people, the video replay of Fallon's ride looked desperate. On Monday, 29 October, at approximately 2.20, Murrihy, a tall, thin figure with a pedantic turn of mind befitting a chief steward, came to race five of the twenty-seven. The video was played again and again. Fallon led comfortably coming into the straight, looked over his shoulder, began to ease down, looked over his shoulder again and only began a frantic ride for the line when Rye, who won the race, came to challenge. It looked worse with each rerun. Fallon looked on impassively, barely a flicker of recognition crossing his face.

'Would you have called a stewards' enquiry?' Jonathan Caplan asked Murrihy.

'Yes, yes, I would,' came the reply. Murrihy went on, 'This was quite an extraordinary race. I don't think I've seen in my experience a horse eased down like that in that part of the race. It cost the win.'

Under prompting from Caplan, Murrihy runs through the tape. 'I saw Ballinger Ridge in the early and middle stages of the race having a commanding lead, six to eight lengths in front, travelling quite keenly. In the early part of the straight he's still four or five lengths in front and leading up to that there's some movement in Kieren Fallon's hands, but then the movement slows quite dramatically, you see his hands drop and see his horse slowing under him. Ballinger Ridge loses momentum, Rye improves and you see Kieren Fallon look around again, presumably he sees Rye and begins to react, but he's never riding with a great deal of vigour, but he does react. It's a race that cries out for questions to be asked at any level.' Had Fallon ridden his horse out, Murrihy added, Ballinger Ridge wins the race. 'He lost because the rider slowed the horse up.' The court was told earlier that Rodgers had won £27,000 after laying bets totalling more than £72,000 on Ballinger Ridge to lose.

If Fallon did intend to lose the race, it was a brave, even foolhardy, way of doing it, but the video presented the defence with its major problem. How to persuade the jury that this was, quite simply, a blunder? John Kelsey-Fry took perhaps the only option in the circumstances and told the court that this was just an 'horrendous blunder', and he was helped in his assessment by the testimony of Andrew Balding, trainer of Ballinger Ridge.

'Kieren's made a mistake,' he said. 'It's cost us a winner. I was disappointed, more so for the owners, who only had a couple of horses. I was disappointed and a little bit angry but it's only a two-thousand pound race. If it'd been a bigger race, I would have been more upset. This sort of incident might happen once or twice a year.'

In fact, by the time Kelsey-Fry had shown the jury eight different incidents of jockeys dropping their hands and losing races, they might have thought it was an everyday occurrence, which was the point. And Murrihy would not suggest that Fallon had deliberately thrown the race.

Ballinger Ridge was, as Justice Forbes noted later, the 'high point' of the prosecution's case. Murrihy's reticence made it the turning point. Justice Forbes was beginning to feel uncomfortable with the validity of the case. Yet Murrihy's evidence, although widely ridiculed within racing, was more logical and relevant than many were prepared to admit. 'I look at races and I call it as I see it,' he told the court. 'I was asked to give advice on whether I thought there was anything wrong with the ride or the horse.' In other words, he hadn't expected to be grilled for five days on the draw bias at Southwell or the location of the best ground on wet days at Newcastle. Asked whether he knew what the best draw on the one mile and two furlong course at Southwell was, he answered: 'Show me the track and the position of the barriers [starting stalls] and I'll tell you.'

Refreshingly, Murrihy refused to be tangled up in the web of semi-expertise that is wrapped around British racing and makes the whole industry so impenetrable. His subtext was that, whether racing on the moon, Abu Dhabi, Australia or Kempton Park, the job of the jockey was to get the horse from the start to the finish by the quickest route, that it wasn't rocket science and that everyone in England seemed to regard it as more complex than splitting the atom. He didn't seem to set much store by the draw bias at Southwell nor the temperamental quirks of the horses, refusing to admit, for example, that a horse swishing its tail was a sign of quirkiness.

He was right on another matter, too. 'Jockeys,' he said, 'are not committed in every circumstance to follow the instructions if they are ridiculous or against the rules.' Murrihy was referring to the instructions given to Fallon by Vince Smith, the trainer of Beauvrai, before a race at Yarmouth in August 2004. Smith had wanted the jockey deliberately to miss the break and hold Beauvrai up at the back of the field until the last moment. Fallon followed the instructions to the letter and won the race comfortably, but Murrihy told the court the instruction was 'simply not appropriate'.

But, after five days on the witness stand and two days under interrogation from three of the sharper legal brains in the land, Murrihy's credibility had vanished into the outback. The prosecution case was lost. Jonathan Caplan knew it, John Kelsey-Fry knew it and Fallon sensed it too.

After a long adjournment, during which rumours about impending collapse spread quickly through racing, Justice Forbes halted the case on Friday, 7 December. There was no case to answer and the jury were instructed to bring a not guilty verdict.

Outside the court, Enda Brady, a news reporter with Sky in Ireland, mentioned that, after the collapse of the case, Fallon would return home a conquering hero, able to do no wrong in the eyes of his countrymen. Not only had he beaten the system on the track by rising from nowhere to become an Irish champion in England, acknowledged as one of the great jockeys of the post-war era, he had now wrung justice from an English court and embarrassed the whole establishment along the way. A vigorous protester of his innocence throughout, he had been proved right and Ireland would celebrate a famous victory right alongside him.

In contrast, the British racing authorities had been made to look foolish at best and downright vindictive at worst, while the City of London Police just looked plain incompetent. At no time during the eleven weeks did any of the police witnesses sound convincing, either in the witness box or on paper. Notebooks were lost, surveillance operations were bungled and the probe evidence was easily dismissed as inaudible and inconclusive by the defence.

In hindsight, the Jockey Club should have attempted to deal with Fallon in the same way that they dealt with Robert Winston, Robbie Fitzpatrick, Shane Kelly and all the other jockeys suspended under the rules of racing. The sense that Fallon was the prize, that he was being victimised for his celebrity and for his careless attitude to authority through two decades, was skilfully exploited by Kelsey-Fry and never fully addressed either by Mark Manning of the City of London Police or Paul Scotney, head of the BHA's security department. The ability to monitor betting patterns of individuals under the Memorandum of Understanding set up with the betting exchanges was in its earliest stages at the time the then Jockey Club called in the police. Bedazzled by their ability to analyse the private accounts of high rollers, the Jockey Club acted too quickly. The MoU has proved to be a useful tool in tracking suspicious betting patterns but not the smoking gun so desperately wanted by the racing authorities. Instead, they are back at square one, at least in their relationship with the courts. It will be a long time before the law is lured on to racing's patch again.

Ever quick to seek a profit, one bookmaker, Paddy Power, offered 8–1 on Fallon winning the 2008 Derby in the aftermath of his discharge from the Old Bailey. Given Fallon's genius for comebacks, it seemed a decent bet. By the morning, it did not seem so attractive. For once in his life, Fallon's timing was wayward. The rumour mill works quickly in racing because news does not have far to travel round its global village. Journalists had already heard the whispers from France that Fallon had failed another drugs test in the summer of 2007, just months after the end of an initial six-month ban imposed on him by France Galop for a positive test for cocaine in June the previous year. France Galop had strenuously denied that there was any such test, let alone any positive outcome, but once the trial had finished, they could keep the lid on the story no longer. Inside Court 12, Fallon was protected by the strict regulations of court reporting; outside it, he was fair game again.

The *Daily Mail* broke the story of Fallon's positive test on Saturday morning under the headline: 'Fallon drugs shock' and the details were soon confirmed by Fallon's hard-pressed lawyer, Christopher Stewart-Moore. Fallon had just ridden a horse called, ironically, Myboycharlie to victory in the Group One Prix Morny at Deauville in mid-August when he was called for a random drugs test by the authorities at the course. The results of the positive A sample were received by France Galop several weeks before they were released, but were withheld for the duration of the trial. By Sunday, although the B sample had yet to confirm Fallon's guilt, racing's mood had switched from sympathy for their harassed champion to disbelief, despair and downright condemnation. Fallon may have been wronged by his accusers from the City of London Police, but he was a fool to himself, no longer worthy of the sustained admiration and support of the sport he had dominated. Racing's capacity for forgiveness, which is almost unlimited for winners, had run dry at last.

In Hong Kong, Aidan O'Brien, the master of Ballydoyle, who had defended his jockey's character and talent so passionately through a long and trying season, was lost for words. A friend had rung from London early on Saturday morning as soon as the news had broken. O'Brien must have heard the rumour, but had hoped that it was just another piece of racecourse gossip. It was, the bearer of the news recalled later that day, like hearing the air leak out of a punctured tyre. O'Brien was speechless, confused, depressed and, although he would not admit it openly to the journalists who had gone to Hong Kong to report on the self-styled World Turf Championships, he must have felt deeply and utterly betrayed. No less than Fallon, O'Brien is a complex and introverted character, shy and to the outsider's eye almost diffident. O'Brien gave most of his winning interviews to his shoes. Yet in recent months, he had become eloquent and passionate on two subjects. One was George Washington, the brilliant winner of the 2006 2,000 Guineas, whose highly strung temperament and limitless talent stretched O'Brien's patience to the limit, and the other was the obvious wrong being done to Kieren Fallon.

O'Brien's defence of Fallon was based not on any inside knowledge of the case, nor necessarily on the truth according to Fallon, but on instinct. 'It's all such a waste,' he said on one occasion. He was right. The morning after news of the second drugs test had been confirmed, the *Racing Post* carried a transcript of a conversation between O'Brien and their reporter, Lee Mottershead.

LM: What does Kieren do now?

AO'B: I don't know, I haven't been at home since...

LM: But you know him well. You said during the week that this [trial] has taken a toll on him. What should he do next?

AO'B: Listen, everyone has to go home and talk. That's the way it will have to be.

LM: Given that Coolmore has stood by him throughout the court case, for there to be another drugs related issue, is there any sense of disappointment in the camp that he has done this?

AO'B (after fifteen-second pause): I don't know how to answer that.

LM: Do you feel he has let you down?

AO'B (after five-second pause): I'm just trying to think which way I'll answer. (ten-second pause) Listen, everyone knows that Kieren has an addiction problem, that he had one before he came to us and that he had it when he came to us. Obviously, anyone like that deserves help rather than anything else.

LM: Presumably, the camp will give him that help?

AO'B: Everybody always has – John and Sue [Magnier], Michael and Doreen [Tabor] and Derrick and Gay [Smith] have stood 100 per cent behind him all the way. I can't see why it would be any different.

O'Brien was furious at the presentation of the interview, including the extent of his pauses for thought, and rang the paper to vent his anger. Actually, O'Brien's agonies in trying not to let down either his employers, his jockey, himself or the truth, were poignant and admirable. Here was a man in turmoil. O'Brien knew he had to pick his words carefully. Livelihoods were at stake. The subtext to that difficult interview was that, yes, Coolmore and O'Brien felt desperately let down by Fallon and yet still felt a responsibility to a jockey they had employed in the first place, knowing full well of his addiction to cocaine, which was a startling admission. They could not cast him out now; equally, they needed to find a stable jockey – with the emphasis on the word 'stable' – who was available to ride their horses on any day of the week in every corner of the globe. Fallon's days at Coolmore were numbered. As if reading the mood of the Coolmore camp in Hong Kong, Dylan Thomas finished his epic season with a listless performance down the field in the Vase. For both horse and trainer, it was one race too far.

Coolmore, to their credit, had done all they could to help their stable jockey. This was not an entirely philanthropic gesture; Fallon was by some distance the best jockey Coolmore had ever known and they were understandably anxious to keep him on the straight and narrow. In 2005, Fallon had lifted Coolmore out of a trough and right back to the top. Within a few months of taking over his new job, George Washington had won the 2,000 Guineas and Virginia Waters the 1,000. The winners had continued to flow and, as O'Brien nobly pointed out after each one, Fallon's contribution to the revival had been incalculable. But, deep down, Coolmore's joint owners – John Magnier, Michael Tabor and Derrick Smith – knew that Fallon lived life on the edge. In the winter of 2005, Coolmore approached David Walsh, the chief sports writer of the *Sunday Times*, who had become one of Fallon's closest confidants. Walsh knew of Fallon's weaknesses, but knew enough of his strengths to want to help. The plan, formulated over several months, seemed to work well for everyone. Walsh would be employed by Coolmore to organise Fallon's life. If that meant becoming a golfing buddy, squash partner, counsellor, mentor, personal assistant, whatever was wanted, that was fine. Fallon stood to benefit from the greater discipline instilled in him by someone he trusted and respected; Coolmore would have a stable jockey at the top of his game every day of the week. But when the time came to implement the new arrangement, in time for the 2006 season, Fallon backed away. Had he made the commitment, who knows what he might have achieved or how long he may have ridden? He had the best job in racing, but changing his way of life to preserve it seemed a sacrifice too far. Credit should go to Coolmore for their optimism in trying to reform the unreformable, for their humanity, too. Many would have cast adrift a man of Fallon's wayward nature long before he could damage their reputation. Walsh never worked a day for Coolmore and went back to the *Sunday Times*. He is still friendly with Fallon, still a little sad at the opportunity lost.

It was bad enough that the moment after his triumphant vindication in the courts, he should be hit with news of another positive test for cocaine, in an instant polluting the water of well being flowing through his country, but there was a tragic context to the revelations. At noon on the day that the positive test had been revealed in an English tabloid, a young man called John Grey died in hospital in Waterford. He had attended a party in Ballybeg in late November where cocaine had been freely available. Another man who attended the same party had already died from swallowing cocaine and fifteen others had been taken to hospital. Katy French, a 24-year-old model, had died at almost the same time, also as a result of taking cocaine.

Ireland was shocked by the apparent extent of the cocaine epidemic and RTE, the national television network, ran a primetime programme highlighting the increasing availability and use of cocaine, particularly among young people. Reporters had found traces of cocaine in nine out of ten clubs and pubs they had tested nationally. Dr Chris Luke of the Mercy Hospital in Cork spoke on national radio about the scale of the 'cocaine crisis'. He said it took the death of 'beloved celebrities' for people to start paying attention. Into the national bout of soul-searching walked Kieren Fallon, a very particular Irish hero. Writing in the *Irish Independent*, Declan Lynch defended Fallon's right to keep on riding. Punters, he said, judged a whole person, not just the weak fragments of a man.

'They did not look to jockeys for moral leadership,' he wrote. 'Callow commentators will hear the name Kieren Fallon in the same sentence as the word cocaine and start sermonising about the state of the world, in which any story seems to be a story of cocaine.' He went on, 'As Aidan O'Brien explained last week, Kieren Fallon has needed to deal with his addictions for a long time now, and this is well known.' It was a tortured and largely illogical argument, based on the premise that punters love him, therefore all is right with the world, and it was not a view widely expressed at the time. Pity, sympathy, understanding, frustration, anger, every emotion had been vented on Fallon's behalf, but brushing the whole thing back under the carpet where racing, in Ireland and England, had consigned it for too long, was no longer an option, for Coolmore or, more importantly, for Fallon himself.

There was another poignant footnote to the eleven-week trial. In mid-October, Julie Fallon also appeared in court, charged with assault following an incident in a pub in Suffolk. Mrs Fallon explained to the court that she had felt another woman in the pub was making fun of her because of Kieren. She was provoked, she claimed, and confronted the woman. She was found guilty of assault by magistrates in Bury St Edmunds and was ordered to pay £400 in compensation to her victim.

Happily for racing, the duel for the jockeys' title diverted some attention away from the turbulent past of one of its own champions. Up hill and down dale, up to Catterick and down to Folkestone, Seb Sanders and Jamie Spencer pursued each other, winner by winner, to the very end of the road. It was a truly epic battle between two contrasting characters on and off the track – Spencer, the young Irishman to whom race-riding came easily, and the Birmingham-born Sanders, a stalwart of the weighing-room who had to graft for every break in his slow-burning career. And, as is the way with these things, racing relished the combat as Spencer and Sanders, like two boxers at the end of a twelve-round title fight, rode themselves to the point of exhaustion and trainers searched their stables to find a winner for their favoured champion.

Sadly, there could be just one winner, except that there wasn't. A winner behind his rival going into the final race of the season at Doncaster, Spencer needed to coax the far from straightforward seven-year-old stayer, Inchnadamph, round the whole field in the closing two-mile handicap to take a share of the title – 190 apiece, the first joint champions since Steve Donoghue and Charlie Elliott in 1923. Tellingly, Spencer went home to bed and vowed he would never be drawn into such an exhausting schedule again. Sanders flew to Wolverhampton that evening to ride one for his boss, Sir Mark Prescott. He was home by midnight and absolutely no one begrudged him his share of the title.

Fallon doubtless smiled at the fact that Tim Fitzgerald, son of his old mentor, Jimmy, had provided Spencer with his final victory, and recognised the exhilaration, thrill and exhaustion of the season-long chase. The race for the title largely obscured the farewell of Kevin Darley, an old rival of Fallon's, particularly in the north. On the day Darley announced his retirement in early November, the *Racing Post* carried a picture of him handing over his jockeys' championship trophy to Fallon at the end of the 2001 season. Darley had usurped the title the previous year after Fallon's season had been cut short by his shoulder injury. 'The title's only out on loan,' Fallon said. He was right, but in the unrelenting greyness of a December day outside the Old Bailey, there were only distant echoes of such bravado.

17

FLAWED GENIUS, FALLEN IDOL

'At their best, the great ones are not only jockeys but horsemen and gentlemen. They have it all.'

Pete Axthelm, *The Kid*

It is hard to know when the drama of Kieren Fallon turned into tragedy. It might have been that moment outside the Old Bailey when the little boy who'd swung his legs from the stool in Jim Regan's front room and talked about his dreams of becoming a jockey looked suddenly very old and very tired. This was supposed to be his hour of redemption, his epiphany, his vindication against all the critics. But he knew his hour would not last sixty minutes. Fallon had been to see Jim Regan back in Gort. Regan, his old mentor, knew something was wrong long before the truth emerged. He didn't ask any questions and Fallon gave him no answers, but there was no spark in the boy, just a terrible sadness. By the morning, a national hero had been damned as a fool. Cecil, Stoute and Coolmore. The three best jobs in racing and Fallon had been through the lot, losing the first and last by his own fecklessness, forsaking the second for the lure of a fat contract and a quieter life. Only in the little enclave of Crusheen was the well of forgiveness still wet.

The French authorities patiently listened to two appeals by Fallon's lawyers against the eighteen-month sentence initially imposed for a second positive test. Neither had any realistic chance of success. The final court of appeal for France Galop belatedly released its findings in

March 2008. It firmly rejected the claims that Fallon's sentence was disproportionate both to the crime and to the ban handed down to the Irish jockey, Dean Gallagher, for a similar repeat offence in 2002. Ironically, Fallon had helped Gallagher financially in his time of need. Now Gallagher was the precedent in Fallon's own suspension. Fallon's own finances, his defence claimed, were a cause for concern because his ability to pay substantial alimony to his ex-wife and support his three children was now diminished. He had, his lawyer said, been tested on many occasions since in France and had been positive once only, and had been to see a psychotherapist to help with his treatment. That one lapse was caused by depression. France Galop remained deaf to the pleas.

In his own hour of need, Fallon turned to the one person in racing who, he felt, had truly appreciated his worth. One story, probably apocryphal, suggested that when Michael Stoute returned from a holiday in Barbados he found his old stable jockey sitting in his kitchen. It certainly did not take long for Fallon to return to his old haunts at Freemason Lodge in a bid to pick up the pieces of his shattered career. Fallon was so bullish about his new job as work rider and general factotum that Stoute swiftly had to issue his own statement denying any suggestion that Fallon was about to become his assistant trainer. The owners of Coolmore might also have raised an eyebrow at Fallon's description of his life in Ireland as a 'nightmare'.

'For the first time in three and a half years, I am feeling really happy and feeling really good about life,' he told the *Racing Post*. 'I want to go where I was happiest and that was at Stoutey's. I am going to spend this year getting myself right and I will do whatever Sir Michael wants. But I want to sort myself out first. That's very important. I'm thinking about going to America and getting my life back together.'

Fallon did go to America, back to the Rehabilitation Clinic in Phoenix, which he had visited once before, in the winter of 2006, but the insistence that this time it would all be different had, by the spring of 2008, become a tired old refrain. Fallon is always about to reform his ways, like a naughty child promising his parents he will be a good boy. Tomorrow. For Fallon, tomorrow never comes. Christopher Stewart-

Moore, his lawyer, likens Fallon to the Winslow Boy, the semi-fictional hero of the Terrence Rattigan play of 1946, who ultimately proves his innocence while leaving a trail of emotional devastation behind him. Fallon is no different from Lester Piggott in his inability to see himself as others might see him, but he is very different in his need to have people around him. Despite his frequent protests to the contrary, Fallon cares deeply what people think of him and is genuinely hurt if their views, for some strange reason, do not coincide with his own.

'The first time I had anything to do with him was at Beverley in my second year as racing correspondent,' recalls Alan Lee of *The Times*. 'I asked if I could talk to him. He didn't know me from Adam and fixed me with one of those dreadful stares, seemed to ignore me and stalked off. Eventually he came out, sat down and started asking me personal questions. It was pre Royal Ascot, but he didn't want to talk about horses. He talked to me for half an hour and at the end of it asked me if I wanted a game of golf the following morning. He's got a persecution complex and it comes through in a distrust of anyone in authority and people he doesn't know. In some ways, he's indestructible, in others he's hopelessly insecure.'

It's the insecurity that brought Fallon to the point of dependency, initially on alcohol to see him through the day and then on drugs to make him feel better about himself. It was in the course of another conversation with Alan Lee, at Salisbury races, that Fallon revealed the depth of his addiction to the bottle.

'He asked me, "Do you drink?" I said, "Yes." He said, "Be careful then. I used to drink a bottle of vodka every day after the races." He suddenly goes into this mode where he wants to talk about it.'

The confessional instinct in the good Catholic boy? It's tempting to believe so, but the real Kieren Fallon reveals himself on the racetrack in the way he rides and the decisions he makes, in the power and gentleness of his jockeyship and the aggression and anger of his competitive will. There is, as Fallon said himself, a 'bit of wild' in his soul that makes him a great rider and a dangerous human being.

Pete Axthelm defined the qualities of a great jockey as precisely as anyone in the opening pages of his book on Steve Cauthen.

He must have the strength and guile to control an animal ten times his weight and the courage to face possible bone-crushing catastrophe every time he breaks from the starting gate. He needs a keen sense of timing, split second reflexes, and ability to communicate with his mount. Some of these traits are taken for granted by screaming bettors at trackside, but they will never be taken for granted by anyone who has ridden a headstrong thoroughbred. The task demands formidable skills and the race rider is a formidable little man.

The words were written about The Kid, but they could have described Fallon. What Axthelm did not mention was that the jockey must master all those skills while existing on a diet of air and water. Cauthen, like Fallon, Walter Swinburn and Johnny Murtagh, was driven to the edge of reason by the constant battle with his weight. Fallon has had other battles to fight, with the lingering pain in his left shoulder after his injury and with a fickle, addictive personality. It is no coincidence that Fallon's two positive drugs tests came when he was deprived of the supreme octane of winning every day of the week. If he was winning enough, as he was during his six years as the champion, he could control the addictive side of his nature.

Stoute describes Fallon as a 'flawed genius' while apologising for the cliché. Michael Bell, who trained Motivator to win the 2005 Derby, describes Fallon as 'definitely a genius' without any apology. In terms of statistics, Fallon cannot match Sir Gordon Richards, Lester Piggott or Pat Eddery for sheer volume of winners, but only Piggott, of those three, has ridden more Classic winners. Richards and Eddery have 14; Fallon has 15, crammed into barely a decade. Frankie Dettori, the only contemporary jockey who can come close to matching Fallon's verve and skill on the track, had 12 by the start of the 2008 season. Fallon has an astonishing record for a man who was still a five-pound apprentice in his early twenties. In the decade since he joined Henry Cecil, Fallon has become the master of all occasions, big and small, as driven, as cool and confident around Hamilton Park as he was around Epsom. Ever conscious of his own upbringing, Fallon particularly enjoyed riding winners for the smaller trainers, such as Eric Alston, who had supported him from day one, and especially back in the north where he first made his living. Fallon's domination in the saddle either side of the millennium turned as much on his ability to clean up in the north as it did on the support of his powerful stables in the south. He would always give a horse a ride and, pretty well always, return to the unsaddling enclosure with some positive words for the trainer and the owner.

If there is a stylistic parallel to be drawn, it is with Sir Gordon Richards, who, like Fallon, was never taught to ride except bareback on his father's pit ponies and who never compromised his deep-seated, long-reined way of riding for the sake of fashion or mere effect. But Fallon's will to win is more reminiscent of Piggott. Fallon loves the challenge of taming difficult horses and of educating them in the art of winning, a process that begins on the way to the start and often continues to the last furlong of a race. In general, Fallon wins the battle of minds, but it is always a conversation, never just a brutal imposition of will. Although, for most of his career, Fallon has found horses as easy to understand as he has found humans puzzling, there is a common denominator. On horseback and in life, Fallon thrives on danger. If there is a wall of horses in front of him, how long can we wait? If there is a rule to be pushed, how far can we push it? 'Kieren has never liked having too smooth a passage in life,' says Jack Ramsden. 'He is the sort of person who is at his best when things are against him.' Where Piggott treated the world with lofty disdain, in part a reflection of his deafness, Fallon attacks it with the restless energy of a child. Neither have an ability to back down or any understanding of how the world outside might view them. In that blinkered perception of the world, they reflect their sport. But Fallon never had Piggott's personal self-discipline, nor does he have his inscrutability. Piggott's smile was always nervous and false, less so now in his mellower days; Fallon's is broad and winning. Michael Bell did not just enjoy having Fallon ride his horses because he knew he was hiring the best; he liked having Fallon on his side for the confidence and the sense of fun he exuded. No one ever employed Lester to have a laugh.

In *The Kid*, Axthelm also quotes the well-known American trainer, Buddy Jacobson, who had a healthy disdain for the input of his jockeys.

'If riding is so complicated,' asked Jacobson, 'how come some of our best riders didn't even learn to get up on a horse until they were sixteen years old?' That's Fallon, too. But the smartest jockeys also work out what's missing from their armoury, on and off the track, and put it right. McCoy is the prime example in Britain; Shoemaker, Pincay and Cordero in the States. Roy Keane worked it out eventually. Fallon has never made any attempt to find out what's missing from his character, let alone making any compromise with it. 'I always lived with the truth that nobody gives you anything for free in this game,' Fallon once said. 'Nobody hands you a thing. You have to earn it all – and you have to do it by your own efforts and skill and determination.' In other words, take him or leave him as he is.

There is no doubt that the racing authorities in the UK want Fallon off their patch. Why wouldn't they? At a time when the sport is fighting hard to restore its credibility and market itself to sponsors, Fallon is not the ideal symbol of change. By the time he is eligible to return to race-riding again, the 2009 season will be drawing to a close and Fallon will be 44. He will take heart in the comeback of Lester Piggott, who returned at the age of 55 after a year in jail and two years in retirement, to ride a Breeders' Cup winner and win his thirtieth Classic, on Rodrigo de Triano. Fallon has already told Jim Regan that not only will he come back, but he will win the jockeys' championship again. With Fallon, anything is possible.

Appendix One
CAREER RECORD

UK JOCKEYS' CHAMPIONSHIP
(TURF AND ALL-WEATHER)

Year	Winners	Year	Winners
1988	31	1998	204 (champion)
1989	28	1999	202 (champion)
1990	39	2000	59
1991	29	2001	166 (champion)
1992	45	2002	149 (champion)
1993	60	2003	221 (champion)
1994	47	2004	200
1995	92	2005	70
1996	136	2006	27
1997	202 (champion)		

Source: www.jockeysroom.com/www.racingpost.co.uk

ENGLISH CLASSIC WINS (15)

1,000 Guineas, Newmarket (4): Sleepytime (1997), Wince (1999), Russian Rhythm (2003), Virginia Waters (2005)

2,000 Guineas, Newmarket (4): King's Best (2000), Golan (2001), Footstepsinthesand (2005), George Washington (2006)

The Oaks, Epsom (4): Reams of Verse (1997), Ramruma (1999), Ouija Board (2004), Alexandrova (2006)

The Derby, Epsom (3): Oath (1999), Kris Kin (2003), North Light (2004)

ROYAL ASCOT WINS (27)

1996 (2): Yeast (Royal Hunt Cup), Dazzle (Windsor Castle Stakes)

1997 (3): Bosra Sham (Prince of Wales's Stakes), Yashmak (Ribblesdale Stakes), Canon Can (Queen Alexandra Stakes)

1998 (2): Dr Fong (St James's Palace Stakes), Royal Anthem (King Edward VII Stakes)

1999 (2): Pythios (Britannia Stakes), Endorsement (Queen's Vase)

2000 (4): Kalanisi (Queen Anne Stakes), Dalampour (Queen's Vase), Caribbean Monarch (Royal Hunt Cup), Celtic Silence (Chesham Stakes)

2001 (2): Medicean (Queen Anne Stakes), Cover Up (Ascot Stakes)

2002 (2): Riyadh (Ascot Stakes), Cover Up (Queen Alexandra Stakes)

2003 (3): Mr Dinos (Gold Cup), Russian Rhythm (Coronation Stakes), Cover Up (Queen Alexandra Stakes)

2004 (3): Iceman (Coventry Stakes), Favourable Terms (Windsor Forest Stakes), Mandobi (Britannia Handicap)

2005 (1): Indigo Cat (Hampton Court Stakes)

2006 (3): Ad Valorem (Queen Anne Stakes), Yeats (Gold Cup), Papal Bull (King Edward VII Stakes)

OTHER MAJOR GROUP ONE WINNERS – UK

Cheveley Park Stakes, Newmarket (1): Embassy (1997)

Coronation Cup, Epsom (3): Daliapour (2000), Boreal (2002), Yeats (2005)

Eclipse Stakes, Sandown (2): Medicean (2001), Oratorio (2005)

Fillies Mile, Ascot (1): Red Bloom (2003)

King George VI and Queen Elizabeth Stakes, Ascot (1): Golan (2002)

Lockinge Stakes, Newbury (3): Medicean (2001), Russian Rhythm (2004), Peeress (2006)

Nassau Stakes, Goodwood (3): Islington (2002), Russian Rhythm (2003), Favourable Terms (2004)

Racing Post Trophy, Doncaster (1): Motivator (2004)

Sun Chariot Stakes, Newmarket (1): Independence (2001)

Sussex Stakes, Goodwood (1): Ali-Royal (1997)

Yorkshire Oaks, York (4): Catchascatchcan (1998), Islington (2002, 2003), Quiff (2004)

OTHER MAJOR WINNERS

UK

Ayr Gold Cup (1): Grangeville (1999)

Cesarewitch, Newmarket (1): Top Cees (1999)

Chester Cup (1): Top Cees (1995)

Chester Vase (1): Papal Bull (2006)

Dante, York (3): Dilshaan (2001), North Light (2004), Septimus (2006)

Dee Stakes, Chester (3): Oath (1999), Dr Greenfield (2001), Gypsy King (2005)

Ebor Handicap, York (1): Tuning (1998)

Geoffrey Freer Stakes, Newbury (1): Dushyantor (1997)

Gimcrack Stakes, York (2): Chilly Billy (1994), Josr Algarhoud (1998)

Jockey Club Cup, Newmarket (1): Cover Up (2005)

July Stakes, Newmarket (3): Bold Fact (1997), Nevisian Lad (2003), Ivan Denisovich (2005)

Lowther Stakes, York (1): Russian Rhythm (2002)

May Hill Stakes, Doncaster (1): Midnight Line (1997)

Mill Reef Stakes, Newbury (1): Arkadian Hero (1997)
Predominate Stakes, Goodwood (1): Asian Heights (2001)
Rockfel Stakes, Newmarket (1): Name of Love (1997)

Ireland
Irish Derby (2): Hurricane Run (2005), Dylan Thomas (2006)
Irish Oaks (3): Ramruma (1999), Ouija Board (2004), Alexandrova (2006)
Irish St Leger (1): Yeats (2007)
Irish Champion Stakes (3): Oratorio (2005), Dylan Thomas (2006, 2007)
Moyglare Stud Stakes (1): Rumplestiltskin (2005)
National Stakes (1): George Washington (2005)
Phoenix Stakes (3): Damson (2004), George Washington (2005), Holy Roman
    Emperor (2006)
Tattersalls Gold Cup (2): Shiva (1999), Hurricane Run (2006)

France
French 2,000 Guineas (1): Aussie Rules (2006)
Prix de l'Arc de Triomphe (2): Hurricane Run (2005), Dylan Thomas (2007)
Grand Prix de Paris (1): Scorpion (2005)
Grand Prix de Saint-Cloud (2): Gamut (2004), Mountain High (2007)
Prix de la Foret (1): Tomba (1998)
Prix d'Ispahan (1): Falbrav (2003)
Prix Jean-Luc Lagardere (3): Hold That Tiger (2002), Horatio Nelson (2005),
    Holy Roman Emperor (2006)
Prix Marcel Boussac (1): Rumplestiltskin (2005)
Prix Morny (2): Elusive City (2002), Myboycharlie (2007)
Prix de l'Opera (1): Zee Zee Top (2003)

Australia
A.J. Moir Stakes (1): California Dane (2006)
Hong Kong Jockey Club Plate (1): Polar Bear (2006)

Hong Kong
Hong Kong Vase (1): Ouija Board (2005)

Germany
Grosser Preis von Baden (1): Borgia (1997)
Preis von Europa (1): Youmzain (2006)

Italy
Italian Oaks (1): Guadeloupe (2002)

United Arab Emirates
Dubai Sheema Classic (2): Fruits of Love (1999), Fantastic Light (2000)

USA
Arlington Million (1): Powerscourt (2005)
Breeders' Cup Filly and Mare Turf (2): Islington (2003), Ouija Board (2004)

Appendix Two
DISCIPLINARY RECORD

SUSPENSIONS/FINES – YEAR BY YEAR (UK)

Month	Course	Offence	Result
1988			
April	Newcastle	whip	1 day
August	Newmarket	whip	7 days
1990			
April	Carlisle	rule 161 (ii)	£150
July	Hamilton	whip	2 days
1992			
July	Beverley	rule 220 (ii)	£240
July	Beverley	rule 162 (iv)	£200
Oct	Leicester	misconduct	£100
Oct	Leicester	no medical book	£60
1993			
July	Redcar	fail to arrive in time	£95
July	Pontefract	rule 220 (ii)	£250
August	Nottingham	rule 151	£700
October	Redcar	whip	2 days
1994			
June	Thirsk	improper riding	7 days
June	Pontefract	whip	2 days
July	Southwell	irresponsible riding	7 days
July	Newcastle	accidental interference	4 days
1995			
May	Ripon	whip	5 days
August	Pontefract	abusive language	£400
Sept	Haydock	irresponsible riding	8 days
Oct	Redcar	improper riding	7 days

Month	Course	Offence	Result
1996			
May	Thirsk	irresponsible riding	6 days
June	Thirsk	whip	2 days
August	Haydock	careless riding	2 days
Oct	Nottingham	not ride to draw	4 days
1997			
April	Ascot	no medical book	£70
May	Doncaster	not ride to draw	4 days
July	Windsor	whip	2 days
July	Goodwood	irresponsible riding	5 days
Oct	Leicester	starting	£125
Oct	Pontefract	no medical book	£70
1998			
Jan	Lingfield	whip	2 days
Feb	Lingfield	no medical book	£100
Feb	Wolverhampton	careless riding	3 days
May	York	careless riding	3 days
July	Haydock	whip	2 days
July	Sandown	careless riding	2 days
August	York	whip	3 days
August	York	careless riding	2 days
1999			
May	Sandown	careless riding	2 days
June	Yarmouth	abusive language	£350
June	Epsom	breaking the parade	£1000
July	Ascot	breaking the parade	£1250
July	Newmarket	whip	4 days
August	Ripon	careless riding	5 days
Sept	Bath	careless riding	3 days
2000			
May	Chester	abusive language	£110
May	Bath	careless riding	4 days
2001			
May	Leicester	not riding to draw	£150
May	Ayr	irresponsible riding	3 days
Oct	Newmarket	irresponsible riding	5 days

Month	Course	Offence	Result
2002			
May	Chester	careless riding	2 days
May	York	whip	1 day
May	Haydock	irresponsible riding	2 days
June	Newcastle	irresponsible riding	2 days
July	Chester	irresponsible riding	2 days
July	York	whip	1 day
August	Goodwood	irresponsible riding	3 days
August	Newmarket	irresponsible (referred)	13 days + (4 deferred)
Oct	Lingfield	irresponsible riding	2 days + (4 deferred)
2003			
March	Doncaster	not riding to draw	1 day
April	Kempton	careless riding	2 days
June	Epsom	careless	1 day
June	Ascot	careless	1 day
July	Doncaster	careless	1 day
July	Ayr	careless	2 days
Sept	Pontefract	careless	1 day
2004			
March	Lingfield	rule 156 (referred)	21 days
April	Newmarket	careless	2 days
June	Windsor	not riding to draw	1 day
July	Lingfield	careless	4 days
July	Goodwood	careless	1 day
Sept	Goodwood	whip	1 day
Sept	Salisbury	careless	1 day
2005			
July	Sandown	whip	2 days
July	Newbury	not riding to draw	1 day
July	Goodwood	careless	1 day
Sept	Yarmouth	careless	1 day
Sept	Newmarket	careless	2 days
2006			
June	Newbury	careless	1 day
June	Ascot	careless	4 days

DISCIPLINARY HEARINGS

Date	Offence	Result
Sept 1994	Violent conduct	6 months (Stuart Webster incident)
July 1996	Medical Book	failed to attend
July 1996	Medical Book	£500 plus 5 days for failure to attend
Nov 1996	Lying in previous hearing	£1,500
Sept 2002	Interference	17 days, of which 4 deferred
July 2003	Careless riding appeal	1 day
Oct 2003	Careless riding appeal	1 day
March 2004	Rule 156 (i)	21 days (Ballinger Ridge incident)
Oct 2004	Mobile phone use	£250

INDEX